"Now, Let Me Tell You Something…"

The Autobiography of James E. Rogers

LAW COLLEGE
ASSOCIATION

"Now, Let Me Tell You Something…"

The Autobiography of James E. Rogers

with introduction by Peter Likins

Law College Association   Tucson, Arizona

Now, Let Me Tell You Something…
The Autobiography of James E. Rogers
by James E. Rogers

ISBN 978-0-692-27107-0 (hardcover)
ISBN 978-0-692-27108-7 (softcover)

Organized and edited by Heather Lusty
Interior design by Emily McGovern
Cover design by Renee La Roi

Cover photo courtesy of
James E. Rogers and Beverly Rogers

Internal photos courtesy of James E. Rogers and Beverly Rogers,
UNLV Photo Services, KSNV-TV in Las Vegas, Mark Whitehead, and
Heather Lusty.

Tucson, Arizona
www.law.arizona.edu/alumni

CONTENTS

ACKNOWLEDGMENTS

We would like to thank the dozens of busy community leaders, educators, administrators, university faculty, and friends who made time to be interviewed for this book. They were wonderfully supportive, offered helpful insights, referrals, and suggestions for the project, and made the process of building the narrative a genuine pleasure. Thanks also to Melisé Leech for assisting with interviews and much needed encouragement during this two-year project. Also, the staff at KSNV-TV were wonderfully supportive and interested in the project along the way. Jim loved to tell stories about other people – friends, coworkers, and local figures – but his own story is just as interesting, as entertaining, and as important to the development of Nevada, to the growth of education, and to the transformation of media. We hope you enjoy reading it, and hear Jim's voice and humor in the tales.

Heather Lusty and Beverly Rogers

"Now, Let Me Tell You Something…"

The Autobiography of James E. Rogers

Introduction

by Peter Likins, President Emeritus,
University of Arizona

I first knew Jim Rogers as the extremely generous, passionately committed primary benefactor of the College of Law at the University of Arizona, where I arrived as president in 1997. I soon knew Jim in a much deeper way as a close personal friend for whom I feel genuine admiration and honest affection.

Our kinship developed very early in our relationship, perhaps because we both appreciate the kind of straight talk that leads to absolute trust. I know down deep that Jim Rogers means what he says, and he knows that about me too.

We don't always agree. I think I earned Jim's respect by respectfully disagreeing on rare occasions with his forcefully expressed opinions. I discovered that Jim loves a reasoned argument, so we both take pleasure in those rare, quiet times together when we can try to hammer out an agreement on questions that separate us initially.

For example, when Jim insists that "the principles of management are transferable from one type of institution to another," I can agree only if he differentiates "management" from "governance," which defines the locus of power, and recognizes the need to transfer management principles within the constraints established by governance systems, which exhibit sharp differences among such categories as public universities, private universities, publically held companies, privately held partnerships, and sole proprietorships. I've been deeply involved professionally in every category but the last, in which Jim has functioned for most of his career. Jim was very successful in moving across this entire spectrum, from sole owner of a television network to Chancellor of the entire Nevada System of Higher Education, not because he transferred management principles but because of his remarkably forceful personality, his impressive powers of persuasion and the respect that he has earned as a prominent citizen of the State of Nevada.

On another point of friendly disagreement, Jim has proven me wrong. He loves to tell the story, in this book and elsewhere, of my reaction when he called me in high spirits and told me that he had accepted an invitation to become the Interim Chancellor of the Nevada System of Higher Education. I said, "Jim, you are not a patient man." He ignored my warning and kept talking about his new job, so I said again, "Jim, you are not a patient man."

I was wrong. Well, Jim can be impatient, but he is so persistent in pursuing distant goals over long periods of time, overcoming countless frustrating obstacles along the way, that I have to give him credit for extraordinary patience when that's what's required to achieve highly valued objectives. When you read in this book about his lengthy pursuit of the Channel 3 license and his prolonged defense of Bob Maheu, you will marvel at his patience.

Another discovery for me in this insightful autobiography is the early age at which Jim acquired his attitude toward money. It's not uncommon for a twelve-year-old to make a little money mowing the neighbors' lawns, but Jim borrowed from his father the funds needed for a capital investment in a gasoline powered lawn mower and made a lot more money, even after retiring his debt. In high school he became an entrepreneur in the janitorial business (again with start-up costs advanced by his father), employing as many as five people in the JR Janitorial and Lawn Service Company. Jim had an early appetite for money and a determination to create the means to earn it on his own.

I find interesting parallels in Warren Buffet's childhood, as described by his biographer, Alice Schroeder. Warren sold packs of chewing gum from door to door at age five, moving on to bottles of Coca Cola and the *Saturday Evening Post*. When at ten he was caught selling used golf balls, his parents were impressed by his initiative. Neither Buffet nor Rogers was from an impoverished family, but in early childhood they both found ways to make money.

Jim has obviously found satisfaction in discovering ways to make money, often exposing himself to high risk. But he has also found perhaps even greater satisfaction in giving away money to institutions and causes he finds worthy in their value to the larger society. He seems not to be afflicted with the common compulsion to accumulate a great fortune to secure in his private vault; he enjoys making money honorably and then using that money to improve the society that made his success possible.

Although Jim and his very understanding and supportive wife Bev have contributed significantly to many worthy charities, their passion has drawn them to support higher education most generously, focusing especially on public universities in the western mountain states where Jim's television stations are located. The primary beneficiary by far is the University of Arizona, where Jim earned both undergraduate and law degrees, with commitments rising to such a level as to justify the name "James E. Rogers College of Law," but his intellectual and moral commitment is to all of higher education, which he sees as critical for democracy and prosperity in a globally competitive environment.

As you read this book and reflect upon the man whose story it tells, I want you to know that this guy is real, and he means what he says. Even if you don't agree with his every observation, you will know that Jim Rogers has been true to his principles, which are honorable and deserving of universal respect and admiration.

Chapter I

LIFE'S FIRST LESSON:

KNOWLEDGE IS CRITICAL, BUT JUDGMENT

IS EVERYTHING

If I were to describe the first 17 years of my life to you, from my birth in 1938 through my 17th birthday, you would believe that I spent every waking hour with my father and that I had no mother, so great was my father's impact on me. In fact, my relationship with both my parents was somewhat remote; after living in Costa Rica with them from age two to six, I went to stay with my grandparents, Dr. and Mrs. James E. Savage in Paintsville, Kentucky, for a year; then I moved to Los Alamos, New Mexico, in 1947, where I lived with my parents until 1953, when we came to Las Vegas, Nevada. While most children spend their summers with their parents, I spent each of my summers from the time I was seven to the time I was 14 with my grandparents in Kentucky. And upon moving to Las Vegas, at age 15, my life until the end of high school was spent working fairly hard in school and working part time in businesses that I organized and ran.

I never went on a vacation with my parents, and while I was a minor athlete in school to say the least, my father never came to see the basketball games I played in, the track meets I ran in, the all-state chorus I sang in, or for that matter, any school activity in which I participated. Both my parents were incredibly talented musicians, and yet neither pushed me to play an instrument, or to vocalize. My father never asked me what classes I was taking in school, how I was doing, what my grades were, what courses I liked, or what I was going to pursue in college. He gave me no advice as to which college I should attend, what to study, whether to join a fraternity, or what my responsibilities should be in school and after school. His only advice was to get myself a profession and put myself into a position where I would never have to work for anybody else. Other than that, he never gave me any advice of any sort unless I asked for it – and I seldom asked for it.

My father was distant, stoic, tough as nails, yet very kind. He worked well with people. The hundreds of employees who worked for him had great respect for him, and he always seemed to care about his employees' professional and personal lives. I'm not sure if my father knew much about being a father; he was the eighth child of his parents and was probably raised more by his siblings. His father (my grandfather) was reputed to be a very stoic, stern, tough, smart, successful businessman. I'm not sure of all the effects the distance between my father and me caused, but I do know that early on I had a need and desire to go into my own business, to be on my own, and make as much money as I could for myself.

I don't like to depend on anyone for money. I love running my own business. Put those together and you can understand why at the age of 12 I told my father that I wanted to go into the lawn mowing business, and if he were to buy me my first gasoline lawn mower, I would pay him back. He bought it, I cut a lot of lawns, and I repaid him. When we moved from Los Alamos to Las Vegas in 1953, I was 15 years old. I went to work at Charlie Weaver's Chevron station where my boss was Bob Faiss, senior and class president at Las Vegas High. He's probably the leading gaming attorney in the world at this time and a senior partner at Lionel Sawyer. After the summer of 1953, I decided to go into the janitorial business. My father advanced me start-up costs and from my sophomore year through graduation from high school, I never employed less than two people or more than five in the JR Janitorial and Lawn Service Company. I bought a brand new car and while I didn't support myself, I was able to provide for all of my recreational needs. When I left for college in 1956, I'm sure I had $5,000 in the bank.

After my freshman year in college, I had performed adequately enough to be a grader and teaching assistant in the economics and accounting labs at the University of Arizona. I was paid enough through that effort, plus my efforts in tutoring students, to live very well while in college. I did one other project each of my years at

Arizona that made me a lot of money. In the accounting department, students are given a one-semester project to do an entire set of books for "x" company. It takes the entire semester to do the project. When the assignment was passed out, I spent every waking hour over the next two weeks doing the entire set of books, which I then sold to the accounting students. I probably should have been expelled for doing other students' work, but for some reason no one ever bothered me.

I don't have a lot of specific stories to relate about my father; in fact, I'm not sure that I ever came to really know him. We never became close; we seldom, if ever, confided in each other about our inner-most thoughts; and we seldom, if ever, sought advice from one another. And yet I worshipped him. He was intellectually and absolutely honest – there wasn't a false bone or fiber in his body. While he was known to exaggerate, he had a reputation for absolute honesty, and while not being a product of great intellect or education (though he was a college graduate), his greatest characteristic, which I considered to be the most valuable attribute any human being can have, was *JUDGMENT*. Judgment was the key to every aspect of Frank Rogers' life, and it certainly was the key to my attempt to understand and use judgment to formulate every action I took.

Very few people are able to take an issue with a hundred varying facts and prioritize those hundred facts from the irrelevant to the most important, then reach a decision that moves the project forward. Most people's minds are cluttered with the irrelevant aspects of a problem and the desire to look at an issue with 100 factors and fully analyze each and every one of those factors to reach a decision on how to move forward in one decisive step. My father could eliminate 95 of the factors in any decision to be made, take the remaining five, put them in proper perspective and order, and come to a conclusion that allowed him to move forward. I marveled at that ability. I never had a discussion with him in which he said he would think about something and revisit it the next day or next week. By the time we finished a discussion over any issue, we had a decision made and moved forward.

The decisions we made were not always right, but we both agreed that if a decision was right 80 percent of the time, the other 20 percent of the time we could repair the damage and move forward. His motto was that the worst decision a person could make was no decision; the second worst decision a person could make was a slow decision.

Being the only child of parents who were remote, to say the least, set me on my own from an early age. Not knowing any differently, I assumed that was the way things ought to be, and that is the way my life has been built. I had no inside close relationships, at least family wise; and although my grandfather Savage and I were close as grandchild and grandparent, we had little, if anything, in common. I will say this for him – he was a brilliant, highly-educated minister raised in the south, and a preacher in Kentucky for over 50 years; he was a man who had absolutely no prejudices, at least none I could ever recognize. In the seven summers I lived with him, I never heard a negative remark about any person, race, color, creed, or any difference between our family and another's. Not only was intolerance not tolerated – it was never an issue in our lives.

As you read through this book, you will note that the concentration of descriptions of people with whom I dealt reflects my belief that mentors are a critical part of anyone's success. I attribute my success – and my success has been far greater than my intellect or work ethic merited – to the outstanding intellectual people with world-class judgment who advised me on solving problems I ran into. In cases where I single out an individual, whether it be my father, Leo Gelfand, Irving Haut, Bob Maheu, Lou Weiner, Pete Likins, or others, you will note that most of these people were at least 25 years my senior. I received advice and counsel of the highest quality from each of these individuals, and while I tend to be a lone ranger and not mindful of the thought processes of those around me, my method of solving problems is a method founded upon the advice and experience of these six core individuals. All of their advice boiled down to one single concept – good judgment. Mentors are everything.

*

I enjoyed an audience at a young age – in fact, my family called me "the deacon," and that nickname stayed with me. My career as a crusader began in high school in Las Vegas, when as a junior, I joined on the staff of the Desert Breeze, my high school newspaper. During that year I assisted the editor, Jim Joyce, who went on to a big political career in Nevada. At the end of the year, in June of 1955, I was appointed Editor in Chief of the newspaper. Naturally ambitious, I felt that if something could be done once, it could be done twice and done twice as well, so I determined that the weekly newspaper should be published twice a week. One of the things I most enjoyed doing was writing editorials for the paper. I was known for being more than a little critical – I remember very clearly taking on a couple of the teachers and their various policies, as well as issues around town.

From time to time my father was called to the principal's office to discuss a particular editorial. I remember one scathing exposé of a teacher there, Mr. Ed Knapp (a graduated law student who had never actually practiced law), a history professor and one of the students' favorites. Mr. Knapp had a very bad habit: he started everyone with a C in Citizenship and he made it nearly impossible to earn an A. Straight As with a C in Citizenship kept students off the Honor Roll. I wrote a scathing editorial about how unfair he was, which he didn't appreciate at all; he went to the principal, my father got a phone call, and I was asked to come to the principal's office to explain. It seemed rather obvious to me. I was in hot water most of the year – not because I misbehaved, but because I felt obligated to expose the dishonest and unfair. This has been a lifelong pursuit.

Although I wasn't at the top of my class, I did fairly well in high school and decided to go to the University of Arizona. My father was a first-class business administrator, and he wanted me to learn how to operate a business and watch money, so I entered the University of Arizona as an accounting major in the College of Business. I was close to the top of my class and graduated in 1960, by which time I had also finished my first year of law school. I graduated from the University of Arizona College of Law in 1962 and passed the bar that year. I went on for a Masters of Law in taxation at the University of California, graduated in 1963, and then worked during the 1963-64 school year as a teaching fellow at the University of Illinois College of Law. Then I returned to Las Vegas and began the practice of law, which was a financial struggle. For the next several years I took in any work that I could get, and it was not until 1968 or 1969 that I got a lucky break.

*

I've made some unfortunate decisions in my life. I've made several mistakes that affected many people. My first wife Cheryl and I grew up and went to high school together and then to college together, but didn't really know each other well. We didn't know what ambition was or what risk-taking was, and how much each of us would be able to endure. We didn't know how our relationship would develop as we got into the real world. When I was going to law school, she taught high school. When I graduated from law school, Cheryl came back to Las Vegas for me to start a law practice. There was never any question that Cheryl was smarter than I was. She made far better math grades than I, and I was pleased that she did. She got a degree in education and for several years taught high school and eventually became an assistant principal. She retired when we had children. Years later she suggested that she'd like to go back to school because she hadn't fully developed a career. I said to her, "Why don't you do something that is really substantive? Why don't you take accounting courses and sit for the CPA?" She got a degree in accounting from UNLV and took the CPA exam and passed it. I was an accounting major, and I don't think I could ever have passed the CPA exam. I was delighted for her to do something that I could never have done. She practiced accounting for some time, and then decided it wasn't something that she really wanted to do.

After a few years of marriage we realized we didn't have many interests in common; we didn't share the same values. Our ambitions and aspirations were totally contradictory. I used to joke that I voted yes for everything and that she always voted no. We started a family and stayed married for 25 years, but eventually my risk-taking in business and finance drove Cheryl to the edge. She didn't want to keep living on the edge of ruin, and I couldn't change my approach to life. Our divorce was probably the most peaceful divorce of all time. It took us about half an hour to figure out the property settlement; we wrote up a document, my law partner accompanied us to court, and we have remained good friends ever since. She's a wonderful person and a wonderful mother. We probably should have separated much sooner, but we've both gone on to be happy.

I got married again after Cheryl and I divorced. My second wife, Janet was an attorney. She was very, very bright. She was at the top of her class, graduated number two out of a very large class, and passed the Nevada bar. She became an assistant public defender. At the time, I was attempting to put my first television station on the air, and I needed all the help I could get. I didn't feel threatened that she was out in front where I should have been. She was also very creative, very ambitious, and very intense. She had the drive to work 20 hours a day when she got onto a project. The projects she completed getting Channel 3 on the air were monumental. Once again I had married someone that was much smarter than I. It's unfortunate that we didn't get along very well, but that's another story.

My third wife, Beverly, put herself through school at UNLV. She worked in sales and marketing at Channel 3, and had been a salesperson for Channel 8 and Channel 5 in Las Vegas. After we married it became apparent that it would not work if both of us were at the station. We decided that she would work outside the station and do those things that she did best. Beverly went back to college and got a Masters in English literature. Many people tend to look down on intellectual endeavors. People make a big mistake if they believe those courses have no substance and do not add to the value of life. I don't know how many books I've read in my entire life that were not related to a project I had. You could probably count them on two hands. Beverly consumes information and reads more than anyone I know. Back to my original point – all of my wives have been much smarter than I am and much better educated. I have been trained, not educated.

*

I have fortunately made a considerable amount of money, probably more through luck than talent. I just happened to be in the right place at the right time. I have noticed with my friends who have a lot of money that the worst thing they can do for their children is to leave them that money, or give them a lot of money when they are growing up. I told my children early on that I would pay for their educations, take care of them and cover any emergencies that arose. But whatever money I have upon my death, assuming I have anything, will go to educational institutions.

> Jim was always a generous man, but he always had this concept that you had to give back, and make your own way. He knew he wasn't going to leave a lot to his children, but give it away to charity. But he didn't have the major financial resources to get involved in philanthropy until he got the TV station. He was very successful as a lawyer and he did donations; he would focus on UNLV in those days – but it was after I left the firm that he got involved in the TV station in a big way and started making major donations.
>
> Bruce Woodbury, Attorney

I explained to my children that there are several problems with inheriting money. First, you haven't earned it; secondly, all of your friends will wonder if you could have made it on your own. People will wonder why you turned out the way you did since someone else's money made you a success, and not anything you've done. I've told my own children I will not leave them any money, but that if there are any emergencies, I will take care of them. I don't know whether that's had a good or a bad effect. I think it probably caused a bit of distance between us because they may not have felt an important part of my life.

> Jim is an interesting man. He has told me on more than one occasion, his goal is to give away every penny he's ever made by the time he dies. He isn't one who's trying to accumulate a giant nest egg. He is a voracious seeker of knowledge. That's

why he does that. A lot of that is because of his being a curious person.

Harry Reid, U.S. Senator

I also told my children early on I would not bring them into my business. Whenever you bring family in, regardless of whether it's as janitor or president of the company, their fellow employees believe the only reason they got the job is because their father owned the company. People with inherited wealth are frequently considered worthless, and I've acted on that assumption and tried to avoid having my own children labeled with that stigma. There have been instances, of course, when they have had emergencies or they have had needs, and I've given them cars and necessities, but never a lump sum of money. As I said, I told them early on that any money left upon my death would go to charities, mostly educational institutions.

> We've had talks about what money can really accomplish. I know one of the things we talked about was the fact that you don't want to leave money to your children, as much as you'd like to, because it'll become a reductive; you'll never know who your friends are. That was a constant comment that he would make about that. He just felt that not only was it giving back to the community in Las Vegas, but to the people that helped him along, that he may not have known, who helped establish the schools in Vegas, and the great institutions that he attended, USC and Arizona. Jim is more of a steward of what he'd been given.

Bob Savage, M.D., Family Physician, Cleveland Clinic

*

I've never felt the problems I had were caused by anyone other than me. I've spent a lot of time recently thinking about the mistakes I've made over the years, and the bad things that have happened to me. I can't remember any one of those bad results that I didn't cause. Every mistake I made, I've paid for in some way. If I made a bad business deal, it was because I miscalculated the numbers or I acted too hastily. Sometimes I've relied upon my instincts rather than the facts. I learned early on that surrounding yourself with people who have high intellect and creativity is the best formula for your own success.

I mentioned that mentors are everything. In my case, there have been several very important men who have helped me become who I am, and from whom I learned very valuable lessons. These mentors appear throughout this book at critical times in my life, my practice of law, my acquisition and development of the television station in Las Vegas, and my experiences and service in education both locally and nationally. My single, most influential mentor was Louie Wiener. Before I begin relating my experiences and accomplishments, I want to give you a bit of background on my other mentors to connect their wisdom and savvy to my own success in life.

The first of the men I mentioned is Leo Gelfand. I entered the Master of Laws program (LL.M) at the University of Southern California (USC) in the fall of 1962, after having taken and passed the Arizona bar exam following my graduation from the University of Arizona law school that same year. Going through the USC graduate law school catalogue, I noticed that there were courses taught in medico-legal problems, and that the professor was Leo Gelfand, who had been a practicing physician (internist) for more than 25 years before going to law school. He entered the full time practice of law specializing in medico-legal problems, which included medical malpractice, various problems with drug-company products, and other areas in which anyone engaged in the medical profession who had injured someone else through fault was responsible to injured parties.

I signed up for Dr. Gelfand's course and was absolutely mesmerized by this giant of a scholar and practitioner. After finishing my master's in the summer of 1963, I entered the JSD (Doctor of Juridical Science) program at the University of Illinois where I served as a teaching fellow for the 1963-64 school year. After finishing that program in the summer of 1964 and returning to Vegas to practice law, I had occasional medico-legal problems come to me through a client in Las Vegas. I called Dr. Gelfand and asked him if he'd be interested in associating with me on one case. He said he would and he

came to Las Vegas, where we joined forces to handle that case and
several others that came to us over the next decade.

Ours was a fascinating relationship, and eventually resulted in the
formation of a law firm called Gelfand, Berggreen, Feinberg, and
Rogers. I was the least educated of the four. Berggreen, before going
to law school, had been a practicing pediatrician for over 20 years.
He'd graduated from both the University of Maryland School of
Medicine and the University of Maryland School of Law. Feinberg was
also a medical doctor, having graduated from both the USC medical
school and law school. To say that this group had a distinct advantage
over most defense lawyers in handling medico-legal problems would
have been a gross understatement.

Leo was not just my partner – he was like a second father to me.
He had an unbelievable interest in sports, especially USC football, and
both of us became great fans of the USC football program. Leo died
in 1993, one year before my father died. The firm had been dissolved
for some time by then. Leo taught me much about the art of
negotiation: He taught me about when to make an offer, when to
make a demand, how not to show one's cards too early in the game,
and how to negotiate. His principles of negotiation were sound in
every sense because they could be applied to any transaction in which
there were adversaries. He was shrewd, tough, impossible to read, and
he always seemed to be five steps ahead of the game in the negotiation
process. I learned more from him in the art (and I mean *art*) of
negotiation than I've ever learned from any other associate or partner
I've had over the years.

Another enormously important mentor was Irving Haut, CPA.
When I returned to Las Vegas in 1964, having I believe the only
Master of Law in taxation degree in the state, I coincidentally came to
know him. In 1964, I was 26 years old, and Irving was 63. He had
retired as a certified public accountant and income tax expert in San
Francisco after having practiced there for more than 35 years. He
knew more about the internal revenue code than the commissioner of
the IRS himself. Irving was shrewd, clever, creative, aggressive,
fearless, and loyal to his clients in ways I had never before seen – nor

would I see thereafter. Having a master's in tax law did not prepare me to deal with IRS agents. I had no idea of the power they wielded – of the tremendous patience they have in getting their man and prevailing with their cases. Dealing with IRS agents takes a special talent, because they are smart, they are well-educated, they know all the tricks of the trade, and there's nothing new you can think up – period. They've seen it all, they've listened to every story possible, and you can see the smiles on their faces when you begin to lay out what you think is a new approach and realize they've already heard your brilliant strategy many times before. Irving knew how to handle all of these issues. He became my initial mentor, and it was Irving who sent me Bob Maheu as a client when Maheu came to see him about the Hughes-Maheu breakup and potential tax consequences of that breakup.

Irving and I worked very closely together from 1964 through September of 1971, when he and I organized the group that would file for the Channel 3 television broadcast license in Las Vegas. There were four major shareholders: Irving and I and two of Irving's clients. Irving and I saw the license application come to fruition in 1978-1979, and it was he and I who put the financing and the corporate structure together to provide the ability for our station to go on the air. My former wife, Janet Rogers, served as our chief counsel at that time and played a major role in the financial structure of the station.

Unfortunately Irving, having been born in 1901, did not see the station really produce its potential value during his lifetime. Sometime in the early 1980s Irving decided to sell out. Irving was more of a combination fatherly-grandfatherly figure to me rather than simply a father figure, in that he was nearly one generation older than both my father and Dr. Gelfand. When I add his strengths in business to those of my father and my client Bob Maheu and my partner Leo Gelfand, I know that I was blessed with a group of mentors I believe could not have been matched.

To this group of outstanding mentors, I would add my latest mentor, Pete Likins. Of my first few mentors, none was less than 21 years older than I – except for Pete, who is only two years my senior. As the first four mentors had already left this earth, I was blessed to meet a new mentor, Pete Likins, Ph.D, who probably had all of the various talents of my earlier mentors in one package – intellectually he was superior to all four. While Gelfand had a medical and a law degree, Likins' education was exceptional. A Phi Beta Kappa graduate of Stanford University, recipient of a master's degree from M.I.T. and a Ph.D in science from Stanford, he is in a class by himself. He'd been an academic all his professional life, but having been educated in the sciences, he'd been involved with NASA. In fact, when he was chosen to be the president of the University of Arizona, he was introduced by the president of the faculty senate, who said: "After all these years, we're convinced that it will really take a rocket scientist to run this place." He was right. Likins had been the president of Lehigh University for 15 years, and had also been the provost at Columbia University for 11 years.

My 15 year relationship with Pete Likins is probably best described in the advice that he gave me when I was appointed chancellor of the NSHE in 2004. I sought advice from Pete about how to handle the challenges of the job; Pete told me: "Let me remind you Jim – you are not a patient man." I believe Pete thought I hadn't heard him, because I kept on talking. Pete interrupted me, saying again, "Jim – remember – you are not a patient man." There were numerous times during my five-year stint as chancellor that I shot off my big mouth and ended up in newspaper headlines. In each case, I sought the advice of Pete Likins – and only Pete – on how to handle those problems. I was confident that Pete's advice was all I needed. To this very day, while Pete Likins might not be my closest friend, because we do not communicate on a regular basis, he's certainly my best friend. I know that his judgment is so fundamentally sound that I never need a second opinion. One interesting note about Pete is that he came from a very poor family, entered Stanford on a full scholarship, was an all-American wrestler for Stanford, and set records in his weight class that still stand as of the date of the printing of this book. Even in his 60s, Pete had the strength to go onto the football field and lift the cheerleaders up onto his shoulders. He may only be five feet seven, but he is a giant of a man.

The friends I've made both personally and professionally have been far more important to my success than my education or my intellect. I would have had no success if not for the support systems these people created for me. They taught me the difference between right and wrong in dealing with people. They taught me the difference between telling the whole truth and the minimum truth during a business deal. They taught me how to deal with people: how to be straight, honest, organized, to simplify issues, to make decisions, to move forward, to straighten out bad decisions, to look at the long game, and to really put balance in my life. Society can only succeed with everyone supporting everyone else, and while this idea may sometimes be branded as communism or socialism, the fact is no one can make it alone. All of us need each other because we all have very different abilities, different backgrounds, different environments that affect and motivate us. Many of those factors can prevent us from reaching our full potential.

Each of us has an obligation to everyone that we deal with to be fair, to be forthcoming and honest, and to consider the good of both parties in any transaction. If a deal isn't good for both parties, it eventually will fall apart. We have become a nation driven by greed. My friends did not get ambition and greed mixed up; they did not get ambition or success mixed up with dishonest transactions. I certainly made my share of mistakes, but the mistakes I made were my mistakes, not anybody else's. I'd have rather made those mistakes than have been caught doing something dishonest. My mentors have been critical to my success and in making me who I am today. Had I not had their help, support, education, training, and the benefit of their experience, I would not have been as successful in the various things that I've tried.

Chapter II

THE LAW AS A PROFESSION

A legal education is designed to enable its graduates to solve complicated problems. When I went to law school, professors told us that whatever processes we'd previously used to solve problems would be scrubbed out of our minds. The laws learned in law school are only used to challenge one's creativity and ability to think logically. Law school is not the accumulation of an encyclopedic knowledge of the rules of law. Students aren't tested on how many rules they know; they're presented a set of unfamiliar facts and evaluated on how they use the legal thought process to solve the problems presented. At the end of the third year, students take bar exams in the state or states in which they wish to practice. That bar exam often contains areas of the law the student has never come across or studied. A question about community property that has never actually been determined by a court may be posed to a student. Students who have not studied community property don't get up and leave the room – they find a solution.

Successfully completing law school does not guarantee that a graduate has the ability to solve any complicated problem, and graduates are often disappointed to realize that merely knowing the rules doesn't mean they know how to apply them. The day-to-day practice of law is fact driven, not law driven. Knowing all the different rules of law in 35 different states is of no help when you are trying to solve your client's problems in one state. Knowing how to use the rules makes one a good lawyer; just knowing them isn't enough. Knowledge is important – but judgment is everything. I was frequently surprised to learn that many law clerks I had could quote the law verbatim, but had absolutely no idea how to use those rules.

A legal education is not limited to use in the formal practice of law. In fact, I believe that a legal education can be of greatest use in all other areas of life – politics, education, finance, corporate building, and international relations. When I entered the University of Arizona law school, I had never met a lawyer. When I graduated from the University of Arizona, I had still never met a lawyer. I'd gone to law school because I thought it would give me great independence after graduation and would give me economic bargaining power. I had no idea what I would do or where I would go after graduation. I did know that I would follow my father's advice: "Never work for anyone." He always said, "If you work for someone, you'll never control your future."

In June of 1962, I was 23 years old, had just graduated from law school, and was hardly mature enough to practice law. I felt I could invest in another year of law school and obtain a specialty that would give me greater opportunities in the world. Having an undergraduate degree in accounting, which had given me some understanding of finance, I thought I would expand on that knowledge and get a Law Master of Laws (LL.M) in a specialty – tax law.

In 1963, I graduated from the University of Southern California Law School with a Master's in tax law. I thought this would set me apart from other attorneys. When I moved to Las Vegas to practice in 1964, there were about 110 lawyers, and I was the only attorney with a Master's in tax law. Tax law was a new specialty at that time. Even though I had taken numerous courses, I still didn't know much about tax law, or how to deal with the IRS or clients who had tax issues. Fortunately, by mere chance, I met Irving Haut, an expert in U.S. tax law who had had years of experience dealing with the IRS. He was then 65 years old, as I mentioned, and became a grandfather, a father, a brother, and an advisor to me. He liked me, and I think he was rather amused by my naivety.

Irving took me under his wing to teach me how the tax code worked and how to deal with IRS agents. I learned how to deal with financial problems when a taxpayer had not paid the right taxes, had misunderstood the code, or was in a very legitimate battle with the Internal Revenue Service. Income is easy to calculate, but expense deductions can be very complicated. Issues were subject to interpretation, and usually at least two interpretations – that of the client's standpoint and that of the IRS. Irving taught me how to deal with the IRS and clients. He taught me the "theory" behind various sections of the Internal Revenue Code, even though certain sections conflicted or contradicted others.

As I became more involved in the practice of law and in the operation of a business, it confirmed the early lesson about never working for anyone else. But as time went on, I learned that flying solo also didn't work. Because the law is so broad, a sole practitioner finds he is one inch deep and five miles wide. The practice of law is 98 percent fact driven and two percent law driven. I knew the two percent pretty well, but I didn't know anything about the other 98 percent. I concluded I needed to join a law firm, and needed to deal with real live clients. I joined Ralph Denton and Earl Monsey in the practice of law. After I was there 90 days they made me a partner. They did so because business was so bad that they didn't want to pay me a salary. That firm dissolved three years later. I then founded a law firm that over a period of 15 years grew to 17 partners and became very successful. That firm dissolved when I went into the TV business full time.

These partners were all very smart men. I want to talk about their legal abilities and talents. Earl Monsey, my partner for 35 years, is a Stanford graduate. Absolutely brilliant, he was an undergraduate in English literature. He is a true intellect, a solid thinking lawyer. His legal agreements were second to none. He was a specialist and expert in the English language.

Bruce Woodbury was a county commissioner for 25 years. Bruce is a graduate of Stanford Law School where he was on the Law Review. He managed to be a full time student and be on the Law Review while he held down two jobs to support his wife and two children. One of those was Bruce Woodbury, Jr., a Stanford Law graduate. Bruce and I remained partners for 14 years until he decided to become a politician and had to break from the firm because of potential conflicts.

I met Jim [in 1969] when I was a law clerk for Judge Howard Babcock in the district court of Nevada. Jim was a practitioner, so I saw him in the courtroom; we met and he looked into my academic background and decided he had an interest and tried to hire me. So while I was a law clerk for the judge he asked if I could do research projects for him on the side, and the judge allowed me to do that after hours and on lunch breaks. I started working for Jim a bit; then, after several months of that, he offered a partnership (there were four of us; two of us were just starting out, one of us just a year into practice, and Jim had 4-5 years in). When I passed the bar in the fall of 1970, I had some other offers, but I decided to go into partnership with Jim.

Jim focused a lot on personal injury and wrongful death and medical malpractice. One case was a wrongful death case, about a blowout; I think it was against Firestone, and Jim really worked that case and turned it into a huge success. I know it was a very challenging case, with a lot of very high-powered lawyers on the other side. He got a very good settlement.

Bruce Woodbury, Attorney

Our firm did medical malpractice litigation. Ray Berggreen from our firm in Los Angeles came into the Nevada partnership. A graduate of the University of Maryland Medical School, he practiced medicine for 20 years before going to law school. Jack Perry was a Harvard undergraduate and graduated from Harvard Law School. When you looked at the lineup of our partners and the associates, we looked like a pretty smart group.

I was the managing partner and directed the way the law firm grew from 1971. (It was during the period we practiced together that I filed the application for the license for the Channel 3 television station in Las Vegas.) I felt very comfortable working with all of these lawyers, and I admired all of them. They were all bright, had world class educations and outstanding experience. The firm was formidable in the practice of law in Nevada.

Jim went to work for Ralph Denton and I think they had maybe two or three lawyers. Things were really slow in 1964, it was kind of an over-building crunch – almost a recession in town. Ralph's law firm couldn't afford to give him his monthly pay check, so they said "We'll make you a partner" and they made him a partner – right away, his first year. That means you don't take any money home unless there is something to be divided up.

About two months later there was the Bonanza air crash – [Bonanza Air Flight 114, crashed November 15, 1964, 29 fatalities] – on top of one of the mountains. They got a huge payout and that put Jim on the track to personal injury and that was just a treat. I was still teaching at the time, but we still didn't have any money to speak of and when they got this settlement, that was just great. He stayed with Ralph for a number of years and they did lots of personal injury cases and also he got involved with Leo Gelfand [1914-1991].

Leo Gelfand was a good mentor for him, like Louie Weiner. He was a doctor/lawyer out of Beverly Hills and their family became quite close to us. […] Leo was really the one who put him on the medical malpractice [track], because he could always have Leo come in to help him. Then [Jim] started his own firm and he did quite well, but he always said that though he liked law he never saw himself staying with it forever. Then he took on Bob Maheu as a client.

Cheryl Purdue (formerly Rogers), Family

When I started to practice law, I had no idea what the sources of income were, but I soon came to know that grinding out legal opinions on an hourly basis had little economic future. Financial success for a lawyer was having ownership in the product the lawyer produced. If you gave legal advice to a business, you needed to convert that legal advice into your having an ownership interest in that business. If you could arrange for fees to be based upon a percent of the profit in a business venture or a percent of the recovery in a personal injury action, that would not only create income but would create capital.

I needed the experience of lawyers with clients who gave them the possibility of obtaining a financial interest in that client's business.

I was a law partner with the late Ralph Denton. Jim had graduated from law school and somebody introduced him to Ralph. That's how we met; Ralph brought him into the practice as a partner – that was a peculiarity of his; he never took on lawyers as employees – only as partners. So, we three were partners – Denton, Monsey, and Rogers (and others). That went on for a long time. Then Jim split from the partnership and formed his own firm. I was still a partner with Ralph, but after a while I left and joined Jim. For the most part we all remained friends.

Jim had a great talent for making money. Ralph and I were not so good at that – but Jim was and when he joined us, he sort of became the business partner. That talent led him to a lucrative field of law and that was personal injury law. He was good at plaintiff cases. I liked transaction law – drafting of documents and agreements. It takes some skill. I never tried many cases and I was all right with it. But you had to try cases then or nobody had any respect for you.

Earl Monsey, Attorney, Retired

I don't think that Ralph or Earl had any idea of the economics of the practice of law. You can't work enough billable hours to make a good living. At some point, unless you get a "piece of the action," you'll be working until your dying day to just make enough money to feed you. My father always told me that it was not the cases that would make me wealthy, but the people I'd come to know who would make me wealthy. Hourly work has no future. Gambling on outcomes of legal cases, like contingent fees, is where the money is. A personal injury case worth $250,000 would probably not require more work than an injury case worth $10,000. It's easy to see why lawyers prefer to pursue bigger cases. In the 1960s, young attorneys trying to develop a reputation for handling "big cases" had a difficult time. It was against the rules to advertise, and ambulance chasing got you disbarred.

I won a couple of large, important cases that made me a well-known figure in Nevada law. In 1966, a Bonanza Airlines plane crashed outside of Las Vegas. Through a series of coincidences, our firm got the case. Although there was an international treaty restriction on the amount of damages a foreign traveler could obtain against an American airline, the amount of the award was substantial and we earned far more on the contingent fee arrangement than we would have on an hourly basis. In the early 1980s, we were hired to pursue a wrongful death case against the Firestone Tire and Rubber Company. A tire had blown out at a high rate of speed where two of the layers of rubber came unglued. The settlement was $1,500,000, the largest to date in Nevada. The attorneys' fees were substantial.

In 1981, Las Vegas was a very small town. The number of attorneys was in the hundreds, not thousands. If there were many specialists in Las Vegas, I can't remember them. Neil Galatz was the only world-class personal injury attorney. Lionel Sawyer had begun to grow to 20 lawyers and was the leading business law firm. I was not connected with the Strip at all. The older firms, that is the Lionel firm and some northern firms, handled all Strip business. I never got any, but I remained intent on building my own law firm because I thought I had the business acumen to build a very financially sound law practice. I knew one incontrovertible fact – the practice of law requires the best talent. I recruited the best and brightest.

*

Bob Maheu, Chief Advisor to Howard Hughes

My most important and interesting venture was representing Bob Maheu against the Internal Revenue Service and the United States for Bob's alleged stock manipulation of the Hughes Air West stock. I was representing several of Irving Haut's clients when the case between Bob Maheu and the IRS came to Irving. Bob Maheu had moved to Las Vegas in 1966 as the chief operating officer and closest aide to Howard Hughes. I'll give you a little background about Hughes to set up the context of my long relationship with Bob Maheu.

When Hughes came into Las Vegas in November of 1966, Las Vegas was bankrupt. Several of the hotels had closed and there was no money. Las Vegas had 70,000 residents and eight to ten hotels, the majority of which were bankrupt. Hughes decided to stay in Vegas and buy every hotel. Maheu urged Hughes to pay all the creditors, even though Hughes could have put the hotels into bankruptcy and eliminated all their debt. If Hughes had done that, what little was left of the economy in Las Vegas would also have been destroyed. That would not have been good for Hughes, nor would it have been good for the town. For example, The Landmark Hotel owed $18 million dollars to contractors. Maheu convinced Hughes to pay off all the construction debts even though Hughes did not want to do so.

Hughes was brilliant and was a ruthless, very wealthy businessman. He moved into the Desert Inn in November, 1966, took possession of the 9th floor, and decided he wasn't going to move out. Howard Hughes was an insomniac. He had the windows covered so that it was impossible for him to see out; he saw no sunlight, and was assured that no one could see in. He lived as a total recluse in filth. He had serious narcotic addictions and did not take care of himself; his hair grew down to his waist and his fingernails got very long.

Even though Hughes was a total recluse, he still wanted to know and he did know about every construction project in Las Vegas – anything that would affect his holdings. He looked at all of the building permits requested in Las Vegas during the years he lived here. He would ask Maheu, "I don't understand this. How did you allow this company to get an increase of three slot machines in its gas station? How did you allow the zoning to go through on this other hotel that is going to be a competitor of mine? How did you allow an automobile agency to be built on that property?" Every day reports were sent to Hughes about building permits, gaming permits, etc. He followed everything down to the most minute detail. As he was a recluse, he could devote 24 hours a day to his psychosis.

The battle between Hughes and Kirk Kerkorian began to escalate. Kerkorian decided he was going to build the Hilton Hotel, originally called the International, off the Strip. Hughes did not want Kerkorian to build the International Hotel because he didn't want the competition. Hughes did everything he could to torpedo Kerkorian's project, including having studies made that showed the damage done to the proposed building site from the bombs detonated at the Nevada Test Site in the 1950s. Hughes tried to prove that the proposed site would not be safe and that once the hotel went over "x" number of stories, it would collapse. The battle between the two continued for some time, but Mr. Kerkorian finally built his hotel.

Maheu was abruptly and publically fired, and Hughes moved unannounced to Mexico. The initial accusation, made by Hughes in a press conference, alleged that Maheu had robbed Hughes blind and the IRS should look into the case. When I first talked to Bob Maheu, he was devastated by the allegations. Hughes was the richest man in the world and Maheu knew that with these accusations, he would be unemployable; he would never get another substantial client. During his years of employment with Mr. Hughes, Maheu had never seen Hughes or spoken to him face-to-face, although they talked nearly every day by telephone. Hughes left Las Vegas, moved to Mexico and refused to talk to Maheu. Hughes claimed he had discovered that Maheu had embezzled money from him, and had made secret deals and stashed away millions of dollars. The IRS was sent to investigate Maheu.

This breach came suddenly, from out of the clear blue. Until that time, Maheu had been trusted with all of Hughes' business, including some very questionable transactions. Hughes thought that money could buy anyone. He had no qualms in bribing politicians via "campaign donations" (before the current campaign finance laws were instituted) or directly. For example, Hughes was incredibly interested in the 1968 presidential campaign, and he was particularly worried about the testing of nuclear devices at the Nevada Test Site and how those tests would affect the structure of his hotels in Las Vegas. Maheu goes into more detail about this in his book, *Next to Hughes*. It's worth looking up to get an idea of what Hughes was capable of. Nixon was Hughes' favorite, but Nixon had taken a position in favor of nuclear testing. Humphrey, however, was not in favor of the testing, and Hughes decided to contribute $100,000 to both the Humphrey and Nixon campaigns (with an extra $25,000 to Robert Kennedy, just in case). The larger donations were divided into two payments, one in cash, the other via check (payable through Maheu's own account).

Maheu arranged a meeting with the vice president (May 9, 1968) at the Denver Hilton Hotel. During this meeting, Maheu told

Humphrey about Hughes' concerns about testing, and his desire to see it end. Humphrey thought that a committee of scientists should be formed (all of whom he knew personally) to explore the consequences of nuclear testing. At the end of their conversation, Maheu told Humphrey that Hughes intended to contribute $100,000 to his presidential campaign. That apparently surprised Humphrey, who was very happy with the support.

Although Hughes was impatient, he went along with the plan, and promised $300,000 to fund the study. He instructed Maheu to deliver the campaign contributions so that both Nixon and Humphrey would be "in his debt." Maheu was given a briefcase with $50,000 in it, and was told that Mr. Humphrey would arrive in a limousine at the Century Plaza Hotel in Beverly Hills, California, for a $5,000-a-plate fund-raising dinner (July 29, 1968). Bob got the briefcase; the limo pulled up in front of the hotel with Mr. Humphrey and his wife in it. Maheu got into the car, set the briefcase down, told Mrs. Humphrey how radiant she looked, and got out of the limo without the briefcase or the money.

At a later time, Mr. Humphrey admitted in his account of the story that he had received the briefcase from Maheu, but there was no money in it. The only conclusion Hughes could reach was that Bob had stolen the money. After Hughes decided to cast Maheu off, this incident was one of the several accusations by Hughes against Maheu. Bob swore to me that he delivered the money, and I believed him. You can reach your own conclusion as to who ended up with the money; mine is that Humphrey got it.

*

The Hughes Helicopter Issue

Another story Bob told me about Hughes' political dealings isn't in his book – for good reason. Now that both men have passed on, however, I think relating it will give you a good idea of Hughes' business practices. I never saw a copy of the memo from Hughes to Maheu about Hughes wanting the Vietnam War extended so that

Hughes could recover his investment in the Hughes helicopter, which had been used in the war, but this is the story I got from Bob:

Hughes had invested hundreds of millions of dollars into developing the Hughes helicopter that had been used in the Vietnam War, and the only way he could recover his investment was for the war to continue and for the U.S. government to continue to buy more helicopters. To that end, Hughes was concerned that Nixon would close the war down, and that the purchase of Hughes' helicopters would cease. Hughes sent Bob a memo which said, in effect: "It's essential that the Vietnam War continue for me to get my investment out of the helicopter. Take $3 million in cash – go to Washington and meet with Mr. Nixon. Give him the $3 million if he will promise to extend the Vietnam War long enough for me to get my money back on the helicopters."

Bob, being the bright man that he was, got the $3 million in cash, put it into the suitcase(s), flew to Washington, checked into The Washington Mayflower Hotel, and stayed in the room for three days, but made no attempt to see Nixon. Maheu returned to Las Vegas, told Mr. Hughes he had made contact with Mr. Nixon, but that Nixon had refused to continue the war and certainly refused the money. Bob returned the money to the Hughes camp. Unfortunately Bob, as bright as he was, and as accustomed to double crosses as he was, did not have the foresight to realize that later he would be a victim of a conspiracy between Chester Davis, Hughes' attorney, and the various Hughes aides to de-throne him.

The breakup of the Hughes-Maheu business relationship came five years after Hughes moved to Las Vegas. Because Maheu never saw or spoke face-to-face with Hughes, Hughes gave all his instructions in daily written memos or on phone lines that were direct from Hughes to Bob. At the end of the week, those memos were picked up and returned to Hughes. What happened to those handwritten instructions is not known to me. The first night I met Bob Maheu, he was paralyzed by Hughes' allegations that he had stolen millions. The next jolt came when the IRS notified Bob that they intended to move into his office and go through all of his files in response to these allegations by Hughes. The large home, planes, and other assets Maheu had access to during his period of employment with Hughes suddenly became financial burdens for him. When I told Bob I needed a retainer, he told me he didn't have any cash. I said we'd work that out later.

Maheu was a peculiar man. He was ambitious but his ambition did not involve greed or a never-ending quest to build a large estate. He lived well. He had several very important talents. He had a great sense of the strengths and weaknesses of all the people with whom he dealt. He had a flawless instinct for determining who was honest and who was not. His training as an FBI agent under Hoover taught him never to leave a paper trail in anything he did.

It's amazing how many people, when their ego is running amuck and they are pulling off a "deal" that has criminal implications, believe that somehow they are invisible or immune. Putting actions in writing is generally a greater liability than an asset, and Maheu understood that one is far better off not putting things in writing. That led me to my first conclusion: there was no paper trail in Bob's dealings with Hughes that could in any way prejudice Bob's case with the IRS.

Bob had always told me that he maintained no bank accounts for which he had the right to sign. I didn't have to worry about a paper trail of checks to come home to haunt him. He wrote no letters. He felt the less you put in writing, the better off you were. He had no foreign bank accounts, and in spite of representing several billionaires during his professional life, Maheu never had an income of more than $500,000 a year. If he had any assets that he concealed from Mr. Hughes, I could not figure out how he could have secreted the funds.

As I looked at Bob's exposure to the IRS, nothing made me uneasy. In fact, when he told me he couldn't pay me because he had no funds, I believed him. That's one instance when not having money was a great disappointment to me. When the IRS asked me for all of Bob's records for the past ten years, I felt very comfortable in giving those records to the IRS because I felt no exposure existed and in fact, I was right because as things proved, Maheu was not in any way vulnerable to a claim by the IRS that he had received income on which he paid no taxes. When Don Skelton of the IRS asked to see Bob's records, I felt comfortable giving him access without a subpoena. Bob didn't know what was in those records because he never looked at them, and 99.99 percent of those records were trivial receipts for airplane rides, dinners, payment to employees and so forth.

Settling with the Internal Revenue Service took 18 years, and that 18 years was spent in total frustration because of Nixon's intervention. Had Nixon not stuck his nose in the matter, the IRS would have completed its audit in a six-month period and would have decided that many of the benefits Maheu enjoyed as a contractor to Hughes were personal income to Bob and, therefore, that Bob owed taxes on that income. Those issues involved the personal use of the Hughes planes, and use of a 10,000 square foot house on the golf course that had been built and owned by Hughes for Hughes' convenience, but which the IRS also determined was for the benefit of Maheu (the fair market value of the "rental" value of that house was charged to Maheu as income). No allegation of income tax fraud was ever made by the IRS against Bob. The income tax liability that it found was no more complex than the IRS might find in 98 percent of those who operate their own businesses.

People ask me what records I keep and my answer is "none." I do not write letters. If I have something to say, I call that person and say it. I do not use e-mail because I believe that people are not able to accurately put in writing what they think or believe to be the facts. I do not know where I bank. I have not signed a check in more than 25 years. I believe the fewer paper trails I create, the better off I am. These are the lessons I learned from Bob Maheu.

Bob was one of the most interesting people I've ever met. He was not an intellect; he didn't have a mathematical or scientific mind, but he had an ability to understand people. He understood what made them tick. He understood their shortcomings and their strengths. He understood how to deal with everyone. Bob Maheu had more understanding of people, their needs, wants and how they reacted to every situation than anyone I have ever known. He never forgot a name; he never forgot that everyone wants to be important. He was interested in all of his employees, where their children went to school, who they were marrying, what problems they had, and what he could do for them. He had an uncanny memory about people. I went to Washington to appear with him before the Securities and Exchange Commission. We got into a taxi. The cab driver said, "Oh Mr. Maheu, I haven't seen you in 20 years," and Bob replied,

> "Oh Bill, it's very good to see you again. My recollection is the last time you drove me across town your brother was in law school at George Washington Law School. How did he do? Did he graduate?"
>
> "Oh yes Mr. Maheu, he graduated."
>
> "And what's he doing now? As I recall you had two or three small children, what are they doing now?"
>
> "Oh, Mr. Maheu, they have all graduated from college."

When we got out of the cab I said, "Bob, it's uncanny how you remember these things. How do you do that?" He said, "I'm truly interested in everybody with whom I deal. I'm interested in their jobs, I'm interested in the people they know, I'm interested in their families, and I make a mental point to take notes on those things. When I can, I use the information. The most important thing to a person with whom you deal is that you recognize their value. If you recognize their importance and their family's importance, they have great respect for you. When you treat them as equals in a deal, regardless of what the deal is, you come out much better." In all the time that I represented him, a little more than 30 years, this attention to detail in his personal interactions was steadfast.

Bob was very simple in his approach to everything. He did not complicate issues; he did not throw temper tantrums. He understood the faults of people and their inadequacies, and he tried to deal with those inadequacies or make sure they didn't adversely affect his business. Maheu might say: "Gentlemen or Senator, whatever your questions are, if I tell you that this is Mr. Hughes' position, that is his position and you can rely upon it. You will not get a letter from him next week saying, 'I don't give a damn what Maheu said, that's not my position.'" Hughes always kept his word because Bob always made sure that he spoke carefully with Hughes before he made a deal, and he always made sure that Hughes lived up to the deal. There were times when Maheu made a deal and Hughes didn't want to honor it, but Maheu prevailed knowing that if he ever broke his word, or if Hughes ever broke his word, the business relationship would end. Bob Maheu had the same ability that my father and Irving Haut had – to simplify every issue, cut through the clutter and come to a very sound decision, which, if not perfect, was as good as you could get. Moving forward was the cornerstone of all three men's beliefs.

Once I'd been retained by Maheu, the IRS called and told me they were going to investigate Maheu from the beginning of his relationship with Howard Hughes. When I talked with Maheu about any potential liability, he assured me he'd never embezzled any money, never misused any money, and that he'd tried to communicate with Hughes several times since Hughes left Las Vegas for Mexico. Bob went on television asking Hughes to call him and work things out, because he could assure Mr. Hughes that none of his money had disappeared or had been misused.

This request never got a response. The agent from the IRS, Don Skelton, informed me that allegations had been made against Maheu for hiding, embezzling and misusing money, and inaccurately reporting his income from Hughes. Skelton wanted to see all the files related to the relationship between Hughes and Maheu. I called Maheu and told him I thought the best way to handle that was to move all of Maheu's files into my office. I could contact the IRS and they could come to my office and examine the files. As I recall, there were about eight 5-drawer file cabinets. Mr. Skelton later moved in and asked if there was anything that I did not want them to see that might be privileged that they would need to subpoena. I told Skelton that Maheu had absolutely nothing to hide, and that his accounting had all been done by people who worked for him. Maheu had not had a personal checking account for at least 25 years, and didn't even know where his funds were deposited; he didn't know how much money he had. He was a very poor administrator of his own funds. Anything they could find they were welcome to take.

The IRS moved into my office and started going through every document. Over a period of time, they went back and attributed income to Maheu that he did not consider income. For example, one question was whether a house that had been built on the Desert Inn Golf Course was there for the convenience of Maheu or the convenience of Hughes. When Hughes moved to the ninth floor of the Desert Inn (in fact, he had taken up the entire floor and most of the eighth floor for his aides), he was very reluctant to communicate by regular telephone lines. He worried that the lines might be tapped, and he didn't want anybody to know his business. After Hughes bought the Desert Inn and the Desert Inn Country Club, he decided to build a house for Maheu on the southeast part of the Country Club, and then dig across from the Desert Inn for a private telephone system that could not be tapped. This way Maheu and Hughes could use the line without fear of having their privacy invaded. The house built was a mansion. Hughes insisted that his chief executive officer live in a home befitting his position in the Hughes empire – it was over 10,000 square feet. Maheu was required to entertain business clientele and host various public office candidates. The house, built to suit, cost well over a million dollars in the late 1960s. Mr. and Mrs. Maheu moved in and entertained often. Maheu was as social as anyone. He had great charisma. When he walked into a crowded room, he captured everyone's attention. He had a walk like Henry Fonda, Gary Cooper, or Jack Kennedy; it caught the eye. He had great presence, and Hughes liked that.

Hughes communicated with Bob in several ways. He talked with him on the phone daily. But when Hughes wanted something done he would write a memo by hand, and it would be delivered to Maheu by one of the seven or eight aides who worked directly for him. The memos gave instructions on what to do about various projects. For example, Hughes told Maheu to buy the Desert Inn hotel because Mo Dalitz wanted Hughes to vacate for the high rollers coming in for

Christmas and New Year's. Hughes did not want to move out. He instructed Maheu to go talk with Mr. Dalitz and buy the hotel, which he did. They communicated half a dozen times a week. There were times when several memos per day were sent, but all of these memos were returned to Mr. Hughes at the end of each week. In my discussions with Maheu, I asked him if he'd ever made copies of the memos from Hughes, because they were in Hughes' handwriting and some of them were rather damning. Maheu said he had not; he'd never thought about needing those memos to confirm anything between the two. The only real records that existed between Howard Hughes and Bob Maheu were Maheu's recollection of specific transactions.

The IRS decided that the specially-built house was not for the convenience of the employer, and that even if it were, the greater convenience was for Mr. Maheu. The IRS felt that the Maheus lived lavishly in the home, had servants and everything necessary to entertain whether for personal or business purposes. At the same time, Maheu had several children under the age of 18 living in the house, which the IRS felt qualified it as a personal residence. The IRS analyzed Maheu's use of a jet and questioned whether the aircraft was for his personal use, or Hughes' use. The IRS wanted to determine whether Maheu should pay taxes on the fair value of all the trips he took on that plane. They decided that a great deal of the travel was personal for Maheu and his family, so they calculated the fair value of that travel and charged Maheu with that value as income.

The audit continued for years. There were times when Skelton would not appear at my office for months, and then all of a sudden he would come back and go through more documents that were related to the financial records between Maheu and Hughes to determine if there was additional income Maheu had not reported. They investigated around the world to determine if Maheu had any other accounts – checking accounts, savings accounts, or accounts of any other sort, into which Maheu could have deposited funds that he had allegedly stolen from Hughes.

Hughes had been asking Maheu for years to become an employee, as executive vice president in charge of everything. Maheu had never wanted to work for anybody as an employee; it had always been his desire to work as an independent contractor. He preferred a retainer, which was $10,000 a week. Of course in the late 1960s that was a lot of money. Out of that retainer, approximately $500,000 dollars a year, Maheu paid the salaries of his own employees, including his oldest son Peter. After covering these expenses, the retainer was not a tremendous source of income for Maheu. He was also required to give up his other clients. At the time, this had included international heavyweights in the shipping business, like Niarchos and others who had employed Bob because of his friendships with Congressional members.

Maheu also got stuck with an expensive boat that was being bought for Hughes. Although Bob had the boat in his name, it was owned by Hughes, and $400,000 was still owed on it. Hughes wanted the boat built for himself, but he didn't want it in his name. Hughes suggested to Maheu that they design what's known as a fisher – a boat that has three engines, two of which run the boat and a third used solely for idling when trolling for fish. It was a 77-foot boat built of wood that took several years to construct. It cost more than a million dollars. When the breakup came, Maheu owed the balance of the purchase price. I went to Los Angeles and made a deal to sell the boat. Maheu lost over a million on the boat.

There were other financial problems for Bob. He had invested several hundred thousand dollars of his own money in deals that were really Hughes' deals, which then failed. Maheu didn't have the money to pay off expenses that were really Hughes' obligations. Maheu had no finance education or experience. After Hughes fired him, Maheu was unemployable. Over a period of time I met with all of those people that had invested money in many deals and convinced them that Maheu could not buy them out – that they should take their losses and move on. My job became solving all of Maheu's problems. Bob was paralyzed by the destructive impact of Howard Hughes. He said to me, "Jim, you do whatever you think is necessary and update me from time to time. The deals that you make I'll be happy to support." I negotiated and finalized every settlement between the investors who

Maheu had brought into various deals because these people had relied on Bob's relationship with Hughes. Over a period of time we eliminated all of Maheu's debts. Bob's real problem was he had no assets. He didn't even have an automobile. He had to move out of the Hughes home. Getting new clients proved impossible. Bob couldn't generate income. I put him on the payroll at the television station to help him.

Agent Skelton moved into my office and was there on a daily basis for weeks. He went through every document and made copies of many. We had no objection because most documents were very routine business receipts and bills. The IRS decided Maheu had received income he didn't report, but there was no fraud. The IRS added up all these perks, for a period of about 20 years, including part time work Maheu had done for Hughes before Hughes came to Las Vegas. The assessment of Maheu's tax bill was $1.5 million dollars. At the time, Maheu was broke. The amount of the assessment was irrelevant – he couldn't pay it. We began to negotiate a compromise with the IRS, under which Maheu would, over a period of time, pay several hundred thousand dollars. Negotiating this was very difficult because there were rules requiring upper-tier government officials to approve any substantial settlement. Local and regional agents couldn't compromise any assessment over $1,000,000. Anything above that amount had to go to Congress. The reluctance of the IRS and officials to compromise on the bill was because of Hughes' political clout, which he used to hurt Maheu. Hughes was willing and eager to use his political weight when he didn't like somebody.

For years the proposed settlement sat dormant. When the IRS informed us that our proposal was not acceptable, I said, "Tell me what to write in this proposal. There's no sense in me continuing to write something if you know from the start that it's not going to be accepted." Skelton and I drafted a proposal that he thought would be accepted. It included payments totaling several hundred thousand dollars. There were politics involved and various interpretations about financial transactions during the relationship between Maheu and Hughes. There were no actual allegations by the IRS of any fraud; yet, as I mentioned, the IRS claimed that transactions between the two of them had created taxable income for Maheu. We disagreed. We fought with the Internal Revenue Service for 18 years before we finally closed the matter. We later found out that there were several tapes released from the latter years of Nixon's administration referring to this case. On one of them, Nixon stated, "Let's get that son of a bitch Maheu. He screwed my friend Howard Hughes and he stole all this money from him, and nobody can find out what happened to the money. Let's sic the dogs on Maheu and see what we can do." Bob eventually paid off the settlement.

*

The Hughes Air West Stock Manipulation Case

Compounding the problem of the IRS audit were the documents totally unrelated to Bob's finances that came from Hank Greenspun and George Crockett. They claimed Hughes owed them for the losses they had suffered when they "dumped" their Hughes Air West stock to drive the market price down, so that Hughes could buy Air West at a low price. When a document from Greenspun was discovered and I showed it to Bob, he said he'd never seen it. I assume he was telling the truth because I can't imagine anyone receiving such a document, reading it, and then putting it in a file that every employee would have the opportunity to see given enough time.

I cannot imagine Bob Maheu being foolish enough to be involved in a stock manipulation scheme for the benefit of Howard Hughes. There would have been nothing in it for Bob, and that certainly was proven because the stock was dumped; Hughes got a better deal than he originally thought, and Bob got nothing. Bob's only reward in this stock manipulation scheme would have been to be accused of a very serious crime. It's interesting to note the arrogance of a human being, who over a period of time, finally comes to believe he is immune from prosecution for criminal acts because he believes himself above the law. I cannot imagine anyone being ignorant enough or arrogant enough to write a letter saying that he might have committed a felony by dumping stock to drive down the price of the stock for another person – that is, Howard Hughes.

When it came to dangerous documents that put the author at risk of serious criminal exposure, Maheu always felt secure because he didn't put anything in writing. He was an honest man and never did anything illegal. But sometimes people write things down that later prove to be damaging. No one ever claimed Bob was dishonest until the Hughes Air West case surfaced. Maheu never kept any documents about any transaction. He felt very confident that the files in my office were unimportant records relating to finance. Unfortunately, he was wrong.

As the IRS was going through all of Maheu's files, they found a letter from Hank Greenspun. The letter said that when Hughes was buying Air West, Hughes was concerned about the high stock price on which the deal was based, and hoped to depress the market at the time the sale closed. Greenspun reminded Maheu that he had been asked to sell much of his stock to drive the price down to lower Hughes' cost of acquisition. Greenspun claimed he had been assured he would be reimbursed for any losses. Hughes closed the deal at a price far less than initially expected. Greenspun claimed he lost more than $100,000 on his stock dump, and told Maheu he was waiting for a check. Greenspun was frustrated that no payment had been made and no one was answering his calls. He asked Maheu to send him the promised funds.

Under previous IRS rules, agents were only allowed to search for and use materials related to the deductibility of expenses and reporting of income. If the IRS found something not related to its task, it was required to disregard it. The rules changed. If the IRS was examining an income tax issue and ran across documents on a separate matter pertaining to criminal acts, the IRS could and would pursue that issue. As the IRS went through Maheu's files, they found the letter from Greenspun asking for the promised compensation. I doubt that Bob ever saw the letter and I doubt Greenspun ever got his money. The issue was not whether Greenspun was paid for the losses he incurred, but rather whether the conspiracy between Greenspun and Hughes to drive the stock value down was illegal. The federal government indicted Hughes and Maheu, but did not indict several other people involved in the conspiracy, including Greenspun.

There were two other primary parties in this stock dump. One was George Crockett, a long-time friend of Hughes. Crockett owned the fixed-base operation at McCarran Field and had been Hughes' friend since the 1940s. The Attorney General's office decided that to make a case against Hughes and Maheu, the feds needed Hank Greenspun to testify. They didn't indict Greenspun, although they called him an unindicted co-conspirator. Because Greenspun died before the trial began, the U.S. attorney decided it needed George Crockett to testify. He too had been asked to dump his Air West stock and was promised reimbursement by Hughes for whatever he lost. Whenever Hughes had flown into McCarran airport in the 1940s, George Crockett and his wife had greeted him and they would have a good time. George had a son with whom I went to high school – George Crockett, Jr. This was how I got to know George, Sr.

At the time Maheu was indicted, he had no money. I was making enough money to eat and pay my rent. My loyalty to Bob was such that I knew I would be the only person to take his case without a retainer, and that I would also be the only person determined to go through the whole case to get him acquitted. After Bob's indictment, my whole life was consumed by the Hughes Air West case. The government has endless time and unlimited money. It is very patient and very thorough, and it built a strong case. There were so many depositions that it took a truck to transport them. For eight months I did nothing but read depositions of people involved, directly or indirectly, with the sale of Hughes Air West. I went through all the documents. Larry Semenza, the Assistant U.S. Attorney at that time, decided the case should move forward against Maheu and Hughes, but that Crockett and others involved in driving the price down, although co-conspirators, would not be indicted.

The case was to be tried in Reno. I rented an apartment in Reno because I knew it would take a month or two to try the case. I would be in court every day and there was no sense staying in a motel. When the hoard of attorneys representing Hughes and I arrived at the courthouse, we were surprised to find that one of the co-conspirators, George Crockett, was not available to testify. Semenza informed the court that Crockett was in Mexico, and although the U.S. Attorney had made every attempt to get him to return to the United States to testify, Crockett had told them he wasn't coming back. Crockett sat on his boat, just far enough off shore so the federal agents and the FBI could see, but not serve him. Because of the legal restrictions regarding bringing in witnesses from foreign countries, the United States was unable to force Crockett to come back to the U.S. to testify. Semenza made a motion to continue the case for at least 30 days while the U.S. tried to persuade Mr. Crockett to come back. Although there were two or three other people involved in this stock manipulation, Crockett was a central figure. Obviously, the federal government felt his testimony was essential to its case. They were particularly interested in the conversations Crockett had had with the Hughes people, and whether Maheu had acted on Hughes' behalf. In response to Semenza's motion to continue the case, I argued that I couldn't afford to come back. I'd spent the last six months of my life – morning, noon, and night – reading depositions and looking at the financials of Maheu and Hughes and Air West. I hadn't been paid anything. Maheu didn't have any money and I had been working gratis 60 hours a week. I couldn't afford to return to Reno when the new trial began. The judge was sympathetic, but he had little choice. The Hughes people simultaneously filed a motion to dismiss, saying that the allegations of stock manipulation, even if true, were not a crime.

Judge Thompson was a highly respected Federal District Court judges. He had dismissed the case on legal grounds, but the Ninth Circuit had reinstated it. The Ninth Circuit ruled the actions of Maheu and his cohorts could be considered criminal under an obscure law. After being reinstated, the complaint and the indictment against Maheu went forward. I drove back to Las Vegas and did not think about the case for a week. Then I started to re-read all of the depositions and review the law to prepare for the trial, which was to resume in 30 days. I had no idea if Mr. Crockett was going to appear at the next trial. I hoped that he wouldn't.

About two or three weeks later, I got a phone call at my office in Las Vegas. The voice on the other end of the line said, "Hello there, Jimmy" (a high school nickname). "This is George Crockett and I need to talk to you about whether I should come back to Vegas and testify." I said, "Well, George, there is NO WAY I'm going to talk to you about that. If you decide not to come back, I could be indicted for interfering with the criminal prosecution. I want nothing to do with this, and I don't want you to call me again. I want you to leave me alone. It's your decision whether you show up or not. You know what's in the transcript. You and your people have gotten copies of everything and you know what you're going to do." George then said, "I really don't want to talk to you about this over the telephone, because for all I know your phone is bugged by the federal government. You know, you grew up with my family and you've known me for a lot of years [I think I was 30 at the time], and I want to do what's right, but I don't want to get involved in this thing." There were notations by Crockett on calls made to Maheu's office, which indicated Crockett called a second time, to say that he had lost $100,000 or $150,000 and he wanted to know when he was going to be reimbursed. Maheu told me that he had never asked Crockett to take the loss, and he didn't even know about it until the federal government got involved. Maheu said he would never have been stupid enough to suggest to anyone that they dump stock to drive down the price. Maheu also swore he never told Crockett to stay away from the trial.

Crockett suggested that I come to the Gulf of Mexico and he would row in to discuss what he should do. He pleaded, "Please come down, I just want some advice. I don't understand any of this; you know I don't have any education about these types of matters. I don't know what to do, and I don't know who to talk to, Jimmy. Please come down so we can talk about it." My ego was flattered. He talked about what a good lawyer I was and what a great relationship he and I had had for 25 years. I thought perhaps I should get on a plane and talk to him to find out what he knew that could hurt Maheu. But I thought before taking action I should go to ask a local judge and friend of mine for advice. I consulted District Court Judge John Mendoza, whom I had known for many years, because I knew that I would get good advice from him. I walked into Mendoza's office and I told him the whole story about Crockett calling me and asking that I come down, that he would pay for my time, and that he just wanted to talk to me to find out my feelings on the strength of the case. I asked John Mendoza, "Should I get on the plane and go?" He told me, "If you go, you're going to end up in jail because no matter what you say to George Crockett, they'll allege he's not at the next trial because you told him not to come back. Even if you go down there and say, 'George, it's your duty as a public servant to come back,' no one will believe you."

Mendoza assured me that no one would believe I'd gone to persuade Crockett to come back. I called Crockett and said, "George, I just consulted with John Mendoza and John says I'd be out of my mind to come see you because no matter what I say to you, even if I tell you to come back to Las Vegas, no one on earth will believe me. If in fact you don't come back to Las Vegas, everybody sitting in that courtroom, including the newspapers and your family and friends, is going to believe you didn't come back because I told you the federal government really didn't have much of a case without you." So he asked, "Is that your final answer?" and I said, "I'm not coming."

Every Saturday morning for many years I had gone into my office to go through the mail, to relax a little bit and give some thought to the previous and coming weeks. One Saturday morning I went to the office and George Crockett was sitting on the front steps. I yelled at him, "What the hell are you doing here? You're going to get us both thrown into jail! I told you I wasn't going to talk with you or give you any advice as to whether you should come to this trial." He said, "Oh Jim, I just have to talk to you." I said, "Well, come on into my office," so he came in. We went through exactly what he did, what he was asked to do, his loss of over $100,000 in the transaction, and that he had been promised reimbursement for his losses. He understood that

Hank Greenspun had the same kind of deal and there were two or three others who did also; none of them got their money.

I said, "Well, George, you need to call a cab, go to the airport and fly back to Mexico and decide what to do. I'm not going to advise you in any matter. Come to the trial or don't, but that's your business – not mine. I'm not your lawyer." He asked me, "Is my testimony very important?" and I said, "Well, it must be – if it weren't, the government would have gone ahead with the prosecution in this case a month or two ago when you didn't show up." George made some excuse about having an infected foot and not being able to come to Las Vegas for the trial. I had no idea whether he was going to appear at the new trial later that month. The Hughes lawyers appeared en masse, and I was with Maheu, not knowing what was going to happen. During the trial opening, Semenza stated, "Your Honor, we can't get Mr. Crockett to come up here. We've had agents down in Mexico and they can see him in his boat; in fact, they wave to him and he waves to them, but they can't serve a subpoena on him and they don't have any way to get him back here. We're not ready to proceed without him. If we had another 30 days, maybe we could persuade him to return."

At that point the Hughes lawyers, who were sitting next to me, knew I was going to protest another continuance. They said, "Jim, the only one who can get this case dismissed at this point is you because of hardship. Obviously we can't get up and say that it's a financial inconvenience to Mr. Hughes because this court knows what Mr. Hughes is worth and that he can come back 100 times without affecting his net worth. You have to get this thing dismissed." I stood up and said, "Your Honor, I can't do this anymore. I've done this twice and it's bankrupting my law firm. I haven't been paid anything for my months on this case. I've paid all the expenses out of my own pocket. When I tell you Mr. Maheu doesn't have any money, I know he doesn't because I've been through all of his records. He doesn't have a nickel, but I've come back for a second time. I've rented a second truck. I've gotten a second apartment. I can't do this again." The judge asked Semenza, "Must you have Mr. Crockett here in order to proceed with the case?" and he replied, "Yes, he's absolutely essential to our case." The judge then asked, "If you are given more time, can you assure me he'll be here?" Semenza said, "I can't assure you, your Honor, but we're making every effort to get Mr. Crockett here. We know where he is, but we just can't grab him to get him to come here." The judge said, "That's just not good enough, Mr. Semenza. If you tell me you can't proceed without him, then I have to believe that you can't. I can't force you to proceed without him. But he's your witness and if you can't get him here, I'm going to dismiss the case."

The case was dismissed. When I went back to my chair, one of the Hughes lawyers leaned over and asked, "Jim, how much money do you have in this case at this point?" Although my memory may be a little fuzzy, I think I had about $155,000 or $160,000 in time, plus my expenses. They said, "Give us the bill." I happily presented them with a bill and I received a check from them for that amount. They were obviously very pleased that I had accomplished what they weren't able to do. The case was never reinstated. It just went away and we all left not knowing what would have happened had we actually gone to trial. We didn't know if the Ninth Circuit would have deemed the allegations a crime. It was a real learning experience.

I learned a lot from Maheu and the Hughes lawyers. One of the most important lessons was that people are really stupid in terms of what they believe they can do that is obviously illegal. People with Hughes' kind of money believe they're bulletproof. Looking back, this stupidity is evident in the existence of documents nobody in his right mind should have written or kept. When I look back over the Maheu/Hughes Air West case, I realize how young I was and marvel at the fact that I was playing ball with all of these big shot Harvard lawyers and experienced Securities people. They regularly dealt with issues that were far more complicated than any I had ever encountered. My youthful arrogance led me to believe that I could actually try that case against the federal government, which had unlimited funds and time to prosecute. I learned my lesson – don't play with the truth, and don't take on the federal government unless you have unlimited resources. In the end, they're going to get their man through persistence and unlimited financial resources.

*

I was in active law practice from 1964 through 1991, although much of the time from 1981 through 1991 was spent in the development of the television station. I never realized how boring and unproductive the practice of law was until I made the transition from practicing law to owning a television station. While a majority of businesses are no more challenging than the everyday practice of law, the television business had all the excitement possible for a young man of 33. My legal training was invaluable in helping me deal with situations in the television business that I'd never imagined could exist.

It's been over 30 years that I've been in the day-to-day excitement of the world of information and the broadcast industry. Every year I speak to graduates of various law schools. I know how hard they've worked to finish law school. I know how difficult it has been for their families to see them study 60 hours a week, to not have time for their children, and to have no life outside the study of law. It is difficult to tell them to consider using their legal education for something other than the day-to-day practice of law. When I graduated from law school, I had no idea that my education would provide me the ability to do anything other than write agreements, settle disputes, and try cases.

Knowing each and every law is of little importance compared to the ability to analyze and solve problems. If I stood in front of the graduating class of my law school and suggested they use their legal education for something other than practicing law on a day-to-day basis, mouths would drop – and yet I feel compelled to do just that. The title of this chapter should be, "The Practice of Law: Not the Best Use of a Legal Education." In my experience, one may be far more successful in ventures that require the analytical abilities honed in law school than in knowledge of the rules of law.

Chapter III

TAKING ON BROADCAST MEDIA

I never had any idea I would enter the telecommunications business. It was a bit of happenstance that set me on a life-changing career path. I was talking with Bob Maheu over dinner one night regarding Hughes' peculiarities about watching television. Hughes paid absolutely no attention to what time of day it was, not having any sunlight in his office or home. Hughes frequently called stations, Channel 8 in particular, and complained: "I don't like that programming. I want you to change it." They would reply, "Well, we're sorry to tell you we can't change that programming. That is CBS programming and we don't have any choice. They pipe it to us and we have to run it." Maheu also had to call Channel 8 and tell them Mr. Hughes did not like the movies it was running. This produced little effect. Hughes finally got so disgusted with the programming that he bought the station.

The FCC's intent in licensing was to ensure local ownership of stations that would respond to the needs of their communities. This meant running stories about local problems and solutions. It would have been beneficial to have an editorial policy for those television stations. The stations in Las Vegas at that time did very little for the community. They concentrated on advertising car dealerships. Hughes had used the television station he bought for his own entertainment and with total disregard for the welfare and needs of the community.

> Hughes owned Channel 8 in Las Vegas and ran it like his personal toy. For example, it was widely reported that Hughes sometimes called Channel 8 if he didn't like the movie they were running and told them to change it, and occasionally called and told the station to run one of the old movies he himself had made years earlier. Not surprisingly, other viewers in Las Vegas did not appreciate Channel 8's stopping a movie in the middle and starting a new one.
>
> Jerry Rourke, Attorney

I understood that FCC licenses were issued for a short period, usually three to five years. During the renewal process, a licensee has to show the FCC that it had participated in solving community problems. I understood Channel 8's license was scheduled for renewal, so I informed Maheu that I intended to file an application for the Channel 8 license. I assumed Hughes would not appear at the hearing. We would be unable to take his deposition about his poor response to the needs of the community, which would cause him to lose the license. Maheu assured me that Hughes would never appear at any hearing before the FCC, but it was always understood that Maheu or someone like him would speak for Hughes, and Hughes' failure to appear would be excused. The FCC had always been comfortable dealing with whoever appeared on Hughes' behalf.

I thought Bob was wrong, but he very quickly convinced me that I didn't know what I was talking about. He went on to say: "You know Jim, there are a whole new set of rules and regulations that have been adopted by the FCC that relate to the local ownership of television throughout the United States." The FCC wanted local people to own local television stations, radio stations, and local newspapers. The FCC had no authority over newspapers, but it could put almost any conditions it wanted onto licensees for television and radio. Maheu explained a new set of regulations that emphasized the importance of local ownership and response to local problems. He suggested that the Donald W. Reynolds license in Las Vegas was vulnerable to attack under the new regulations.

> [Ed] Morgan told Maheu it would not be a good idea for Jim to challenge Channel 8 – Howard Hughes had too much political clout in Washington to lose the station in a license challenge, even if he would not appear at a hearing himself. In those pre-Watergate days there were no laws governing campaign contributions. Morgan had heard of too many briefcases full of cash "contributions" that had been delivered to the Nixon White House and various offices on Capitol Hill on behalf of Hughes for the FCC to ever take the Channel 8 license away from Hughes. Morgan told Maheu that if Jim Rogers were thinking about filing a license challenge in Las Vegas, it would be better to file against Channel 3 than

Channel 8, and if Jim were interested he should come to Washington and talk to Morgan about it.

Jerry Rourke, Attorney

Don Reynolds owned 131 newspapers and was very powerful politically across the United States. He also owned many television and radio stations; he owned the NBC station in Las Vegas and an AM/FM station in Las Vegas; he owned the *Las Vegas Review-Journal*, the most powerful newspaper in Nevada. This concentration of power in one person was something the FCC did not encourage. Maheu suggested that if someone put a local group together and filed an application when the Reynolds license was to be renewed, the government might take the license away from Mr. Reynolds. Maheu suggested that I seek the advice of Ed Morgan, of the firm of Welch and Morgan, in Washington, D.C. Morgan had gotten several clients across the country to file competing applications for licenses as they came due when he felt those licenses could be wrested from their current owners. I went to see Morgan in Washington, D.C. He had been one of Bob Maheu's closest friends for some years; they had been in the FBI together. Welch and Morgan was one of the most powerful and influential law firms in Washington, and Morgan and Maheu remained the closest of friends. Morgan had represented both Maheu and Howard Hughes in various ventures.

I told Morgan that Maheu had suggested I call him about filing a competing application against Don Reynolds of Donrey Media for Channel 3 in Las Vegas. In an FCC comparative hearing, diversification of media ownership was an important factor that would favor a competing applicant without other media interests. I suggested that we, as a local group, would be more suited to respond to the needs of the Las Vegas community. Even though Mr. Reynolds lived in Las Vegas, he never participated in anything related to the community. He was, for all intents and purposes, as reclusive as Howard Hughes. Morgan agreed that the circumstances were not in Reynolds' favor for renewal. I negotiated with Mr. Morgan to obtain a cap on his legal fees. I knew one could be papered to death by big law firms and bankrupted trying to litigate issues. Mr. Morgan agreed to a $200,000 cap. In hindsight, he had to know that once we filed, the Reynolds people would spend every nickel necessary to defeat our petition.

> There was another aspect of the question of Welch and Morgan filing a competing application against Channel 8 that was not mentioned to Jim at the time by either Maheu or Morgan, namely that Morgan had a conflict of interest that would have prevented his firm from filing such an application in the first place. At some point after Maheu had become Hughes' major domo in Las Vegas, he had gone to his old FBI friend Morgan to acquire Channel 8 for Hughes from Hank Greenspun, a close friend and client of Morgan. In a proceeding that raised eyebrows in Washington legal circles, Morgan had represented both the buyer and seller in the transaction. The result was that Hughes bought Channel 8 from Greenspun, and Maheu retained Welch and Morgan to continue to represent Channel 8 before the FCC for Hughes. In short, Welch and Morgan had represented Hughes at the FCC as the owner of Channel 8 from the time Hughes bought the station. When Maheu was very publicly fired by Hughes, out of loyalty to Maheu, Morgan resigned the FCC representation of Channel 8, although Morgan had had no problems with the station and resigning the representation meant a financial loss to his firm.
>
> Jerry Rourke, Attorney

I ventured forth to find a diverse group of people in mid-1971. The license application had to be filed by September 1, 1971, and it was essential that we have a group together to make a bid for Channel 3. We laid out programs that would be developed locally: cooking programs, teaching programs, education programs, and political programs. We promised to be more responsive to the needs of the southern Nevada community than Reynolds. I called upon many friends and we put together a group of 17 people; no one was wealthy, but everyone had lived in Las Vegas for many years and had participated in the political, social, and education processes of the city.

On September 1, 1971, we filed our application for the license of
Channel 3.

> They all went to work preparing the application for Channel
> 3, which had to be filed in less than two months. It was agreed
> the applicant would be named "Las Vegas Valley
> Broadcasting Company," called "Valley" for short. One of
> the first things I did was to arrange for the monitoring of an
> entire week of the programming of KORK-TV, the call sign
> of Reynolds' Channel 3, from a Saturday at midnight until the
> following Saturday at midnight. The purpose was to enable
> Valley to show in detail exactly how much of a typical week
> of the programming of KORK-TV was devoted to news and
> public affairs, locally originated programs, public service
> announcements, and other programming in the public
> interest. The monitoring had to be done immediately, before
> KORK-TV found out that a competing application was going
> to be filed against it and upgraded its programming. A temp
> firm was hired with a team of people who worked around the
> clock preparing a detailed log of every single item broadcast
> over the air during that week and the exact time it was
> broadcast. As things turned out, the log of that week's
> programming on KORK-TV came in very handy later on for
> a purpose that was never dreamed of at the time.
>
> Jerry Rourke, Attorney

It was suggested to me during this process that I would no longer
be able to find clients in southern Nevada and that I should leave
town, dismiss the application and disappear. I decided we would stay
in the fight and we would go forward with the licensing procedure.
Although the license application was filed on September 1, 1971, it
was not until 1978 that the case got to the United States Supreme
Court. The Supreme Court decided it wasn't going to hear an appeal,
even though the application had been appealed to the FCC and the
district court in Washington on several occasions. In each case, the
decision was consistently in our favor, and we moved forward as the
potential licensee.

> Once there were two mutually exclusive applications on file
> for Channel 3 in Las Vegas, by law the FCC was required to

examine each application to determine whether the applicant was qualified to operate the station. If both parties were qualified, the Commission was required to conduct a comparative hearing to determine which one should be awarded the license to broadcast on the frequency. Given this legal framework there were two kinds of issues that could be raised in the FCC hearing – qualifying issues and comparative issues. Qualifying issues would go to the question whether a particular applicant had the necessary minimum qualifications to be a licensee of the Commission. Comparative issues would go to the question of which of the two qualified applicants would better serve the public interest as the licensee of the station. In such a hearing process, the comparative issues were necessarily conditioned upon both applicants being found qualified.

Since Valley was an applicant for a new station, there were many qualifications it had to meet. Among these were engineering questions such as whether Valley had a studio, a transmitter site, and equipment sufficient to put the required television signal over the entire city of license; financial questions such as whether Valley had sufficient financing available to build the station, put it on the air and operate it for three months; and questions regarding programming, staffing and all the things necessary to operate a television station.

Western, on the other hand, was an existing Commission licensee that had operated a television station on Channel 3 in Las Vegas for many years, so none of the basic qualifying questions Valley faced applied to it. The only qualifying question Western faced was whether it had complied with the Communications Act and FCC policies, rules, and regulations during its last three year license period. Once the Commission completed its review of the two applications it would issue an order designating the applications for a hearing on the issues it had found. The parties would then have a specified period of time to petition for the addition of other issues against the opposing party.

Jerry Rourke, Attorney

Unbeknownst to us, at the time we filed the competing application in September of 1971, the Reynolds people had already committed financial suicide by engaging in a series of ethically dubious acts, which were coupled with acts that would make it impossible for their license to be renewed. All of their injuries were self-inflicted. Had the Reynolds people not been engaged in a practice called clipping and then lied about their participation in those activities, we never would have prevailed. But as with most people who make mistakes, Reynolds compounded those mistakes by not telling the truth about how they happened. Had he told the truth, the court might have excused the misconduct and renewed their license.

Clipping – stealing from the networks to run local ads – was something all the Las Vegas stations did, but Channel 3 had lied about their actions and those lies cost them their license. An explanation of clipping: in a half-hour show, there will be a break at 28 minutes into the program so that NBC and the local television station can run up to two minutes of advertising. There are four 30-second ads in 30 minutes. In syndicated programming, even though the station has purchased that programming, the syndicator has the right to run additional ads. The network that broadcasts the programming retains one or two (or even three) ads for itself. The local station gets what remains. Some of the Las Vegas television stations decided that rather than run two minutes of ads, they would run three or more. To do this, the stations started to run ads at 27 minutes after the hour, cutting off a minute of network programming. Through this practice, the local station got an extra minute of advertising in each half hour. This practice distressed those who were watching the programming, but not to the extent that viewers complained.

A professor at UNLV looked at this practice and was upset by the amount of clipping. The clipping was most obvious to the public during sports events. It is difficult to determine when an inning in baseball will end, because three outs can involve 19 batters. The television network will wait until the third out and then go to break. The two teams playing knew there'd be a two-minute break; play would resume after the advertising spots ran. Local television stations decided they preferred three-minute breaks after baseball innings. When the teams returned to play, the stations continued to run ads for another minute. When the local station came back to the game, a player might be standing on 1st base, or there might already be one or two outs. No one in Las Vegas knew how this had happened, and it was very irritating to local viewers. The UNLV professor started to track these instances, and discovered that all of the stations in Las Vegas were clipping. He filed a complaint with the FCC alleging that this practice was illegal, misleading to the public, and in effect prioritizing ads over programming.

> Clipping of the NBC network feed by KORK-TV in Las Vegas was brought to the attention of the FCC during the station's last license period in a series of events which did not involve Jim Rogers or Valley in any way, and of which Jim and Valley had no knowledge at the time the competing application was filed. Donald Hendon, a professor at the University of Nevada Las Vegas, sometimes watched baseball games on television. It annoyed Dr. Hendon that after a station break KORK-TV would often return to the network broadcast after play had resumed in the game – with a runner on second base, for example. During the World Series in 1970 Dr. Hendon noted the details of clipping by KORK-TV, which prevented the audience from seeing part of the play of the game. He then wrote a letter to the FCC complaining about KORK-TV carrying local commercials that interfered with the network broadcast of the games. Over a period of months Dr. Hendon and other viewers wrote to the FCC on three other occasions about KORK-TV's local commercials interfering with the broadcast of network programming.

> When the FCC received Dr. Hendon's complaint about KORK-TV's failure to return to the network coverage of World Series baseball games on time because of the carriage of local commercials, the FCC followed its standard practice. The Commission wrote to KORK-TV and asked the station to submit to it a written response to the complaint. Western responded, among other things, that the problem was caused by employee error, that it was KORK-TV's policy to "limit the length of commercial announcements to the available break time" and that the interference with the World Series game was an isolated incident. The station said nothing about carrying extra commercials in its network availabilities.

When over a period of months, the FCC received a second, third and fourth letter of complaint about KORK-TV's carriage of local commercials causing it to fail to return to the network feed in a timely fashion, the Commission followed the same procedure. Each letter of complaint resulted in an FCC letter to KORK-TV with a request that the station submit a written response to the Commission explaining the circumstances surrounding the interference with the network programming. In response to each letter KORK-TV continued to blame others for the problem, variously complaining about operator error in switching between the network feed and the local commercials, or about advertising agencies which were "not always careful about meeting precise commercial announcement length requirements." The station continued to claim that it limited the length of commercial announcements to the available break time, and said nothing about carrying extra local commercials.

In keeping with the FCC's standard practice, the four letters of complaint about KORK-TV and Western's four written responses on behalf of the station were routinely placed in the station's license file at the FCC to be considered by the Commission in connection with KORK-TV's next license renewal.

Jerry Rourke, Attorney

The FCC decided it would come to Las Vegas to look at the station's programming, and do something about the clipping. This investigation began after we had filed our application for the television license. None of the other stations considered this practice terribly wrong or felt the public was being cheated. Nevertheless, each of the stations paid a $10,000 fine. Because we were the competing applicant for the Channel 3 license, we highlighted the fact that the Reynolds people had defrauded the network by stealing its time, which violated basic FCC principles, and that this activity should cause Reynolds to lose his license, as it was an act of dishonesty.

The Reynolds people first took the position that they hadn't done anything wrong, that the decision to clip was made by an underling, and they were going to stand by it. We took a deposition from Mr. Reynolds about his programming, in which he said he knew nothing about the station after the case had been going for four fours. Ed Morgan called me and said he'd received a call from Reynolds' lawyers. Reynolds wanted to settle the case, and had a proposal. Ed told me, "Jim, they are willing to give you 50 percent of the station if you dismiss the complaint." And I asked, "How much would I have to pay for it?" He assured me that Mr. Reynolds said I wouldn't have to pay anything up front for it, but they'd work out a final price. I asked, "How am I going to pay for it?" He replied, "Well, I asked Mr. Reynolds' people that and they said it didn't make any difference. You could pay it out of cash flow, and if there isn't any cash flow from the station you don't have to pay anything. You'll never come out of pocket."

We discussed it with our lawyers and decided that 50 percent of a viable, lucrative station was worth a lot of money, so we agreed to make a deal. We agreed to Reynolds' proposal to take the 50 percent stake and the documents were drawn up and ready to be signed when our lawyers got a phone call. Reynolds' lawyer said, "Here is the signing procedure. The documents will be placed in Room B at the Sands Hotel. Mr. Reynolds will be in Room A and Mr. Rogers will be in Room C. Mr. Reynolds will sign the documents first, then Mr. Rogers will sign the documents. It's a 50/50 split, but Mr. Reynolds will never speak to Mr. Rogers.

> Koteen offered Valley 50 percent of Channel 3 in exchange for dismissing its competing application for the station. Bernie Koteen made this astounding offer without giving any explanation as to why Western was willing to give half of a network affiliated television station to a competing applicant for nothing, without a fight, and without Reynolds or any of the senior members of his organization even taking part in the negotiations.

> It was obvious to Valley that Western must be in big trouble of some kind at the FCC, but Valley had no idea what was involved. Not being inclined to look a gift horse in the mouth, however, Valley decided to accept Koteen's offer on condition that Valley would be able to back out of the deal if Western's renewal application, amended to include Valley as a half owner of Channel 3, were not granted by the FCC.

Valley's condition was accepted, the deal was made and the attorneys for the two sides then set about preparing a settlement agreement ending the case and merging the two applicants into one. Western also imposed a condition which Valley accepted: a bizarre arrangement for signing the merger agreement in Las Vegas under which each side would send the people who were going to sign the agreement to a certain room in a certain hotel but at different times – so that the people signing for Western would never even have to meet the people signing for Valley!

In such strange fashion on March 3, 1972, the merger agreement was signed by Western and Valley. On June 1, 1972, the agreement was filed at the FCC with an application to assign Channel 3 in Las Vegas from Western Communications to a new company owned equally by Western and Valley.

Once the merger agreement was on file, Valley did not have to wait long to find out what Western's problem at the FCC was all about. Within ten days the FCC issued an order designating Western's renewal application for a hearing on two issues to determine whether Western was qualified to remain a licensee of the Commission. The disqualifying issues were first whether Western had engaged in fraudulent billing by the "clipping" of network programming, and second whether Western had made material misrepresentations, i.e., had lied, to the Commission about its clipping. Under FCC procedures the Commission's Broadcast Bureau would present the Commission's case on the disqualifying issues against Western in a hearing before an Administrative Law Judge who would decide the matter and issue an Initial Decision.

Jerry Rourke, Attorney

We signed the documents and submitted them to the FCC. During litigation, a very peculiar situation arose. The FCC asked us if we realized that by joining Reynolds, who was being investigated for clipping practices on the current license, we would lose along with him (or win with him, which wasn't likely). When that happened, we said to the Reynolds people, "We're out. We don't know what problems you have, exactly, but if you're going to go down the tubes because of the things that you've done, we're not going to go down the tubes with you. We're out of the deal." At that point we sat on the sidelines and the FCC proceeded with its actions against Mr. Reynolds. Eventually the lower court found Reynolds guilty of not being forthcoming and truthful with the FCC, so the FCC took their license away.

The litigation between Reynolds and Valley lasted from September 1971 until August 1978. The details of that litigation probably are not very interesting because much of the maneuvering by the Reynolds people to postpone what was an inevitable decision were more procedural than substantive. We finished the proceedings before the hearing judge, who was considered one of the most competent judges in the FCC system, and everyone knew the hearing examiner's decision would be upheld. All of the Reynolds maneuvers were made simply to defer what everyone knew would be a final decision. In August of 1978, after seven years of litigation, I came back to the office and there was a note from Ed Morgan that simply said, "You've got it." I called Ed and asked, "What did I get? When did I get it? And how am I going to use it?" He replied, "We have finished all the litigation, have prevailed over Mr. Reynolds, and you are now the licensee. It will take about a year for the decision to come back down through the court system, but a year from now you'll be on the air." I asked, "Oh my God, what am I going to do at that point?" and Ed said, "Two things: we will work out a deal with the Reynolds people to hire their employees because Reynolds wants to make certain their employees don't lose their jobs; secondly, Reynolds will agree we can stay in their building for a period of time until we can build our own. You'll take over all their agreements for programming, and there will be a very easy transition. The public will probably see absolutely no difference in the station."

> It was immediately upon release of the DC Circuit Court of Appeals decision that Ed Morgan called Jim Rogers and said: "You've got it." The case wasn't over yet, but Morgan could see the handwriting on the wall. Reading between the lines of the Court's opinion, further proceedings in accordance with the opinion could only mean for the Commission to accept Valley's new bank letter, acknowledge that Valley now had

enough financing to pay Alta for Western's share of the access road, and thus rule in Valley's favor on the site access issue, the only issue remaining in the case against Valley. The inevitable result would be a grant of Valley's application for TV Channel 3 in Las Vegas.

Jim Rogers' problems were not over; they were just beginning. By the time the DC Circuit ruled, the litigation over Valley's application for Channel 3 in Las Vegas had gone on continuously for some seven and a half years. Given Western's enormous pleading effort to defend its license, Welch and Morgan had long ago used up the $200,000 retainer Ed Morgan had quoted to Jim Rogers at the start of the case. Since Valley now stood to become the owner of the NBC affiliate in Las Vegas in large part because of his firm's efforts, Morgan thought it would be only fair for Valley to renegotiate their fee arrangement. Jim did not see it that way. A deal was a deal. Besides, and more importantly, Jim now faced the problem, and enormous cost, of actually building a TV station in Las Vegas and putting it on the air. Valley simply did not have any more money to pay to Welch and Morgan. The result was that Valley and Welch and Morgan had a parting of the ways.

Jim employed the Washington firm of Dow, Lohnes and Albertson to represent Valley before the FCC, and the firm assigned one of its partners, Domenic Monahan, to handle the case. Dom was an experienced Washington communications lawyer well known and liked at the FCC. He entered into discussions with the Commission's staff while the Western petition for certiorari was pending at the Supreme Court. Dom argued, and the Commission recognized, that no purpose would be served by ordering a further hearing for Valley on the issues remanded by the Court of Appeals once the denial of Western's renewal application became final. To order a further hearing for Valley would mean that Western would have to remain the operator of Channel 3 for an indefinite period after the denial of its license had become final, which would clearly not be in the public interest. Instead Dom negotiated a settlement with the FCC, under which it was agreed that Valley would be granted a temporary license to put a new station on the air on Channel 3 in Las Vegas if it could do so in 60 days. If Valley could not put its station on the air in 60 days the Commission would invite new applicants to file for the facility. If Valley succeeded in putting a new station on the air in 60 days, it would be granted a permanent license.

Jerry Rourke, Attorney

Ed had prophesized: "It may take you 20 years to realize this, but 20 years from now you will realize that this win will completely change your life." He was right. It gave me a new energy to practice law; it gave me an outlet for my thinking; it gave me new, tremendous political influence in the local community and throughout the state. This event was the major turning point in my life.

*

Problems with Fellow Shareholders

None of the 17 individuals in our group owned more than 10 percent. Some owned as little as 2.5 percent. Their obligations were to pay their share of the legal fees, which were capped by Ed Morgan at $200,000. From time to time we needed money and some of the owners could not contribute. We had to handle that in different ways. The lengthy license acquisition process had caused problems we had never anticipated. We had three or four owners in their 70s at the time we filed the application. When we filed they had been eager to get involved in the business, but during the seven-year application period they aged and couldn't be active in the operation of the station. In addition, people originally brought into the group for their money and community involvement wanted to be bought out. When we formed the group, I tried to make sure we would not have a divisive group of shareholders. Even though we were all friends and very compatible in 1971 when we filed the application, people change over time.

When we entered litigation and began to strategize for proceeding against Mr. Reynolds, the lack of sophistication among our group made it impossible to create a plan of attack. We had veterinarians, teachers, authors, people in gaming, an accountant, and an individual who had formerly been in the radio business. We were a group of novices taking on a giant. It proved difficult to keep the group together. Part of the group went together and decided to sell their interests because they wanted out. According to the original agreement, all 17 shareholders were required to consent on all deals. Even those people with two percent of the shares had to agree. We would either stay in it all together or get out altogether.

Over the seven years of litigation, the group became very fractured and contentious. Those of us who were friends found relationships were very strained, and on several occasions I learned that attempts had been made to sell out. In each instance, I had to tell everyone that unless I agreed to a deal, no sale could go through. We were able to proceed financially, but had Morgan not agreed that legal fees be capped at $200,000, we would have run out of funds quickly. I have no idea how much Reynolds spent on legal fees, but the amount of paper work filed by his lawyers could have filled a bus. Every motion filed required a response by Morgan. His billable hours probably exceeded $800,000. Morgan kept his word; he never asked for more money.

We'd filed the application for the Channel 3 license in September of 1971. I was 33 years old and far more ambitious and reckless than I was competent and smart. If I'd thought long and hard, I'd have realized that I would never beat Mr. Reynolds. His vast holdings and undeniable clout with public officials were assets in his favor. Generally, one of the first rules of business is to stay away from newspapers and television stations. If I hadn't been so naïve, I would never have filed an application for the license.

On October 31, 1979, we took possession of KORK-TV in Las Vegas, Channel 3, and changed the call letters to KVBC. We kept all the employees; the public never knew what happened other than the call letters for the station had changed. When we took physical possession of the station, we found it was a disaster. Las Vegas was ranked 129th out of 209 markets. A financial statement we found indicated in the previous year the station had grossed over $1 million dollars. We thought that was absolutely wonderful – until we learned the Reynolds executives had long believed they were going to lose the license, and had therefore stopped putting any money into the station.

The station was still using film, not tapes, for all of the programming it ran. When Dick Gregg, the sports anchor, went out to shoot the film, he brought it back to the station to develop and then probably ran that film the next night or the next morning. The station had 55 employees. We had made a deal with Reynolds to use his building until we could build our own. His building was about 6,000 square feet. Compared to the 65,000 square feet we have now, saying the quarters were cramped would be a gross understatement.

It was a grim start. The equipment had come over on the Mayflower; there was always something wrong with it. When we began to operate the station in 1979, it was only by accident any viewers watched. Channel 8 had a 67 percent share of viewership, and ours was significantly lower than 15 percent. If someone happened to watch Channel 3 it was by accident because they were jumping from Channel 5 to Channel 8 to Channel 13. We were awful. Reynolds leased us his studio for a while after we won the case, but there were important assets missing. We didn't realize there was no signal from NBC in Los Angeles. We estimated what renovations and upgrades were necessary and we borrowed $1,500,000 to purchase equipment. It became apparent, as is usual when estimating the cost of major projects, that we had underestimated the real costs and would certainly need more funds.

The initial loan funds went into our new building's remodeling, and for eight months following the granting of the license, we continued to broadcast from Reynolds' tiny building. As we remodeled, we discovered that purchasing and moving station equipment from the Reynolds building was a waste of time and money. It was so outdated it was literally useless. We borrowed additional money for equipment replacement. Unfortunately, that was the time when usury laws had just been abolished. Carter was the President of the United States and interest rates went to 21 percent. We were paying 3 percent over prime. The loan suddenly jumped to 24 percent interest a year. For a period of time we simply couldn't make the payments. The lender agreed to accept monthly payments at 10 percent interest, plus part of the principal; the remaining 14 percent interest was added to the note. In other words, we'd started the year owing a million dollars of principal, and by the end of the year we owed $1,300,000 in principal on top of the 24 percent interest we were already paying. When they deferred that interest, we were paying interest on interest. We were running like hell to stay in one place. And the harder we ran, the further behind we got.

The station had grossed a million dollars the year before we bought it. Its ratings were rock bottom. NBC was not doing very well; local programming wasn't worth much, and our news was deplorable. We started with a business that was sick and dying. I decided we had to be competitive. Rather than have 12 people producing a mediocre news program, we needed to expand our news. Mr. Reynolds had allowed the station to go into total decay. I assume he thought that if he lost the station, his successors would inherit something of little value. He was right; it was almost worthless when we took over.

From the time we went on the air in 1979 and for the next several years, things were terrible and we had to keep going back to our shareholders for more money. In addition to construction costs, we were putting money into new programming because the station had very little worth running. Those shareholders who didn't have the money couldn't pay and others didn't want to put more money into the project. Fortunately, the purchase agreement stipulated that if additional funds were necessary for construction or operation, shareholders would meet a call for funds or take a reduction in their interest in the company. That caused a lot of grief and hostility toward me as we continued to need more and more money to build the station. We always came up with the money when we needed it, though.

Many of the investors, who had no experience operating a business and didn't understand income, investment, and operating costs, panicked and wanted out. I felt if we stayed with it, eventually the station would be worth an incredible amount of money. In addition, we had gone on record with the FCC that we wanted to satisfy the needs of the community rather than make a profit, and there was a three year prohibition on our being able to sell the station.

There came a time when the hostility in the boardroom, toward me mostly because I was calling all the shots, was overwhelming. I'd slowed down my law practice to spend my time operating the station. Mike Gold (who had been in the radio business for some time) and a few other shareholders, who by then were in their 70s, decided I shouldn't be the president anymore. They tried to sell the station unbeknownst to me. The information got back to me and obviously, because I had veto power, I stopped it.

The shareholders' frustration became so great they hired an attorney to see if they could oust me as the president and chief operating officer, or at least take the operating power away from me. They retained attorney Lou Weiner to, at the very least, reign in my aggressive expansion. Louie came to see me, and said, "Jim, you have 17 shareholders, and 16 of them are mad as hell and want you out. They think you're recklessly aggressive, that you've got too many people involved in news and that you're spending too much money on equipment. The station is in bad shape and not yet competitive. They don't think you'll ever make it."

I thought about the trouble the other shareholders were causing, and suggested that Lou come on board as their representative. There wasn't a smarter businessman in Las Vegas. He understood the dollar better than anyone. I said, "You come on board and you and I will run this place. If after six months you think I'm crazy or don't know what I'm doing or have unsound plans, I'll quit and you can take over." Lou thought that was a good idea and that it would at least stop a lot of the chaos. Everything we were doing required 17 people to vote in agreement, and when things dragged I generally just did what I thought best without waiting.

Lou took the place of the shareholders as members of the board. He came on as a member. In 1981 he bought a doctor's stock and became a shareholder for 1 percent. After six months, Louie and I had developed a tremendously close relationship. We spoke the same language; we understood investing money was essential in projects of this sort. If we had to borrow it at outrageous interest rates, we did so because we wouldn't consider going forward without being competitive. Some two or three years after Lou and I partnered in running the company, we got a phone call from Sam Lionel – an outstanding attorney with total credibility. His law firm was and is the largest and most prestigious in the state. Louie had known Sam for many years. Sam said, "Lou, you and Jim need to come down to my office." There he told us, "Your 17 shareholders have come to see me. They believe the two of you have taken over the station, contrary to the needs and desires of the other shareholders. They have asked that I represent them against you to get you out of the company. Let me give you some good advice. These people are good, honest people. They've worked hard for their money, but they really don't understand operating a business or the need for capital. They don't understand the things that you two take for granted. I only see one way to resolve this. – You need a divorce – You need to buy them out!"

We didn't have the money to buy them out, but if the station continued to grow as we thought it would, we could have the company redeem their stock and pay for it out of company funds over a long period of time. We decided to let the shareholders decide on a fair price, telling them: "You pick the price because you've shopped this thing all over the country. You pick the price and we pick the terms, and the higher the price, the longer the terms we're going to need, because obviously if you pick $2 it's going to take us twice as long to pay for as it would if we paid $1." The negotiations went very well, and Lou and I agreed to buy out all of the other shareholders. We made deals with various shareholders, who owned from one percent to eight percent to ten percent. We bought every one of them out.

We continued to have problems. Lack of revenue was solved to some extent thanks to the tremendously rapid expansion of Las Vegas. When we bought the station, it was the poorest earning station in town. Rates for television advertising are based upon the number of people viewing the ads, and those rates are fairly fixed. You've got to produce 24 hours a day of programming. You can produce that at a relatively low cost when you are the 130th market. Before the city's rapid growth, our first several years were a real struggle. None of us took any money out of the company. I spent 80 percent of my time at the station without pay. There was no money to pay me any salary; for a period of time we were really under water. Because of the interest rates, the harder we worked the less equity we seemed to have. We had a national sales rep in New York who called me and said, "You know, you haven't made a payment on our commissions in about a year." When I told him I didn't have it, he said, "We believe you will be a success and we have no doubt you will pay your bills. We've watched you grow and have total faith in you." I said I appreciated his support because without that we simply couldn't make it. When I told him I'd pay him as soon as I could, he not only accepted my promise, but said, "I'm going to put a check in the mail to you for $400,000 because we believe in you." If he hadn't done that, I would've been busted.

Once the revenue started to climb, we were able to renegotiate our loan and reduce the interest. The station started to become profitable in the late 1980s. I was spending all my time on the station. In 1986 my law firm dissolved and each of us went our own way. I moved to the television station and took two or three young lawyers with me. We remodeled the upstairs of the building and I practiced law part-time; the rest of my time was spent developing the station. We fell into a very lucky spot being one of the first stations to buy *Wheel of Fortune* and *Jeopardy* – we were the station that *Wheel of Fortune* and *Jeopardy* built. At that time they'd been running during the day and had not done well. They decided to move to evenings, so we bought them. We paid about $125 a week for each of those programs – not very much money considering that we pay $40,000 a week today for those same programs.

NBC started to get stronger and stronger, and as NBC strengthened, so did we. We'd put a lot of effort into news programming and were able to bring on some very talented reporters and anchormen. Slowly but surely, the station captured the number one slot in the market. NBC grew very strong, the station became stronger and more profitable, and those profits were split between us. In 1987 or '88 I decided it was time to expand – I love to build, and I enjoyed increasing our territorial involvement. In July of 1989, I decided to look at Yuma, Arizona. Bates Butler, who was the U.S.

Attorney for Arizona, had a construction permit from the FCC to build a station in Yuma but decided that he couldn't build the station. He'd already gotten several extensions and his license was going to expire on October 1st. I talked with Bates and told him I didn't know how we could build a station between July and October, but we would pay him $40,000 for that license and go from there.

We began the construction of a building designed to be an affiliate on the chance we could bring ABC into the market. The NBC station in Arizona had been owned by the same family for 30 years, and the CBS station was located in El Centro, California. We bought two acres of land, started construction and hoped we could get on the air by the deadline. We called ABC about becoming its affiliate. They weren't quite sure if Yuma was in the United States. They had heard of Yuma from movies, but weren't overly interested in a presence there. Nevertheless, they decided to come take a look. They came to Yuma, walked around the property, and asked, "When do you have to be on the air?" We told them we had to go on by November 1st at 7:00 p.m. and they asked, "How are you going to build a building between now and then?" We replied that construction was underway and pointed to our building. Their response was: "You mean to tell us you built for an affiliation that you don't have and may not get?" I said, "Well, my only two choices were build it and pray, or not build it and lose it." They agreed to take us as an affiliate, and we raced to complete construction.

On November 1st at 6:30 p.m., when we flipped the switch to see if everything was working, we found we didn't have any power in the antenna. These antennas are 300 to 500 feet tall – not an easy fix. We had an engineer, Frank Haynes, who had an uncanny ability to trouble shoot issues like that, and Frank said, "I think I know where that short may be in that tower – let me go check." Thirty minutes before we were required to go live, he climbed that tower and actually found the short. Just 15 minutes before our construction permit expired, we went on the air. If we had gone back to the FCC and said we needed another ten days, we probably would have gotten it, but we ran it this close and were able to get it done. This accomplishment indicates either great stupidity or brilliance on our part, and a willingness to take chances. We had a lot of money in that building and equipment. Had we not become an affiliate, we would have lost it all. There would have been nothing to program at that time.

Once we got the Las Vegas station moving forward, I was interested in buying the NBC station in Reno. I felt if we had a northern station, we could cover the entire state politically and economically. We might be able to bring the state closer together, and if we broadcast southern Nevada news in northern Nevada and vice-versa, we could get additional viewers that no one else had. We would be one of the few companies in the United States that owned stations covering 100 percent of its state's population. I'd made several unsuccessful attempts to buy the Cord Foundation's NBC station in Reno. I had also filed a competing license application, but wasn't able to pursue that. Eventually the Cord Foundation, which owned Channel 4 in Reno, decided to take bids and sell the station. I think there were eight or 10 bidders. We reasoned that having a station in Reno would actually add value to the station in Las Vegas. We bid a rather substantial amount, around $25.5 million, which, looking back, was far more than it was worth. We based our bid on cash flow for the previous two years, which was inflated because of political revenue for the national and local elections. We won the bid, but spent a lot of time digging out of that. This brought our holdings to two NBC stations and one ABC station.

We developed a close relationship with General Electric and the Vice Chairman of General Electric, Bob Wright, who later became the President of NBC. Because of that relationship, we were able to help NBC and the other networks eliminate some financial and syndication prohibitions. Wright asked me if there was anything he could do in return, and I suggested we would love to get rid of ABC in Yuma. We thought having another NBC station would be much more useful. The affiliation was exchanged; the NBC station became ABC and we became NBC.

*

Back in 1981 we bought a building in North Las Vegas, on Foremaster Lane, that was about 17,000 square feet. It had been a roller skating rink used by kids from Rancho High School when I was young. I don't remember exactly what we paid for the building, but it wasn't very much. We redesigned the floor to accommodate our 55 employees, commercial shoots, and so forth. Of the 17,000 square feet, we only used 11,000 feet. The day Ed Morgan called me to tell me we'd gotten the Channel 3 license, I said to him, "What have I gotten? What am I going to do with it?" That was an off-the-cuff statement, but I had no idea or understanding of the impact and power of a television station. I was later able to learn how much power and influence I had gotten.

Over-the-air television in Las Vegas was more successful than other areas of the country because cable was not a competitor. There had been a long-running war between the Greenspuns and Reynolds about who was going to get the cable system allocation for Las Vegas. That fight really was to our benefit, because for a long time the cable penetration, while it may have been 15 percent or 20 percent across the country, remained at about three percent in Las Vegas. The only television game in Las Vegas was the three major networks during the first ten years we had the station, none of which had ever been aggressive in editorial comment. That left editorial comment and public service and education television wide open for us. General information came from newspapers. Unfortunately, most Nevadans didn't read the newspapers and didn't pay attention to television news.

When the networks began a nightly news program, they only did 15 minutes. They were concerned they might not even be able to fill 15 minutes. CBS and Walter Cronkite decided to do a one-half-hour news program each night. There was extensive discussion in the television business about whether the public would be bored and whether there was enough news to fill a half hour. When we began operating the station in 1979, the television stations in Las Vegas had a morning news program, but nothing until the nightly news at six o'clock. The remainder of programming was soap operas, game shows, and other programs of that ilk. News took a back seat to all other programming. Television was all fluff.

At the time we began operating the station in 1979, Las Vegas was the 129th market (out of 206). Las Vegas might have been ready to become a boom-town, but it was not yet there. The station had inherited 55 employees, and a great number of them were sales people. Some were management, but few were in the news. The news department, as I recall, had only about 12 people and those 12 people did a lot of ripping and reading, i.e., they took what other people produced including national, regional, and international news, and rebroadcast it. I believed southern Nevadans should know what was going on regionally, nationally, and internationally. I still believe it is a local station's obligation to inform and educate the people of southern Nevada about issues that affect their lives. I found that even though the Las Vegas station was doing a half hour of news a night at six o'clock and another half hour at eleven o'clock, local television spent much of its efforts following police calls. If there was a rape, robbery or a murder, local news responded. Television news was exciting, but had no real substance.

TV sensationalism abandoned any obligation to the public to inform and teach. It took shortcuts and produced flashy, non-substantive garbage. That was distressing to me. I thought television had done a very poor job of meeting its obligation to the public. News is very expensive to produce. That's why you don't find large news staffs in small towns like Helena, Montana, or Pocatello, Idaho, or Yuma, Arizona, which are markets with very limited revenue. Large markets, those above 100, usually generate enough revenue to have meaningful news programming.

Las Vegas continued to do better. I was able to buy better and more equipment. We never thought of being second rate and we never bought second-rate equipment. Any time Sony developed something cutting edge, we bought it. We didn't have any obligation to maximize the bottom line because we didn't have shareholders to satisfy. As the station improved, the market grew from 129 to its present standing of 40. By 1986 the station was doing very well, and allowed us to expand

into northern Nevada, Arizona, New Mexico, Idaho, Wyoming and
Montana. I believed we could put all of the stations together and
develop an intermountain television network. Because we didn't have
other shareholders, we could do as we wanted and, in keeping with our
obligation with the FCC, we would serve the public interest.

> I was working at Channel 8 at the time; it was the dominant
> local station, the news was number one. After Jim bought this
> station, within a couple of years there was an energy that was
> clear. You could feel it coming from the station. We were
> always watching other stations to see what was going on and
> boy, there was something going on here.
>
> The next couple of decades was a battle between Channel 8
> and Channel 3. They'd be number one for a while and then
> we would be. It was largely because Jim was not an absentee
> owner. He lived here; this was his community, this was his
> town. He knew people. When he went out, he was the
> representative of Channel 3 and people would talk to him
> about the station. It really became a wonderful battle that
> really improved the quality of journalism in this town.
>
> What Jim did was bring the level of broadcast journalism up
> at this station, which pushed Channel 8 even harder and back
> and forth. So the public really was served. Jim invested time
> and energy – but more than that, he invested his reputation.
> He lived here.
>
> Bob Stoldal, Executive Vice President of News,
KSNV Channel 3, Las Vegas, Nevada

In 1995 we purchased the NBC station in Pocatello, Idaho, which
covers that state's eastern half. In 1996 we bought Helena, Montana,
and we built the NBC station in Casper, Wyoming, which covers the
entire state. Our Arizona station covers a very small percentage of
Arizonans because the Phoenix station, one of the finest in the
country, covers five million people. We're a small player in Arizona, a
good sized player in Wyoming, a small player in Idaho, and a big player
in Nevada. We felt that our first job was to satisfy the public needs of
our communities, and that's what we set out to do.

When we bought the station in Idaho, we wanted to become active members of the community. The Idaho station would probably not be profitable, but because Las Vegas was so profitable we could support the operations in Idaho, Wyoming, Montana and western Arizona. We gave money to schools in Montana and Idaho. We developed scholarship programs at the University of Idaho.

> I'm on the board of a group called Valley Pride [in Pocatello], which actually was started by Jim; it was an idea of his. Something he said actually gave it its name: years ago, he used to have Saturday morning phone calls when he first bought the television station here, with leaders of the community and folks in our company. And he got so frustrated one time with what was going on, that he said, "Don't you guys have any pride in your valley?" That's the way Arlo Luke tells the story (one of the old timers here in town).
>
> We back projects – we give people with great ideas help with their projects to come to life. Last year we built Brooklyn's Playground. In one of the worst economic times ever, we built a $600,000 all access playground. One little girl, Brooklyn, has spina bifida, and her dad was pushing her in the swing once and she fell out, so he started looking into these all-access playgrounds, and came to Valley Pride looking for help. I saw his presentation at a volunteer symposium the spring after I got here, and I knew I had to get involved. I found out when they were having their board meeting and crashed it and said, "I've got to help you guys build this thing." So our unsold inventory helped raise funds. We raised the $600,000 in one year, and opened the playground last fall, one week before the snow came. It was a great thing and that's what Valley Pride is about. I don't know if Jim knows he was the inspiration for that group.
>
> Shelley Goings, General Manager, KPVI, Pocatello, Idaho

Television has provided us the ability to provide financial support to students. For a period of ten years, we gave $500,000 a month ($64 million to date). The drop in the economy cut down our giving, but in time we'll return to our previous levels.

*

During the period from 1981 thru 1996 when Lou died, he and I ran everything informally. Our minute book did not have one single page in it. Lou would lend me money or I would lend him money but we never kept documentation. Our meetings were informal. The Board of Directors meetings had no records. We ran the company by going into each other's offices and saying, "What do you think of this? Okay, let's do it!" or passing each other in the hallway or talking at lunch.

We were good managers. We hired the best people and we treated them well. We paid good wages and believed the last thing you should do is negotiate your people down to the lowest possible salary. If you do that you will get the lowest possible production and certainly very little creativity. Our personnel have been strong and outstanding leaders in our industry. There were times when we had financial shortfalls because the station had lost ratings or the market had turned down. In each case, Lou always stood with me. When we got into an adversarial situation with outsiders, Lou stood by. He called me the greatest negotiator he'd ever seen, a great compliment to me because Lou was as smooth and as smart and as cunning as anyone I have ever known. He was also the most honest and forthcoming person with everybody.

Louie came to me two or three years before his death and said, "Jim, you need to buy me out." I said, "It doesn't make any sense for me to buy you out. I don't want your stock." He said, "No Jim, you have to buy me out because you don't want to deal with my children after my death. You don't want them to become your fellow shareholders; you need an agreement that upon my death you will buy my shares." I was very reluctant to get involved in such an arrangement because bad things happen and you can become adversaries rather than partners.

We handled the issue this way: Louie had lawyers from southern California come see us. They met with Lou and me and said they'd been asked by Lou to prepare a buy/sell agreement that would take effect on Louie's death. Lou said I would find the agreement was very fair. I told the lawyers: "Let me tell you something – Lou Weiner and I, over 20 years, have had the closest relationship of any two business partners, or father/son team, or any other type of relationship in the history of mankind. I will not allow this agreement to become adversarial, so here's what I'm going to do – whatever you prepare, I will sign. I have no intention of reading it. I don't want Lou to believe I am questioning his honesty or his integrity or his intentions. Do you understand that?" They said yes.

Several weeks went by and they came to the office and said, "Here's the agreement we've prepared for Lou. Lou believes it's very fair to you, and he would like you to read it and sign it." I said, "Well, I won't read it, but I will sign it because I know how Lou has treated me all these years and I have no reason to believe it would be anything other than absolutely fair." I signed the agreement, Louie signed the agreement, and I stuck the document in a file. Lou died in February of 1996. Louie kept his word – he made me one hell of a deal, didn't put me under any great strain to make payments on the stock, and his 30/31 percent of the stock was transferred to me. His children were the beneficiaries of the agreement; they came out very well. Certainly, I came out as well as they did. The agreement for the stock buyout was actually a long term arrangement to benefit his children. The children came to me and said they didn't want the long-term buyout, and they would discount the note I'd signed if we could pay cash immediately. I bought out Lou's heirs.

I am now the sole owner of the company and have been since 1996 (with my wife, Beverly). We have no other shareholders. This has made it very easy for us to take chances and do what we wanted, rather than do only what would make a profit and pay dividends to the shareholders.

*

The Las Vegas Radio Station

There came a time when the FCC rules and regulations allowed a television station in a market to own a radio station. A radio station became available in Las Vegas and I bought it to support the news programming of our television station. We lost money every month I had the station. But as fate and luck would have it, there was a group that understood radio broadcasting far better than I, and that group came to me and offered to buy the station. Their offer was $17 million. I had paid less than $2 million for it. I thought I had died and gone to heaven. My daughter was then my business lawyer and I called her and told her of the pending sale. She, along with her brother and sister, having bought into the radio station initially, each received a portion from the proceeds of the sale. Fortunately the deal went through and each of my children got checks for $1.4 million.

> When we started [the radio station], it was "news talk" reflecting the station and had another vehicle to get news out. That went okay, but not great. We started incorporating a few different talk shows, which were phenomenal. They were extremely involved in the community and they did a lot of activities; they had good public response. We had some crazy shows – one with Dave Ramsey (the money guy). I think the radio station started falling away from [Jim's] vision because we started getting crazier talk shows that were great for ratings, but had nothing to do with news. It became entertainment. As it became more and more popular, it just moved away from what Jim wanted to do. He sold it off.
>
> Michelle Sanders, Accountant,
> Intermountain West Communications Company

*

Over the years I've made mistakes – some of which almost cost me everything – but I learned something from each of them. As Channel 3 became very strong financially, I thought branching out would be a good idea. I bought several television stations without close examination of the business. I was always convinced that if somebody else was failing in a business, I could make money. My failure to thoroughly examine the history of the business was a serious flaw.

I got caught in a bidding war with several other people who were interested in buying the Reno NBC television station. When we went through the station in Reno we were convinced that it was so poorly run that we could take that station and quickly turn it into a profit maker. We were wrong. The station was far behind the times. It still ran news in black and white when every other station had color. It did not have cameras that developed a picture immediately. The station had to send its film to Sacramento to be developed. The stories that Channel 4 ran were all at least a day late.

I thought that we, being the smartest people in the world, and having turned the worst station in the United States, that is the Las Vegas NBC station, around, could take over Channel 4 in Reno and make it profitable. We took possession, remodeled it, and spent a lot of money. I probably paid twice what it was worth. We paid $25 million dollars for a property that was worth $15 million. I'd thrown away $10 million dollars. If I'd been more thorough in my analysis, I might not have bought it. If you make that kind of mistake, you have no choice but to get yourself out of the hole.

Over the next several years we invested money in the Channel 4 building and the equipment. To give you an idea of how cheap the previous owner had been, when we went into the hallway next to the newsroom, I said "Why is it so dark? There are light bulbs up in the ceiling, but only one of them is on." Cord's employee said "Mr. Cord would not allow the operators to have all of those lights on at one time." The news product was about as bad as it could be. It may have actually been worse than the news product at Channel 3 in Las Vegas when we began to run that station. We turned it around, and eventually Channel 4 became the leader for news in Reno.

Another mistake I made, from a purely financial standpoint, was not to keep *M*A*S*H* as one of our syndicated programs in Las Vegas where we began operation in 1978. It went to Channel 5, then an independent station, and they ran it over and over. Las Vegans loved it. They watched it and bought the products advertised during the program. *M*A*S*H* was the program that made Channel 5 a financial blockbuster.

As we continued to develop throughout five western states, we were mindful of television's political influence. We were aware of the influence we could exert and the power we had to make life better for everyone. When I look back, this was a series of miraculous wins. We were always fighting against the odds, not only from the first venture in Las Vegas but every one after that. Louie used to say, "You know, Jim, you and I aren't really very smart and we're not overly talented. We don't have great business acumen, but we sure as hell are lucky. We both live in a town that has made us rich. We got involved in television purely by accident by filing this competing application for the station in Las Vegas, and through a whole series of quirks in the law we ended up owning it. And then Las Vegas started to grow, no thanks to us, and the market became a monster. We were standing in the outfield with our gloves up and the ball just fell in. We have money because we are far luckier than anybody else. We need to be mindful that we are lucky and that no action of ours, no brilliance on our part, accounts for our success. We didn't invent television, and we didn't invent how the affiliates work; we didn't invent how licenses were granted by the FCC." I've always remembered this.

Chapter IV

Growing Up and Out:

The Expansion of Valley Broadcasting

We pride ourselves in doing accurate, thorough and important news. We take no pride in running programming that has no substance. We have made every effort in the last several years and will continue to make every effort to remove meaningless programs. We will continue to expand relevant news and editorial comment. I have always viewed television as the arena for public service, for being able to inform and educate the public on the issues important to all of us. I have always been open-minded in recognizing the opinion of others. It's been my policy to let everyone have their say and to listen to them very carefully. Whether Republican, conservative Republican, tea party, flaming liberal – no matter the political stance – I believe every one of those viewpoints has some merit and it's important that all of those perspectives be presented to the public by our television stations.

It's been a profitable and substantive relationship our company has with NBC. We're proud of that relationship being in its 33rd year. We are also pleased that *Wheel of Fortune* and *Jeopardy* have done so well for us. But as pleased as we are about the programming we purchased, our mission still remains to provide the states of the intermountain west with programming that improves the lives of all viewers.

My job as chairman is to support my president and our stations. The most important people are those who put our product before the public – the news people. My every effort is to make them look better, to give them the best equipment possible and make them more creative and less afraid to try new approaches. They are pushed to be bold and aggressive in their actions, knowing they will have my support. We are not a company run from 500 miles away. We are a company whose bosses are 20 feet away, and we make decisions very quickly.

One time my chief engineer, Frank Haynes, came to my office and said, "I have 'x' company on the phone [we were going to buy several million dollars' worth of equipment] and he wants to know how long will it take me to get a decision on our purchase." Frank Haynes told me what he wanted to do, and I said fine; I didn't know anything about engineering but because I relied upon his expertise, it was his decision to make. That is the way we have always done business. We don't do things by committee; we don't have meetings with every group in the station every time we have an issue. My goal has always been to distill everything I want done down to 30 minutes of decision making. If I can't make a decision in 30 minutes, something is terribly wrong with the situation.

*

Taking Care of Employees

> Jim is a straight shooter; he's going to tell you what he thinks. He's very up front, but he's also a very caring person. He comes in and he'll ask about your family. He wants to know how everyone's doing. I myself have been extremely active in a few different things and Jim has always been very supportive.
>
> Michelle Sanders, Accountant,
> Intermountain West Communications Company

I have always surrounded myself with the best people. When we entered the television business, it was my opinion that the station could only succeed if we hired the most talented employees and paid them well. The number of employees in our stations increased from 55 people to 535 when we added other stations. We sought the best and we got the best because we paid them well and treated them fairly. I've never chiseled any employee on salary or benefits. I've always believed that if I took care of our employees, they would take care of me. Our employees are experts. All of them are creative.

I learned a lot from my father, and I believe that much of my company's success stems from his approach. Early in my career I had several discussions with him about managing people and projects. One of the concepts he pushed was informality and a reduction of barriers in communication. Too often people view the structure of a project as one divided between management and labor: those who do the day-to-day work and those who do the planning. This approach does not work. Any division between different groups of workers is non-productive.

The chief executive is not necessarily the most important person in an organization. One's position on the organization chart should have little relationship to the money he or she is paid. There was a long period of time when our news anchors made more money than the president of the company because those anchors had a greater effect on our income than did the president. Station managers may be paid $150,000, but a top salesman might be paid $250,000. A news anchor like Matt Lauer has an audience of 25 million people and sells his network's products. He obviously has a tremendous effect on the profits of companies that advertise on NBC.

One of the biggest mistakes executives make is to negotiate the salaries of those who work for them to the lowest amount possible. Chiseling the last dollar out of those who report to you will eventually cost you tenfold the money you think you're saving. An underpaid employee will cut his production by more than the salary saved or leave to take another job. Don't ever believe that all of your employees are not aware of what every one of them is paid, and don't believe that your employees don't know what your competitors pay.

I believe the best managers are those who walk around to manage. It is essential that management have direct contact with all employees, and that all employees feel comfortable speaking to them, and that those discussions make the employees believe the managers are genuinely interested in them. There must be an open and cordial relationship between management and labor. That relationship begins with the employer talking to the employee about subjects not related to their jobs.

> It's been really tough around here the last few years financially, but as long as we know what's going on, it's easier to accept. There have been cuts, no pay raises – but there

hasn't been a time where we didn't know. He lets us know: "This is where we are; this is what we have to do to keep going." There's no surprise or shock or false anticipation. He says, "This is what I'm trying to do to make it better for us" or "This is what it's going to be." We know what to expect and everything is very straightforward. And that makes a difference whether people stay and if they feel you're being honest with them.

We have our Town Halls where they give us all the information they can; as a manager I know there are things that you just can't share. I just take things I hear in stride. Because Jim has a philosophy of being straightforward, there must be a reason they did not share that with us. Employees may look at that differently, but I think if it's information that can be shared, it's shared. And that keeps people feeling in the know, comfortable about where they are and whether there's any security in the job.

Michelle Sanders, Accountant,
Intermountain West Communications Company

In every one of our stations, we have found there are those who simply cannot wait to talk to the competitors about what we are doing. I've always been open with the employees and have tried to keep them in the loop on the company's progress. But I've told them, once they start to give our competitors the information we've confided in them, the communication will cease. Cutting off the lines of communication injures both the employer and the employee. Unless a project must be kept under wraps until the day it's shown to the public, I make every effort to ensure the employees know what the company is doing. I don't always tell employees about all the specifics because I don't want our competitors to create something better. I do try to tell the employees what our future is because I want them to feel secure in their jobs.

Often my management team has been appalled at my openness. That was never a problem because our competitors were never able to adjust to our plans. Too many managers are afraid of getting too close to their employees, believing that the employees will take advantage of the situation. You must communicate with your employees. I do believe that the general health of the company should constantly be explained to the employees – even if that explanation includes telling them that the company is having serious financial problems.

> I've always felt like when management has a plan, they let us know what the plan is, and that's nice as an employee to know where your company is headed. He told me a story early on that really stuck with me. He has a reputation for his rules, certain things he's very strict about, eating in the newsroom and things like that. He can be tough at times, and I think that some people are just intimidated by that. I've always found that if something is on your mind or he has something on his mind, it's an honest conversation, straightforward, and I think that he respects that, and I think that's completely understandable. He's an interesting guy to be around; he's got a lot of stories, so I always find my time with him enjoyable.
>
> Jim Snyder, Journalist, News Anchor, Channel 3

We've spent hundreds of thousands of dollars sending the children of our employees to college or trade school. It's good for the company; it's good for employee morale and it's good for the students. No one can operate a business without the loyalty of the employees. Employees must be your partners; they must feel they have a vested interest in the outcome of every activity of the company. They must feel that you trust them and that you rely upon their integrity and good faith. Your employees must believe if they tell you something that you're going to listen. You may not agree with them or come to the conclusion they'd like, but it is incumbent upon you to make them feel they're part of your thinking.

It is incumbent upon owners and managers to work as hard, or harder, than any of the employees in the company. No one employer can take full credit for a company's success. All of the fortunes that have been made in this country are the result of the work of a multitude of the company's employees. I'm a very demanding employer, but I demand simple things and I'm very consistent. I like order. I do not like to find junk strewn all over an employee's office. I believe that's a good indicator of how they handle their business and mine. I don't want a mistake hidden under a pile of papers on someone's desk.

I do not allow anyone to call me Mr. Rogers. I insist on everybody calling me Jim. I believe that being formal creates a barrier between people. Loyalty is very important, and it must be a two-way street. I expect our employees to be loyal to the company and in turn, I expect the company to be loyal to its employees.

LOYALTY CANNOT BE BOUGHT – but it should be rewarded. It makes no difference how high the salary or how many the perks, if an employee is not loyal, you cannot buy his or her loyalty. Loyalty, as much as competence, keeps the project together. When times get tough, loyalty more than competence will save the company. Loyalty has kept a group of people with us for many years without contracts; they trust us to have their best interests at heart and vice-versa. The managers of our stations have been with us 15 to 20 years. No one has ever had a contract, and no one has ever asked for a contract. We communicate on a very regular basis face to face; we try not to do business by telephone or memo or e-mail. I don't use e-mail because I don't think anybody can really express what they think in an e-mail. I insist that everyone talk directly either by telephone or while looking the other person in the eye.

No one should be terminated for making a mistake; perfection is not a standard requirement. The most damaging mistake employees make is that after making a mistake, they don't tell the people above them. Hiding a mistake is the ultimate sin. When I started to practice law, my senior partner told me the problem with young lawyers was not that they made mistakes, because all of them make a lot of mistakes. The problem was they make a mistake and then cover it up. I am not outraged at somebody who makes a mistake. I ask, "Why did you do it? Can we fix it? Let's fix it now and move on." Employers make just as many mistakes as their employees.

I make a point of knowing as many of the people in the company as I can. As I've gotten older my memory for names has gotten weaker, but where I still have the ability I try to remember everybody's name and their spouses' names. There is nothing more important to a person than being acknowledged and appreciated. It's always been our company policy to reward those who do well for us. If you stand behind your employees and you push them and make them feel appreciated, everyone will be a winner.

*

We had barely begun broadcasting when we realized we were desperate for programming that raised the awareness of Nevadans to our commitment to help solve Nevada's economic and social problems. There are a few different methods we've used to do so. Early on, I decided to do editorials. The contents of the first editorials were pabulum. But the preacher in me took over, and I started getting stronger and stronger with my opinions, especially those that involved political figures.

> [Jim] is the only TV station owner in Nevada that I know of who would personally editorialize, just like newspapers. Other TV stations should do that, but they don't. He has done that for years. I think that's wonderful. He's trying to create a public TV station in the sense that he's trying to get away from as many network programs as possible.
>
> Harry Reid, U.S. Senator

The editorials began in late 1979 and continued for several years. My family had lived in Las Vegas since 1951 and I thought I understood the nature of Las Vegas and the nature of the state, and therefore thought myself qualified to give an opinion on the various issues of Nevada. I did editorials once a week for several years. We began to get traction and increased editorials to twice a week. I think they showed a whole new role of local television.

As Las Vegas continued to grow and I was no longer involved in the day-to-day politics of the state, I lost track of the important issues and the important people in Nevada. Knowing that an inaccurate or unfair editorial can do harm to the person discussed, I thought it essential to be very careful about what I said. If you're wrong in an editorial, apologizing and trying to make things right doesn't work very well. I never wanted to hurt anyone, and therefore I stopped doing them. I don't know exactly how many of them I did, but it was somewhere between 150 and 200. I felt it was important for us to be out front, not because my opinion was the best, but because we hoped the editorial would stir thoughtful consideration of the issues.

You may recall the CBS program *Point-Counterpoint* that Shana Alexander and James J. Kilpatrick did on CBS. She would present a position and he would respond to it. My second wife, Janet, a very good lawyer, very articulate and very knowledgeable on political issues, decided we should do a *Point-Counterpoint* on Sunday evenings. Over this period of time, Janet and I got so involved in confrontations that the public began to react. We also developed other programs to stimulate the thinking of our citizens. We are always looking for new, engaging shows that will interest the public.

> Jim is a news junkie; he watches the news a lot, and he watches every point of view, and I think he wants his station to become principally known for news. I used to go on *The Agenda* once in a while; then I began doing editorials two nights a week. That's a more interesting story, how that happened. Jim called me on the phone and asked, "Are you ever going to run for political office again?" and I said no. He said, "Why should I believe you?" I explained that I liked my life, seeing my family, working on things that interested me, and not feeling obligated to work on things that other people think are important. He called me back later that day and said, "Are there things you wish you would've said when you were in politics?" And I said, "Of course. There are things I wish I would have said and done, but I was ambitious and measured in almost anything I said. I wish I would have said this and that. I was too careful."

> He told me to come down to the station the next morning; he came down to the lobby and took me to Lisa Howfield's office [station manager]. She was sitting there talking with somebody and Jim told him to get out. He said, "I believe in the first amendment. I'm not going to tell you what to say, you can say whatever you want. When do you want to start?" I said, "I have no idea what you're talking about." Jim said, "I need an editorial board. I need you to get on TV and say something. You'll be on the six o'clock news. Say whatever you want. You don't have to run anything by me. I won't

comment on what you say. I just have one thing that I hope you do – I hope you piss a lot of people off. I want you to be provocative." I looked over at Lisa and it was obvious she was surprised and had no knowledge of this.

And that's how the *Weekly Reid* started; 90 seconds to say whatever I want. He wants his station to be a place where people talk about issues that are relevant and things people care about. He's tired of a lot of the programming that's profitable – he thinks it's silly and he wants to get rid of them and just have local news programming. I've talked about how our tax system is ridiculous; most of it was adopted in the 19th century, and we want to have a 21st century economy. I've talked about the north/south issue, how northern Nevada has taken advantage of southern Nevada, not-withstanding that we have 75 percent of the state's population and that this amount of the state budget comes from the South. I've taken specific parts of state bills that have been proposed and criticized the sponsor – on mental health, on guns, some other social issues. So I'm trying to be as controversial as Jim suggested; he thinks it is fun. I'm trying to develop that skill – to enjoy rousing the community.

Rory Reid, Attorney

When I stepped down from the NSHE chancellor's office in 2009, Josh Griffin, who had been the lobbyist for the higher education system, suggested I get on Twitter. I'd never heard of Twitter. I joined a few years ago and started to Tweet about what I believe to be critically important issues. We have about 3,452 followers, but the number of followers is not as important as our ability to read those Tweets on the air. Rather than me doing an editorial once a week, I now read a part of the Tweet on the morning news at about seven thirty a.m. In many cases, I read the entire Tweet to fully explain the point.

He was really supportive in my last campaign. The mining industry was just funding the hell out of my opponent. I think for people he does believe in, he could not be a more loyal supporter. He ran a series on the mining industry (on Twitter), and I knew they weren't going to like it. I appreciated how he stood firm, ran the story with the support of his staff, and I think really helped us change the (time) – like it or not, those people are not like us (educated people), and they get their information from the nightly news. By profiling that series, and then standing firm when there was backlash from the mining industry, he helped deliver our message. It really made a difference. He's really been a critical factor in the passage of this legislature (which is going on right now in the legislature). This is another instance of him standing up for what he believes in. I love those values. He is able to withstand pressure that other people wouldn't be able to handle, and for the right reasons. He truly believes in what he's doing.

Sheila Leslie, Former Nevada State Senator

Our company has been actively engaged in supporting education. I spoke with the leaders of the higher education system and informed them we would be happy to do Public Service Announcements about the higher education system at no cost. We filmed several Public Service Announcements (PSAs), broadcast them, and found they had little effect. We then merged the concept of the PSAs with the Tweets, believing that rather than just a talking about this course or that course at the university, we would have the Tweets written so someone could read them and learn important facts about the information discussed. The Tweets are three or four paragraphs and never more than a page. They can be read quickly and understood easily. To date the most important Tweets have dealt with the funding of the higher education system, the inequitable division of funding between northern and southern Nevada, the question of tenure, and questions about the future of Nevada's public education system. I think the Tweets read very well. They show there has been substantial thought given to every issue discussed. In most instances, I am the author, although I've frequently called on people in the university system, including the chancellor's office, and requested they write a series of Tweets on any aspect of education they choose.

What's interesting is that I got on Twitter because I knew all the legislators are on Twitter and all of a sudden I found Jim on Twitter, which was funny because you wouldn't think someone in his age bracket would be. But I realized he was still engaged – just this time in writing – and he was Tweeting about the governor and the performance pool. And then I saw him Tweeting about how tenure and faculty were the problem with things not changing and that pissed me off – so I contacted Jim and asked, "What the hell are you writing about. Are you talking to faculty? Do you even know what's causing the problem?" And he said, "No, but none of you seem to be doing anything so I'm Tweeting to piss you off."

That's when he asked me if I would be willing to write some Tweets, so I could Tweet about CSN [College of Southern Nevada] and about what the problems are in terms of things changing. I wrote some stuff for him and tried to explain to him that it's not really tenure that is causing the problem; it's seniority that's causing the problem. You need some sort of system at the lower end of the tenure track that protects those people from the senior faculty at the upper ends of the tenure track.

And so, he did re-Tweet a lot of the stuff I gave to him, but he also kept a lot of it for his own reference. If he were going to talk to Mike Richards or Neal Smatresk, he could go in with an informed perspective and tell them that they really needed to get the senior faculty on board with whatever the policy was, as opposed to saying, "We need to get rid of tenure." That way he could understand where the logjams were, where the pushback was coming from and understand how he could help empower newly tenured and untenured faculty. They were in a department with a lot of old-timers.

Sondra Cosgrove, History Professor,
College of Southern Nevada

One of the most interesting subjects in the Tweets is the question of whether Nevada's two major universities, UNR and UNLV, could continue to grow as research universities. The man on the street generally believes that research costs a lot of money and creates no return. Nothing could be farther from the truth. Public universities across this country have seen state support of their systems drop from 80 percent of their budgets to between zero and 20 percent. The leading public universities saw this coming many years ago, and knowing they had to develop other sources of revenue they got into the research business, which has proved to be very profitable. For 25 days, we did Tweets that dealt with the development of UNLV and UNR as research institutions. We hoped they would have a positive effect on the Nevada legislature. We argued that Nevada had to support these institutions not only financially, but support the concept of developing research institutions. As the private sector becomes more active and becomes more interested and understands the importance of UNR and UNLV becoming research institutions, the private sector will continue to invest more and more money in the system.

> I think his presence on Twitter is very interesting. You don't see many people of his caliber writing on Twitter. I think that's interesting because he could be recognized – which is what media is all about. It's not as easy for people to grasp. It's weird at first. I had to have someone come over and tutor me. But he's been on there for a long time, and he uses it to get attention to and promote his ideas. You don't see many people like that on Twitter. You see advocates, you see politicians congratulating themselves all the time, but you don't see any in-your-face advocate saying exactly what he thinks. He's not afraid to take heat, and good for him.
>
> Sheila Leslie, Former Nevada State Senator

When I left the chancellor's office, I thought I might go back to doing editorials. I think those wear thin pretty quickly, though. I think the public would rather have one of the anchors reading the facts and opinions in the Tweets rather than see my face twice a week. We haven't had any complaints about reading the Tweets on air, but we have had positive comments from the people who have said: "I saw this issue spoken about on the air this morning. I didn't realize that was a problem. Let me ask you a question about how that works." If someone writes us on Twitter or just writes the station in general and asks a question about anything that we've said, we respond.

*

Our company's future in television broadcasting depends on having a product different and better than every other television station's product. Even though there are five or six television stations in Las Vegas, only two will survive. The only way to survive is to be able to do something different from what our competitors are doing. I have been preaching for years about the 30-second sound bite. News programming must be substantive. I've begun to drop syndicated programming to shift to a more news-oriented format, but those are major changes that will take years to complete. We've pushed news. We know we have the most talented and competent news people in the state. We believe this team could compete nationally against any other news team. Our reporters are very smart and very well educated. We have hired the best people from the best colleges. We want our news staff to be able to understand the issues they are covering. We want them to cover issues that are more complicated than who ran a stop light or who shot whom or how firemen put out a fire. We believe our theory of providing more and more local news will be successful.

> I think that Jim is a visionary, and people recognize that. Citizens are changing the way they get their news and television is changing dramatically. Everyone's talking about the melding of computer and television and plugging one into the other, and at that point the networks may not need local affiliates as much as they need them today. Between the changing technology and Jim's passion for covering local and state wide politics and issues that matter to Nevada, he's made the decision to reformat the station, get rid of all the insubstantial programming, and just concentrate on local programming about local issues.

> He was quoted in the paper recently as saying the other part of that is strategy, positioning the station to be *THE* voice for local news and local issues, so that no matter what happens with the network relationship, the station will stand on its own. The way things are going, that sounds like a really smart idea. Now of course, we're all wondering "How are we going to fill all that time?" But that's what they're working on with the construction, and Bob Stoldal and Jim are planning together on what will be a newscast, what will be more like a talk on *The Agenda*, like Jon Ralston's show, and what the mix will be. It's exciting to be in a newsroom that's expanding

right now because of what happened with the economy and what's been happening to broadcasting for the past 10 or 15 years (newsrooms have been shrinking). To be in one where they're knocking down walls and expanding – it's exciting. It's pretty rare.

Jim Snyder, Journalist, News Anchor, Channel 3.

News programming must be relevant for a substantial amount of the state's residents. ABC has canceled one of its soap operas and CBS has canceled one or two of its soap operas. I hope that NBC cancels *Days of Our Lives*. I would like to see soap operas go away completely. They are inconsistent with the type of programming we should provide to the community. MSNBC has been brilliant about gathering some of the smartest, best-educated, most experienced journalists I have ever seen. Rachel Maddow is a Rhodes Scholar and has a Ph.D from Oxford. Lawrence O'Donnell is a graduate from Harvard. As you go through the entire group of NBC commentators, you find they are a first class group of journalists. MSNBC took the liberal presentation of news in response to FOX's decision eight or 10 years ago to be the voice of the conservatives. I think MSNBC provides a hell of a service with its programming. I want our company to go one step further than MSNBC and FOX by giving both sides of every argument.

One of our most important functions in the community is to be a mouthpiece for local issues. We're always willing to promote charitable organizations, do stories on local issues affecting kids, high schools, and so on. We established a community outreach position to keep up with all the organizations that needed our help, and to try to efficiently and regularly bring forward their issues and pleas for community support.

When I was doing the Crystal Darkness campaign, we came down to Las Vegas. The first station we came to was Channel 3. He went on record and said we'll play this video (an anti-drug message) this was really what we needed to get out here, we're losing too many of our kids to methamphetamines. He also said we will do a roadblock [when every station airs the same program at the same time] and play it from six-thirty to seven; just pick the day. We picked a day in May (it was towards the end of the school year).

Because Jim Rogers said yes, every station in the state of Nevada said yes after that. Every newspaper in the state said yes. All I had to do was use Jim Rogers' name and they were on board. He really stuck his neck out for us when we were trying to do something positive that had never been done, ever in the country (a roadblock) and it was so successful in Las Vegas and so successful in the state of Nevada that because he owned all the NBC stations in the state –it grew, went all over the United States.

I am very thankful that Jim had this passion for helping people and serving his community. At the time it was 17.9 percent of juniors in Nevada high schools who had tried meth at least once. We turned back those numbers within a year to less than half. We're still involved; we have grass roots people who have still kept that program going.

Dawn Gibbons, Senior Vice President,
Communication and Government Relations,
Intermountain West Communications

Our show *Jim Rogers' Nevada* is another success. We invite people in the community to be interviewed. They're non-confrontational; we don't want heated arguments about whether the school district is underfunded. We know it is. We want to let the community know how to help, what to look out for, and so forth. Those started in September of 2009. People call to ask if they can come on the show. There's a two year waiting list to get on – there are so many local issues.

So many charities, foundations, and organizations that don't have a voice – it's very hard to get them on the news. We have a segment we can put them on Saturdays now, but really Jim Rogers' voice [on *Jim Rogers' Nevada*] has given people who never had a voice a very powerful voice; Jim is a great advocate. He gets them on and he lets them talk. A lot of times when people have these talk shows they do all the talking. Jim does the listening; he'll give them some questions – some write their own questions. But it's a forum where they can talk about their issues and educate the community on those issues. I think that is the gift that he gives to Las Vegas and to the state.

We have various charities on the show: there's a two-year waiting list. Every charity that comes to me we try to squeeze in because they are really doing good work but don't raise a lot of money, like Easter Seals – huge charity nationwide, but people in Las Vegas don't think about them, so they need a little extra attention. Or the organ donor program at the UNR medical school: Frankie Sue Del Papa came on to talk about issues of organ donation. We only have one organ procurement center in the state of Nevada (in Las Vegas). That was a big deal in the press. And I like the way Jim gets involved in politics, because he really makes people better public servants. He holds their feet to the fire.

> Dawn Gibbons, Senior Vice President,
> Communications and Government Relations,
> Intermountain West Communications

/

I was asked by the U.S. Consulate to put together this trip to Israel. I was already going over there to speak at a conference in Tel Aviv, and the U.S. Consulate wanted me to merge this with an international trade exchange trip. One of the first people who came to mind was Jim, because of his stature and his interest in the issue, and his general presence. I took him and Mike Saltman, David Sherer, Jim Thomas, and Steve Wells and a staffer. I got to really know him during that trip. I've never laughed so hard as I have watching Jim trying to use an iPhone.

We taped three segments of *Inside Nevada* right after we went on that trip. We talked about the trip and about community water issues. I did get feedback from a lot of sources about those segments. I think the format of those interviews is really conducive to digging into the issues, and I think people appreciated that. The interviews were a real success.

> Pat Mulroy, General Manager,
> Las Vegas Valley Water District, Retired

Another way in which we're trying to serve the community is to fairly give a voice to all the ethnic groups. Las Vegas is now comprised of more than 50 percent minorities. We believe the Las Vegas television stations have not done a very good job of bringing attention to the problems that minorities face. I asked a group of local citizens to help produce news about the issues facing their respective groups.

> I'm on a team through Channel 3 that deals with various issues and through the TV station we've been able to suggest presenters that deal with matters that matter to minorities, particularly Asians, Hispanics, and African Americans.
>
> Hannah Brown, Community Developer

We are just getting started with the program and not quite sure how to put it together. We'll be doing a lot of testing and probing and experimenting in this project. We may offend people when we start, but you can be sure we will be acting in good faith to make that program accurate and unbiased. We have representatives from the Hispanic, Asian, and African-American communities to start. We will hire more minority reporters and add an assistant news director who will be a minority. I want the public to tune into our stations morning, noon and night, and be informed about the real and substantive issues facing Nevada.

> Jim's philosophy about the station being a part of the community has helped in many ways. One time we did a phone-a-thon for people in mortgage trouble, or highlighting a consumer scam, I always felt like we had a supporter in Channel 3. If it was important for the community to know about something, he made that a priority – without interfering with the news side of it. He would set us up with the news director, simply saying, "Hey, this is important from the community point of view."
>
> Barbara Buckley, Former Nevada State Assemblywoman

As we're expanding, we're getting into more areas that concern the community. I'm always open to ideas for new segments, or ways we can bring attention to areas that affect Las Vegans. We've done a lot of good bits, and some that were less successful. We keep trying though to meet and serve our community.

*

My Venture into the World of Banking

I wanted to know who had the money. I believed there was no better way to learn than to become a member of a major Nevada bank board. In 1981, having been in the television business two years and having become better known in the Las Vegas community, I called State Senator Floyd Lamb, who also happened to be a neighbor of mine, and asked him if he could get me on the board of Nevada National Bank – a statewide bank with 63 branches. He did so and for six or seven years, I served on the board until the bank was purchased by Security Pacific Bank of California. In 1985 through 1987, I served as the bank's chairman of the board. I later became a founding board member of Community Bank and founding member and chairman of Nevada First Bank which later merged into Bank of Nevada. I learned many lessons from those boards. Some of my observations may shock you.

First – I was shocked to learn how many people who lived lifestyles that were very simple and conservative actually had tremendous wealth. I also learned that many Nevadans who lived the good life really had very little. I remember one woman who lived in the same middle-income area where I lived made a simple inquiry at our bank about her account. I learned that she had a net worth of $98 million dollars, all held in blue chip stocks. That made me understand you can't judge a balance sheet by its alligator and diamond cover. The lesson in all of this is "beware of those with whom you deal." You may believe they are wealthy because of their lifestyle, but make sure you check them out before you become their business partner. It may be all air.

I have some observations about bankers, who are a strange lot. I am not sure my characterizations of them are totally accurate, but give these observations some thought. Bankers are not businessmen or entrepreneurs. I've never known one who had built a business, made a payroll, done any long-term financial planning, or had been involved in selling, advertising, and dealing with employees. In other words, they know nothing about business. Don't confuse banking with every other business. Bankers understand banking, but when making loans to your company, they use criteria to determine the strength of the loan that would never occur to you as operator of that business. Bankers have no capacity to understand why your cash flow goes up and down. When your cash flow goes up, for whatever reason, they want to lend you more money. When your cash flow goes down, for whatever reason, they want you to cut expenses and most importantly pay your debt. Attempts to explain the ups and downs of your business to your banker are futile.

There is a very fundamental difference between bankers and all other business people; those in business have a *product*. In my case it is news broadcasting and entertainment. In an automobile dealer's case, it is buying and selling automobiles. A business owners' *by-product* is his profit or loss from his product. Banking is different – bankers have no product. Their product and their by-product are one in the same. Their sole purpose for existence is to make a profit. Their sole driving force is to make a profit for their shareholders. They have no product in which to be paid. In the Humphrey Bogart movie, *Sabrina*, he explains to Audrey Hepburn that his *product* is ship building and the shipping of cargo produces the by-product: profit. He is proud of his product and pleased with his by product. His product is his life. The only thing bankers produce is a profit or a loss. The entire source of their pride is the bottom line – the profit. It seems to me that if your whole being is simply to produce a profit, you don't have much substance.

The bankers of this country, especially the large banks that do business in multiple states and in multiple countries, have damned near destroyed us time and time again. We have always been unable to control this and always will be. They are an industry with little conscience. They are not dishonest – not many would ever intentionally violate a law. But they are more than short of conscience. Beware of your banker's loyalty to you – he has none. As long as you keep that in mind, you can navigate the financial world of your banker.

Banking provides a unique business model; it allows banks to take its depositors' money and make loans of that money. The bank is also required, however, to invest some of its shareholders' money in each of the loans it makes in order to ensure that the shareholders of the bank will carefully monitor loans. The investment by the bank itself in loans usually amounts to 10 percent of the loan total. That is, if the loan is $100, the bank shareholders put up $10 and the depositors put up the other $90. One of the problems that occurred in the 1960s and 1970s was that the regulations on banking continued to reduce the amount of participation by the shareholders. Rather than a 10 percent investment, the investment by the banks of their own money went down to two percent and in many cases, when the loan was really scrutinized, it was discovered that the bank had really put none of its own money into the loan.

Local banks and most national banks make a great deal of their profit not only from the interest charged, but from the fees charged. If you borrow $100 at 10 percent interest for one year, you may pay a two percent origination fee. Because fees are charged when the loan is made, it's in the best interest of the bank to make many short-term loans rather than any long-term loans. It doesn't take a Rhodes Scholar to understand how the reduction of the capital investment by a bank causes it to tend to be careless with "other people's money." Therefore, because most loan officers are paid based upon volume of loans, more and more loans of lower and lower quality tend to be approved. The result is obvious.

I've never known a banker who was a businessman, and that is the problem. When you make loans based only on the balance sheet and profit and loss statement and do not understand the fundamental working parts of the business, there's trouble ahead, because all businesses, given any period of time, will have very serious financial problems. When things start to go downhill in the economy, banks are simply there for the ride. They have little ability to stop the slide.

I have had several occasions where I've had very serious financial problems. The other businesses with which I dealt were supportive of our efforts to solve our problems. Because bankers really have little idea of whether a business can recover, they tend to only look at the profit-loss statements and the short-term trends of those statements and decide whether to pull the plug. For the most part, they tend to panic and because they are trigger happy, they pull the plug.

My reaction and criticism of bankers has in some instances been very severe probably because I entered into a transaction where I should have been more careful in what I was doing. When problems arose, the bankers, like vultures on a power line, were there to make my life miserable. In one instance, I took the position that the bank itself had created part of my problems, so I bought a set of books called "Lender Liability" and I put the whole set up behind my desk on the credenza. When the banker came to see me I immediately noticed that his eyes focused on that set of books, and he seemed unable to forget their presence. This banker was a very young man whose only understanding of money was that $100 was two times $50.

Bankers have no real understanding of the long-term success of a company. They panic when the first problem arises. That panic usually translates to charging higher interest rates, which of course make a business's problems worse. I will say that many of the bankers with whom I have dealt during the last 25 years have been exceptions to the rules. They may not understand my business, but they understand the value of a customer whose overall financial strength is good and whose integrity and reputation for telling the truth is stellar.

*

For the last several years I have been very distressed that the news media seems to be moving more and more toward sensationalism. The public loves rape, robbery and mayhem more than it loves the complicated political process. It is necessary to change that culture and to develop a more substantive culture. To do this, we must have leadership that is outstanding, that has gathered world-class producers. To that end, it has been our purpose over the last 30 years to develop the most effective news broadcast team in Las Vegas.

Our only *product* is news. You can have the most talented management, the most superlative accounting departments, and the best creative departments, but when push comes to shove, it is essential we present a news product the public trusts. The most important people in our company are not our bosses, but those whose work product is on the air. The anchors are those who the viewers must trust. Their credibility is critical to our success. The reporters and anchors must inform and explain to the public the most important issues that affect the community.

Along with the emergence of NBC as a real force in our lives, we learned that although it was good to have the number one news network, we could not take credit for it because we did not produce that programming. If NBC were effective, we would make a lot of money. If NBC were ineffective, that cost us money. More important than money, however, was knowing that we produced news that was important to the decision making of our viewers. We didn't want and could not rely on a national network to perform our job. We invested in our future by investing in the well-being of Nevadans.

I believe 1956 was the first year that the population of Las Vegas was larger than Reno (one had 28,000 people and the other 26,000). Today, the population of northern Nevada is around 400,000 and the population of southern Nevada is 2.75 million. The place to be for nearly every business, especially television, has been Las Vegas. Our revenue is based upon the number of people who view us. If one is buying advertising on a television station with ten viewers, the rates are low; if there are 20 viewers the rate is higher; if there are 100 viewers the rates skyrocket. We are a fixed-cost business. It costs the station as much to broadcast to 1,000 people as it does to broadcast to 100,000 people. When times are bad, we are not able to cut costs because we can't reduce programming from 24 hours to six or seven hours a day. Every television station must program 24 hours a day to compete.

Serving the public has always been our only mission. We served southern Nevada first and foremost because we all lived here. We were interested in maintaining the integrity of the area. Out-of-state companies, some as far away as Virginia, Iowa, and Wisconsin owned all of the other stations, and still do. We looked at the station not solely as a profit center, but first and foremost as a business designed to help improve the standard of living and quality of life in southern Nevada. We poured every cent we had into the station.

> If you think in terms of his role in education, and the media as a tool for education, Jim has really been one of the most influential media people in the history of this state beyond any doubt.
>
> Dominic Gentile, Attorney

It took several years for the Las Vegas station to become a meaningful force in southern Nevada. During the last 30 to 35 years, the station has either been in first place or tied for first place. Our company is driven to produce a quality program – our first concern is not profit, but the quality of the product we produce. We have never been driven by the bottom line. We produce local programming that is relevant and important. The station has been far more successful than any of us ever expected, and the volume of business has been fantastic. We've been blessed.

*

We have now been in business in Las Vegas since 1979. We have been relatively successful, and while we've had a lot of luck, the key to our success has been our talented, hardworking people who have their jobs at heart. We've continued to acknowledge that our employees, the ones on the front line, are the most important parts of our operation. We support them and make sure they are happy, are provided the best equipment and are given the best benefits. We want them focused on what they produce.

We have been through some terrible times. We've made some terrible mistakes and we have only pulled through those because of the trust we have in each other. We operate as 535 people on an equal plane, each with his or her own abilities and expertise contributing to the success of the operation. I view our employees as my mentors, people who have taught me much more than I have taught them. We have an openness that is enviable; we take care of each other. If somebody gets into financial trouble, we make sure they don't suffer for that. If they have health problems we have always made sure we took care of them We've established scholarship programs for their children and have made a big difference in their children's lives; many of them could not have afforded to go to excellent universities without our help.

We had everything going for us in Las Vegas. We had a network that was very strong; we had a growing economy in which money flowed like water. We had the ability to produce a fine product. Over the next several years we began to develop the news programming and we became very competitive. In 1984, Channel 3 actually moved into first place in many areas, and was either equal to Channel 8 or very close. It's good to have strong competition; Channel 8 has been a leading news broadcaster in southern Nevada. It's invested in the community and it developed very skilled and talented people. They gave us a target and a standard we knew we had to meet to be successful. We pushed and pushed and succeeded because we hired the best people. Eventually we became the leader in the market, and have remained so for the last 20 years.

*

Gone Fishing

All of my life's projects have begun with a very limited, specific purpose. With the passage of time and a series of events, both planned and unplanned, small projects have grown into major ones. That certainly is the case with the television station and my interest and involvement in higher education.

The fishing trips began solely as company fishing trips in the early 1990s and developed into education seminars. We started with a small group of my Las Vegas station employees going fishing in Oregon, California and Washington. Team retreats are a very effective way to help people build relationships and enhance their professional careers. Our trips started with seven or eight employees camping under the stars, staying awake because rocks under our sleeping bags made sleeping very uncomfortable. After several trips where we didn't catch one fish, I told Rolla Cleaver, our general manager, that I didn't care what it cost – the next year we were going to go fishing where we could actually catch fish! We went to Alaska the following summer and caught 2,000 pounds of salmon.

These trips grew quickly; catching fish became the secondary purpose. I developed the habit of inviting everyone I know on every trip. On several occasions travelers appeared for the trip and I didn't remember inviting them. Our numbers doubled, tripled, and became events at which discussions began about real-world issues. They became symposia for university, college and professional school presidents and deans to compare notes. The trip became the "Education Fishing Trip" and the "Salmon Seminar." The last trip was in 2007; I had to discontinue them because of my health. In the decade we had them, those trips spawned very productive dialogue about the state of education in this country, and taught every participant valuable lessons, the most important being that all organizations had the same problems. Professionals from all walks of life participated, focusing on discussions on education. The trips lasted four or five days. Three days were spent fishing at the resort. Each night when we returned to the lodge for dinner, we asked one of the attendees to speak about their experiences with the problems, solutions, and future plans for higher education.

In the early 2000s, our group began to visit the Sonora Resort, which is located on a private island off of the coast of Vancouver, British Columbia. It was ideal for these trips because there was no intrusion from the outside world. We discussed business, education, and politics. There were no televisions at the resort – just nature, conversation, and handshakes.

> Jim knew exactly what he was doing – setting up opportunities to make something historic happen. The University of Arizona was granted, very early in the history of these two [Arizona] institutions, the opportunity to build a college of medicine in Tucson. Consequently, we have the only allopathic college of medicine in the state – and a lot of folks in Phoenix felt we ought to have it there. It's a big city . . . shouldn't ASU have a College of Medicine? Well the practical challenges to creating a new medical school are

almost insurmountable: accreditation and hundreds of millions of dollars. Gary realized that the subject had been so hot that the Board of Regents had actually banned discussion of an ASU college of medicine because it was just driving a wedge between University of Arizona and ASU. Gary told us on the first day that we were going to establish a college of medicine residency in Phoenix – and his idea was that it should be an extension of the University of Arizona college, but in collaboration with ASU.

He laid that on us – and that's a very, very big deal – he asked us when we were free at night to respond to his written proposal. So we spent the night, both Mike [Crow, ASU president] and I, separately, responding to Gary's proposal. It came together the next day – a whole day on a boat, right? – We're talking about this and thrashing it out.

Pete Likins, Former President, University of Arizona, Retired

From 2000 to 2003, the group grew each year from 15 to 20 to 35. On the third year of the trip, our group was discussing education and there were so many individuals in the dining room that it was difficult to concentrate and focus. At that point, I decided that if we were going to move forward with these brainstorming sessions, I needed to rent out the entire resort, which I did from 2004 to 2007.

The 2004 trip literally started off with a bang. Coordinating the schedules of 70 to 80 executives, flying from over 30 different cities and arriving in Vancouver, BC within a two-hour window, proved an enormous task. Once in Vancouver, the participants had to be transported by bus from the airport to the seaplane terminal, and then flown to the resort before dusk, when flights stopped. We had some out of town travelers fly into Las Vegas the night before. All 36 were at the Las Vegas airport ready to fly to Seattle to meet their colleagues. Before the plane was to be boarded, it was struck by lightning. The flight was grounded. Getting all 36 people to Vancouver was the first hurdle we had to overcome. We landed after dusk, too late to take the seaplanes to Sonora. The group settled in Vancouver and flew the first thing in the morning. After a year of flawless planning, one storm almost canceled it all. If it had been canceled, I never would have seen

the day when the University of Arizona played basketball against
UNLV. Lute Olsen (University of Arizona) and Mike Hamrick
(UNLV) agreed to schedule a game.

> [The fishing trips] were amazing. Usually three people and a
> guide in a boat, and hours of conversation. Jim started by
> inviting university presidents from all the Nevada schools,
> and then it just got bigger and bigger, like a western
> educational conference. People from schools in California
> and Idaho and Oregon and the whole west were coming. I've
> heard from some of the people who were in education that
> ground was broken there on any number of issues, and they
> said that getting away from their campuses and their
> hometowns and being in that environment – that Jim really
> made something amazing happen. People were able to drop
> the territorialism that can sometimes be a part of education.
> People seemed to get a lot out of it.
>
> Jim Snyder, Journalist, News Anchor, Channel 3

Karl Eller, for whom the College of Business at the University of
Arizona is named, was present, as were Idaho State University
President Dick Bowen and long-time NBC executive, Jean Dietz.
Arizona and Nevada university regents were in attendance, as well as
the Governor of Wyoming. Pete Likins, president of the University of
Arizona and one of my best friends, was also in attendance. He spoke
to the group discussing an issue every other college president was
facing: funding. You could see the faces of all in the group hanging on
each and every word Pete said. All of the schools had the same issues.
Each had the same struggles: legislative cuts and rapidly rising tuition.
In this day and age, more funding is spent on prisons than education!

> Jim saw that the funding of education was changing; and he
> saw this early: state support of institutions was declining, and
> he could see that that was going to continue to decline. A
> good university has got to have a stable funding source, and
> if it's not being funded by the state, it's going to have to be
> funded by its citizens and the business community. Jim knew
> that educators didn't appreciate how important the support
> of businesses was going to be to their future funding. And

business took for granted that education was always going to be funded and didn't worry about it.

The fishing trips were a way to put business people together with educators, and we could talk about common problems, what they saw. From our standpoint, we would talk to the university presidents and deans about the skills that we needed not only now, but ten years from now, where we saw things heading, and what we saw as the talent that was being produced and why their skills matched or didn't match. And it was pretty clear that the ability to work collaboratively was very important. Hiring people who had the ability to write and speak well was very important to business owners. And those skills were in many cases not being developed.

We talked to the educators about funding and what closer relationships with the community could do, and how businesses could help with financial support. On the other hand, we got to understand their struggles, and how they were trying to meet their goals for the university. Our problem of course is that if a community doesn't have good programs, the best and brightest are going to go elsewhere to school. And then we won't have the kind of people we need to hire to be competitive and be able to move forward and attract more business.

Park Price, President, Bank of Idaho

Another important aspect of these trips was the networking. It's rare these deans and presidents and provosts actually get a chance to talk to each other about issues at their schools, and learn from each other's struggles. If they meet at football games or fundraisers, they're in competition with each other. These trips gave them a chance to step out of the office, away from distraction – in fact, I did everything I could to make sure they weren't distracted – no spouses, no cell phones. While the fishing was fun, the opportunity to learn from each other and to work together to make education better for everyone was the goal. Some of the academics I put onto boats together developed real friendships and have stayed in touch. That makes me feel like I was able to contribute in a way that otherwise wouldn't have been possible.

I wouldn't have been nearly as close to some people, like [former University of Arizona president] Pete Likins, had it not been for those trips. It was important in forming and solidifying inter-school relationships. There's something about breaking bread together, flying together, being in a boat together, being away from the work setting together; it's amazing. It was an incredibly important time for me as a dean, and those friendships endure.

We'd get booklets with everyone's bios so we knew who we'd be interacting with, so we'd be prepared. A lot of energy went into these trips, to make them productive, and if Jim saw you sitting down twiddling your thumbs, he'd be really disappointed. This was not a party, but it was a lot of fun. We couldn't access any of our technology there either, which was good, and there were no distractions with family stuff while you were there, and I think that was a smart move. […] It's important to form these deeper relationships; they're what you draw on during the tough days. He put me on boats with deans of other law schools one trip: the deans of Berkeley, UNLV, USC, Colorado, and we talked about common problems. Of course we're all competing in the same space. There's something about figuring out how to negotiate that. There were people from different occupational positions, provosts, presidents, business leaders.

It was always the same weekend, at the end of July. It became cost prohibitive. But that weekend became a big part of my summer. Coming back started off the new school year. Jim made this available to us every year for almost 15 years. There's no doubt in my mind that it would be a worthwhile expenditure for any business, and entity or organization trying to achieve thinking about macro-problems and change. For example, NYU has a villa in Italy and they have high profile gatherings with the Clintons and such.

> Toni Massaro, Former Dean, James E.
> Rogers College of Law, University of Arizona

The 2005 trip was outstanding. Word had circulated through many colleges that the fishing trip was the event of every year. Our guest list grew. Eighty-five guests, including former presidential candidate Dick Gephardt, attended that year. The focus of discussions was the Nevada Health Sciences System. Dr. Trudy Larson from UNR attended, as well as Nevada State Bank president and supporter of education Bill Martin, Fertitta Corporation CFO Bill Bullard, NSHE Vice Chancellor Dan Klaich, NSHE lobbyist Josh Griffin, Nevada State College president (the late) Fred Maryanski, Nevada Regent Mark Alden, Stavros Anthony and Doug Hill, DRI President Steven Wells, Cleveland Clinic cardiologist Dr. Bob Savage, NSHE medical school vice dean Jim Lenhart, Senator Richard Bryan, and UNLV Law School Dean Dick Morgan. This elite group did not focus on what was wrong with the system, but instead asked, "What can we do to make it right?"

> I really got to know Jim on those fishing trips. They were very well done. It was a place, sort of like a think tank, on higher education. He had a lot of great leaders going to the retreat. And it was a real pleasure to me to be a part of that group. I was telling Jim that there were a number of things that we talked about that we actually began implementing: the distributive model of medical education, the importance of the health industry to the universities, ways that we could become more self-reliant, the investment in economic development through the university – those are some of the great issues that all of us weighed in on as educational leaders.
>
> Art Vailas, President, Idaho State University

Each evening a guest speaker would address the crowd. The first speaker was Steve Sample, then president of the University of Southern California. In his 20-year service to USC, he brought that school from mediocrity into the top 25. The school had recently completed the largest capital campaign in the history of U.S. universities, raising $3 billion dollars. Steve Sample's presence has always stayed with me. Suffering himself from Parkinson's disease, he noted that nothing was more important to him than ensuring his students received the highest level of education. He shared his successes with donors. For many years, the College of Engineering had asked an alum for a gift, and year after year the alum declined. Finally, Steve Sample went to meet with the donor. They talked about USC and the alum discussed his true love of the arts. By the end of the meeting, the alum committed millions to the school's arts programs.

This story taught us to go talk to – and listen to – donors, and not to assume what his or her interests are.

The second speaker was the Associate Dean of Yale Law School. Yale Law School has been ranked number one among all U.S. law schools for more than 20 years. The law school alone had, during that 20-year period, raised more than $700 million dollars. Associate Dean Carroll Stevens had been in charge of that campaign.

The third speaker was Congressman Dick Gephardt of Missouri, who had been a contender for the democratic nomination for president of the United States. Dick was a guest on our trip on three occasions. He spoke about the failure of the American higher education system to compete against the universities in other countries and produce engineers, mathematicians and scientists. After his retirement from the U.S. Congress, having served 23 years, he became an officer of Goldman Sachs.

The fourth speaker was Michael Crow, president of Arizona State University. He is the most aggressive university president in the United States. When he became president of ASU, he announced his intention to create the largest university in the United States, with 125,000 students. In a recent visit to my office, he told me ASU was currently at 88,000 students.

Michael, along with Pete Likins of the University of Arizona and the chairman of the Arizona Board of Regents, went out on a boat in the morning and returned that night with a signed memorandum of understanding that the University of Arizona and Arizona State University would join efforts to create a medical school in Phoenix.

> I was paired with the President of the University of Arizona, Pete Likins, and the Chairman of the Arizona Board of Regents at the time. The theme of the trip seemed to be how to resolve unresolvable problems, and what Jim was trying to get going there was 1) How do you get past political impasses? 2) How do you actually solve real problems? 3) How do you make politics a secondary variable and problem solving a primary variable? The thing I was working on there was the design of this joint medical school.

We took [the joint medical school project] to a certain distance and then we discontinued it. It turns out that the differences between the University of Arizona and ASU were pedagogical rather than rivalry, so the University of Arizona went ahead on its own and we paired with Mayo Clinic. We're still obviously allies with the University of Arizona and working with the University of Arizona. What we'll end up with in Phoenix is two new medical schools, one run by the University of Arizona and one run by the Mayo Clinic with ASU.

Michael Crow, President, Arizona State University

The success of these retreats was in creating an environment in which presidents and deans would interact to coordinate their efforts and put aside their competitive and single-institution concerns to move forward on projects.

Nothing frustrated me more than the lack of communication and cooperation between UNR and UNLV. I couldn't understand why two universities under a single Board of Regents bickered all the time about every issue. I put their presidents in a room together and told them not to come out until they reached a middle ground on the Nevada Health Sciences System. Hours later, an agreement was drawn, and the rest is history. I don't mind being called a "dictator" if that means getting people to work together in the interests of the people of Nevada.

On this trip, with an audience of 85, three people spoke about education – but not higher education. All three spoke about this country's most formidable problem – K-12. The K-12 system has, during the last 30 years, eroded to such an extent that it not only fails to graduate 50 percent of its students, but the majority of the 50 percent of those who do graduate are not prepared for college and are not prepared to do the simplest jobs in the business world.

Former Governor and U.S. Senator Richard Bryan, a renowned historian of Nevada history and a teller of tall tales, entertained us on several nights with stories from Nevada's history, which were totally different from those of any of the other 49 states. Kenny Guinn, a former Las Vegas superintendent of schools and former governor of

Nevada spoke about Nevada's future education. USC Provost Max
Nikias, soon to become president of USC, newly appointed University
of Arizona President Bob Shelton, Harrah's Foundation President
Thom Reilly, DC lobbyist Larry Grossman, UNR President Emeritus
Joe Crowley, UC Berkeley Law School Dean Chris Edley, and
University of Arizona alum and heir of the founder of *The New York
Times* Stephen Golden all participated.

> I went twice to Sonora Island, and actually I was a speaker
> both times I went there. First of all, Jim was able to really
> attract a great group of people, presidents, provosts, deans of
> schools, of universities; and also he would bring past senators,
> people with interests in the whole area of American higher
> education. We all got together and did a lot of salmon fishing
> during the day. Obviously you got to meet a lot of people. On
> the boats, we had a lot of interesting discussions. In the
> evenings, there were lectures and Q & A and discussion. They
> were something I enjoyed very much. It was a great
> networking activity, but also you got to meet great people and
> exchange ideas. It was very valuable.
>
> The usefulness of those trips wasn't so much that you called
> people to end up collaborating on a project with another
> university. It was more about sharing "best practices" because
> they were all leaders in education. That was really how I got
> the most out of it – learning something or at least having a
> conversation with someone who faced similar challenges as I
> did.
>
> Max Nikias, President, University of Southern California

The last trip was largely focused on the Health Sciences System.
Medical services in Las Vegas have long been subpar – if you needed a
specialist, you had to go out of state. With almost two million people,
Las Vegas needs a stronger, better-developed health services system.

> That year we were talking about health services and health
> education and it seemed as if we were on the cusp of making
> some very substantial progress – but that was right before the
> economy tanked. Still, the fact that it was a regional and
> national group of thinkers opened the prospect for inter-state
> collaboration. For me, coming into a deanship – and it was

my first one – I went fishing with the deans from Colorado and Arizona and Berkeley. It was a great six hours both days and really helped me situate myself in terms of the challenges. You don't go into a deanship without ideas about what you want to do, naturally, but it's always helpful to hear some confirmation of those ideas from others who have been doing it. It was a huge personal benefit to me – but they weren't vacations – they were work. The times, I think, were marked by the increasing competitiveness between institutions and that was a challenge for everybody to come together and talk specifically about education and how to improve it. Now the challenges are a little bit different – access and cost and budget costs . . . more localized.

> John White, Executive Vice President and Provost,
> University of Nevada, Las Vegas

Various regents, university presidents, law school deans, and philanthropists attended. The man who made the greatest impact was Mr. Bob Wright, vice chairman of General Electric and president of NBC Universal. He ran the largest company in the world – a man who made half a dozen $10 million deals before lunch each day. On the day he spoke to the group in 2007, he was just a grandfather who wanted nothing more than to find a cure for his grandson and the millions of others who are afflicted with autism. He spoke of the challenges in finding treatment and funding for research. Bob began Autism Speaks, a world-wide organization that speaks for those who can't, an organization that has changed legislation and will, someday, find a cure.

There's tension sometimes between higher education institutions, and competitiveness, and those opportunities were just remarkable for people to feel relaxed enough to talk about those challenges and how to get over them. So sometimes there were tensions between my institution (DRI) and UNLV, and those retreats gave us a chance to have a discussion about how to move forward. I found them very useful. There were some significant discussions on the medical school, and ultimately I think out of this retreat came the concept of the Health Sciences Center that Jim put forward when he was chancellor and pushed, and still continues today. And how everybody could work together in a health sciences system. That's another thing that really impressed me about Jim Rogers – he didn't want any campuses left out. He wanted all campuses included in this health science initiative because they all contribute something to that (system). The Health Sciences initiative came out of those trips, and agreements on how it would operate.

Steve Wells, President, Desert Research Institute

Harrah's chairman Phil Satre and Nevada developer and philanthropist Harvey Whittemore attended. The late Governor Guinn spoke of his commitment to education and his creation of the Millennium Scholarships, which he introduced to Nevada in 1999, ensuring Nevada students who meet criteria, will be afforded an opportunity to attend higher education.

*

I have great memories of these trips. An effective CEO knows that to get the most out of his team, that team has to be put in a variety of creative situations to foster development. I'm confident that as more school systems become independent and rely on external support, these relationships will become more important. Some of the people I put together keep in touch, not just in the education arena but also in the business sector, in the medical field, and in communications. Only by working together, and working creatively, can communities develop into stronger, more engaged bodies. The support and participation of a substantive education system can raise the quality of life for everyone.

The following list highlights some of the notable educators that went on the fishing trip (with titles at that time):

1. Mark Alden, Regent, Nevada System of Higher Education
2. David Ashley, President, University of Nevada, Las Vegas
3. Philip Amerson, President, Claremont School of Theology
4. Stavros Anthony, Regent, Nevada System of Higher Education
5. Douglas Baker, Provost, University of Idaho
6. Richard Bowen, President, Idaho State University

7. Richard Bryan, Nevada Governor and United States Senator
8. Don Burnett, Dean, University of Idaho College of Law
9. Dr. Richard Carpenter, President, College of Southern Nevada
10. Joe Crowley, President, University of Nevada, Reno
11. Michael Crow, President, Arizona State University
12. George Davis, Provost, University of Arizona
13. Jill Derby, Regent, Nevada System of Higher Education
14. Carl Diekhans, Interim President, Great Basin College, Nevada
15. Thalia Dondero, Regent, Nevada System of Higher Education
16. Christopher Edley, Jr., Dean and Professor of Law, University of California, Berkeley and Professor of Law, Harvard University
17. Richard Flaherty, Dean, University of Nevada, Las Vegas College of Business
18. John Frederick, Provost, University of Nevada, Reno
19. Dorothy Gallagher, Regent, Nevada System of Higher Education
20. Geoffrey Gamble, President, Montana State University
21. Jason Geddes, Regent, Nevada System of Higher Education
22. Dick Gephardt, Democrat and Majority Leader, United States Congress
23. David Getches, Dean, University of Colorado Law School
24. Milton Glick, President, University of Nevada, Reno
25. Cary Groth, Athletic Director, University of Nevada, Reno
26. Yash Gupta, Professor and Dean, University of Southern California College of Business
27. Paul Jarley, Dean, University of Nevada, Las Vegas, School of Business
28. Mike Hamrick, Athletic Director, University of Nevada, Las Vegas
29. Carol Harter, President, University of Nevada, Las Vegas
30. Meredith Hay, Provost, University of Arizona
31. Linda Howard, Regent, Nevada System of Higher Education
32. Dan Klaich, Vice Chancellor, Nevada Board of Regents

33. Ron Knecht, Regent, Nevada System of Higher Education
34. John Kuhlman, Manager, Public Information, Nevada System of Higher Education
35. Bob Kustra, President, Boise State University
36. Dr. Trudy Larsonle, Professor of Pediatrics, University of Nevada School of Medicine
37. James Dean Leavitt, Regent, Nevada System of Higher Education
38. Dr. James Lenhart, Vice Dean, University of Nevada, Reno Medical School
39. Pete Likins, President, University of Arizona
40. John Lilley, President, University of Nevada, Reno
41. Jim Livengood, Athletic Director, University of Nevada, Las Vegas
42. Carol Lucey, President, Western Nevada College
43. Earl F. Martin, Dean, Gonzaga University, School of Law
44. Fred Maryanski, President, Nevada State College
45. Toni Massaro, Dean, University of Arizona James E. Rogers College of Law
46. John McDonald, Dean, University of Nevada, School of Medicine
47. James Moore, Director, University of Arizona Foundation
48. Dick Morgan, Dean, William S. Boyd School of Law, University of Nevada, Las Vegas
49. Max Nikias, President, University of Southern California
50. Jane Nichols, Vice Chancellor, Academic and Student Affairs, Nevada System of Higher Education
51. Kevin O'Shea, Deputy Director, National Law Center for Inter-American Free Trade, University of Arizona
52. Lute Olson, Basketball Coach, University of Arizona
53. Jerry Parkinson, Dean, University of Wyoming College of Law
54. Paul R. Portney, Dean, Eller College of Management, University of Arizona

55. Mike Reed, Vice Chancellor, Finance, Nevada System of Higher Education
56. Mike Richards, President, College of Southern Nevada
57. Sally Rider, Director, Rehnquist Center, University of Arizona James E. Rogers College of Law
58. Bill Robinson, President, Whitworth College (now Whitworth University)
59. Harry Rosenberg, President, University of Southern Nevada
60. Steve Sample, President, University of Southern California
61. Robert Savage, M.D., Faculty Member, Cleveland Clinic
62. Jack Schofield, Regent, Nevada System of Higher Education
63. Maria Sheehan, President, Truckee Meadows Community College
64. Steve Sisolak, Regent, Nevada System of Higher Education
65. Robert Shelton, President, University of Arizona
66. Matt Spitzer, Dean, University of Southern California Law School
67. Tessa Stewart, Public Relations, Chancellor's Office, Nevada System of Higher Education
68. Carroll Stevens, Associate Dean, Yale University College of Law
69. Gary Stuart, Arizona Board of Regents
70. Maurizio Trevisan, Vice Chancellor of Health Sciences, Nevada System of Higher Education
71. Marcia Turner, Vice Chancellor of Health Sciences, Nevada System of Higher Education
72. Art Vailas, President, Idaho State University
73. Jonelle Vold, Assistant Dean, University of Arizona James E. Rogers College of Law
74. Steve Wells, President, Desert Research Institute
75. Bret Whipple, Regent, Nevada System of Higher Education
76. John White, Dean, William S. Boyd School of Law, University of Nevada, Las Vegas
77. Tim White, President, University of Idaho
78. Michael Wixom, Chairman, Nevada Board of Regents

Chapter V

PHILANTHROPY:

PAYING YOUR COMMUNITY RENT

Louis Wiener, Jr., deserves a special section in this book because of the all-encompassing relationship that he and I had for 20 years. Lou was my closest friend, a great advisor, and like a second father to me. He had boundless energy and an infectious sense of humor. Louie's belief in paying your community rent – giving back to the community that enabled you to make a living – shaped my own view of giving in more ways than I can count.

Lou was born in 1915 and died in 1996, a month and a half before his 81st birthday. He and his family moved from Pittsburgh, Pennsylvania, to Las Vegas in 1931. When he arrived, he was met by an uncle who had been disbarred in the state of New York; I'll call the attorney Uncle Harry. Uncle Harry told Lou that whatever Lou's ambitions were, he should never become an attorney in Las Vegas specializing in the documentation of transactions. He explained to his nephew that Nevadans did not work with signed contracts. The entire business community functioned on the basis of a man's word being his bond, and no further guarantees were needed.

Lou's lifestyle was very simple. Lou's mother, Kittie, and father, Lou Sr., had moved to Las Vegas in 1931 and had brought their two children, Lou and his sister, Katherine. Lou's father had been a tailor and obviously did not have a large income. The Depression broke him. I don't know when Lou's father died, but I do know that when he and I were in business together, from time to time he would wear a suit to the station that had been made more than 20 years before. Lou took care of all of his belongings. He lived in a condominium in a gated area during the 20 years he and I were partners. There was nothing fancy or expensive about it. He didn't care what car he drove and would insist that the station never buy more than a mid-size car for him. In his later years, when Lou traveled, I suggested to him that being nearly 80 years old was reason enough for him to fly first class. Lou refused, saying that that was a waste of money.

> The family was hard hit by the Depression, which resulted in my grandfather's losing such clients as the Mellons and the Carnegies, who didn't need new suits during the Depression. Without telling anyone, they purchased one-way train tickets from Pittsburgh to Las Vegas. Because they already had family in Las Vegas, and because this was the only place in the country where people were working due to the construction of Hoover Dam, they agreed to a covert move west. At midnight one November day in 1931, three generations of my family took that train (also one of dad's grandparents). After arrival, my grandfather opened a tailor shop at Main and Fremont. He designed and made suits without patterns (he actually customized each suit for each patron) for the owners of houses in the Red Light District (Block 16), and my grandmother, a talented seamstress, designed and made the dresses for the ladies who worked in those houses. Dad's sister, Kit, who had planned to attend a musical institute before the midnight move, at least once each week drove the dirt road from Las Vegas to Boulder City to teach piano to the children of the dam's construction managers.
>
> Valerie Wiener, Lou Wiener's Daughter,
> Former State Senator

Lou attended the University of Nevada, Reno with the thought of becoming a school teacher. It was only through a chance meeting with a prominent lawyer in Reno that Lou decided to go to law school. Lou graduated from the University of California, Berkeley Boalt School of Law in 1941 and returned to Las Vegas to practice law.

> When dad decided to go to the University of Nevada, Reno, there was no direct route between Las Vegas and Reno. He was required to go by bus to Los Angeles, then to San Francisco, then Reno. The family had no money in the bank, but spared $5 each month for his spending money. They "gambled" on the number of days it would take to get the check back to the originating bank for payment – this was their buffer time to get money into the account to cover the check.

Dad worked five or six jobs during college. One, in particular, was to donate blood every six weeks or so. When he needed extra money, he'd give blood more often. During his senior year, he couldn't afford the dorm during the winter semester so a friend allowed him to sleep on the floor in his dormitory room. At the end of the semester, one of the administrators saw him and commented, "That floor must be very hard and very cold, Mr. Wiener."

> Valerie Wiener, Lou Wiener's Daughter,
> Former State Senator

When he passed the State Bar, Justice Orr (I believe) called his father, Lou Sr., to tell him the great news. When Lou Sr. asked, "What do we do with him now?" the justice replied, "Take him down to the courthouse and get him sworn in!" Lou was the only attorney from Clark County who took the bar exam that cycle, and the number of practicing attorneys in Las Vegas at that time was fewer than 30. In those times, every attorney knew and regularly dealt with every other attorney several times a year. They all knew each other's strengths and weaknesses. The underlying bond among them was a shared sense of loyalty and truth.

Louie was really one of the finest lawyers in the state of Nevada. Lou's law firm of Wiener, Goldwater and Galatz was probably the leading law firm of the day. Formerly Jones, Wiener and Jones, the firm eventually became Jones Vargas, which I believe is now the largest in the state. Louie quickly became known as the brightest of the Las Vegas lawyers, and as various people moved into Las Vegas to build hotels, Louie became their counsel. When there were just 12 hotels on the strip, Louie was general counsel to 10 of them.

Benjamin "Bugsy" Siegel arrived in Las Vegas in the late 1940s to finish construction of the Flamingo Hotel. He had a transaction that concluded at an hour when no local attorney could get an order from a local judge. Unbeknownst to Siegel, Las Vegas courts were actually open on Saturday. On Saturday morning, Lou Wiener appeared in the Clark County Court and got an order cancelling Siegel's transaction. The next Monday, Siegel appeared at Lou's office and told Lou that he admired Lou's ability to act so quickly and because of that, Bugsy was going to make Lou his local counsel. He told Lou he would never call on him for any action that required advice on illegitimate deals. Lou agreed, and that began a relationship that only terminated when Bugsy was killed in July of 1947 in Beverly Hills.

> Siegel was running race books in town. He controlled all but one of them – a legitimate operation. Somehow, Siegel convinced Western Union to withhold wire service to this lone book, and getting race results by Western Union was crucial. However, real-time wire reporting of the race was not in Siegel's best interest, because he got the results, *THEN* posted the betting odds (knowing the outcomes), and played the results after bets were made. Thus, he controlled the betting outcomes. So his intent was to close the legitimate book. The owner approached Dad to get injunctive relief by requiring Western Union to reinstate service to the book. Dad went to the one judge in town to request the injunction. That particular judge was planning to leave on a 3-week hunting trip in rural Nevada the next morning and told him that if he could get the paperwork to him before he left, he would sign it. Dad spent all night typing it and got to the judge, who waited a few minutes later than his planned departure so that he could sign the order. Because the County Clerk's office was technically open 24 hours/7 days a week, Dad called the clerk and processed everything he needed to get done.
>
> Valerie Wiener, Lou Wiener's Daughter,
> Former State Senator

Louie had not only been one of the most talented lawyers in the state, but he was probably one of the four or five most successful businessmen in Nevada as well. He went to Siegel and said: "Listen, I want to talk to you about gaming and what I think is going to happen with people who visit here. People will not want to gamble a whole weekend or even two or three days. In addition to providing them gaming and entertainment, I strongly suggest that you build a golf course adjacent to the hotel. That will get people out of the casino to enjoy themselves." Bugsy agreed he would do that.

> My mom, Tui Ava Knight, was Dad's first wife and married to him for about 15 or 16 years. She told me about the many evenings they spent at the Flamingo. One afternoon, Siegel

called Dad and told him to bring some extra money that evening because they were going to raffle off a beautiful mink stole and he thought my mom would love it. So, when the bidding began, someone kept bidding up my dad. Eventually, after Dad had the highest bid, he went to Ben's table at the back and asked if Ben would give the "okay" for my dad to go to the cage and get a cash advance to cover the auction bid. Ben said it was fine. When Dad arrived at the cage, the employee was laughing his head off. He told my dad that it was Ben who kept outbidding him.

Another time, my parents were at the hotel, and a cigarette girl slipped a raffle ticket under my mom's plate and told her to hold onto it because "it's a winner." Well, what a surprise when my mom's ticket won a beautiful freestanding, blonde-wood radio-record player. Dad said they couldn't accept it because he was the hotel's attorney. Siegel accepted my dad's decision. Monday, an even more elaborate radio-record player was delivered to our house.

Valerie Wiener, Lou Wiener's Daughter,
Former State Senator

The lawyer-client arrangement between Louie and Siegel satisfied each. Louie required that everything Siegel did in Nevada be "legal." Siegel didn't allow Louie anywhere near a conversation that involved illegal activities (so he didn't have any knowledge of them). Also, Siegel wanted everything in writing and separated by subject. If Louie wrote a legal memo addressing three issues, there had to be three separate sheets of paper so that Siegel could file them exactly where he could find each one.

The Flamingo Hotel was finished and scheduled to open when Mr. Siegel was murdered in his home in Beverly Hills. When Louie went to the new owners, they suggested that he go peddle his ideas about a golf course somewhere else. Lou went to the Desert Inn, to "Mo" Dalitz, the owner, and suggested that if the Desert Inn were going to continue to grow and prosper, it should build a golf course. Lou said that Siegel had thought it was a damn good idea, but he hadn't lived to see it. Dalitz agreed with Lou. The Desert Inn Golf Course was built, and still stands as one of the major landmarks on the

Las Vegas Strip. As compensation for that idea, Dalitz gave Lou a housing lot on the golf course. Lou's wife objected to him being that closely involved with men she (correctly) assumed were connected to the mob. Lou returned the title to Dalitz and didn't build on that lot, although he continued to be Dalitz's lawyer for many years.

Nevadans were known for avoiding income tax. A great number of transactions were handled in cash and no escrow records of any sort ever appeared. In one instance, a two percent ownership had been given to Lou for which he paid nothing (but provided legal services). The ownership paid Lou $35,000 a year, which in 1950 was a lot of money. One day Lou got a phone call and the caller said, "Lou, there will be a man in your office at 2 o'clock this afternoon with a paper bag that has $66,000 in cash. He will give you the money and you will sign over your stock certificate." Lou replied, "You are nuts. You are telling me that I should give you my stock, which has been paying me $35,000 a year, for only $66,000?" The caller said, "Lou there will be a man in your office at 2 o'clock. He will give you the money and you will give him the stock." Lou repeated that the caller must be nuts. The caller's voice then dropped and he said, "Lou, I suggest you pay attention to what I'm saying. There will be a man in your office at 2 o'clock. You give him the stock. Do you understand what I'm saying?" Lou said finally, "I understand." That's how Nevada operated.

Lou was one of the greatest baseball and football fans. There was an unwritten rule in the courts: if Louie Wiener was trying a case, the court would not meet on Fridays – only Monday through Thursday – because on Fridays Louie got on a plane to Pittsburgh and watched his Pittsburgh teams play baseball and football. If you went to Louie's house on any night during baseball season, he had six or seven TV sets on showing baseball games all over the country. He was an unbelievable sports fan. I think Louie probably bet thousands on sports events over his 80 years. When I asked him why, he said he needed to have some interest in the outcome of the game or he tended not to watch the whole game.

One day Louie was in Federal Court before Judge Foley. The matter before the court was being continued to mid October.

Opposing counsel rose to address the court, and protested: "But your honor, 'The Wiener Rule.'" As everyone who had ever met Louie knew, he was an inveterate sports fan. His family was from Pittsburgh and by reputation he never missed a World Series. By longstanding tradition, none of Louie's court appearances were scheduled during the World Series. Judge Foley is said to have replied, "Of course, 'The Wiener Rule.' This matter will be continued to November."

Richard Bryan, Attorney and Former Nevada Governor

The rules for the practice of law in Las Vegas – and probably the entire state – were somewhat different from the rules of practice in more sophisticated areas. For example, in 1946 Lou was trying a divorce case before Cliff Jones (who had been the state's lieutenant governor). Lou's opposing counsel, Gordon Hawkins, was the partner of Howard Cannon (who became a long-time U.S. Senator from Nevada). The law firm was Hawkins and Cannon. Court procedure in Las Vegas allowed cases to be tried Monday through Saturday. In the divorce case that Lou was trying before Judge Jones, it seemed that the parties were very difficult to deal with and both lawyers had become very distressed. Lou suggested to Judge Jones that they continue the case until the next week because the Boulder City Hotel was being auctioned that day, and Lou wanted to bid on it. Judge Jones agreed and so did Hawkins. However, each wanted to know if they could have a piece of the action. Lou left the courthouse, went to Boulder City, and won the bid. Lou always did business in cash and in this case he had the entire purchase price in a shoebox. This may read as an uninteresting story, but a twist to it is that Judge Jones' last day on the bench was to be the final day of the trial. The next day Jones became Lou's law partner in the new firm, Jones, Wiener, Jones (this Jones was Herb Jones, Cliff's brother). The relationship between Lou and Cliff was known by Hawkins, and only in Nevada would Hawkins not have objected to this relationship.

Louie's besting Hank Greenspun, the owner of the *Las Vegas Sun*, is also legendary. Greenspun had written an editorial about District Attorney Franklin being in the black marketing business for baby adoptions. Greenspun refused to print a retraction and Franklin sued Greenspun for libel. Lou was Franklin's attorney and obtained a judgment for more than $100,000 against Greenspun, which was the largest defamation verdict in U.S. history. Greenspun eventually got the decision reversed on grounds that are not relevant here. However, Lou's participation in the case created an enemy for life.

Another funny story is about Roxie's Four Mile, a brothel on the road between Las Vegas and Boulder City, right around where Sam's Town stands today. When I was in high school, all the older boys would talk about going to Roxie's Four Mile. I don't believe any of them ever actually got there. Lou was the attorney for the owner, Eddie Clippinger. The Clark County sheriff conducted periodic raids on the whorehouse, and, supposedly, only he and his staff knew when those raids would occur. Somehow, Eddie always knew when his establishment would be raided. On one occasion, Eddie was in Los Angeles and called Lou to tell him that there was going to be a surprise raid that night. However, Eddie could not get back to Las Vegas before the raid, and he had $75,000 in a safe. Since Eddie believed the money would be confiscated, he asked Lou to go to the house, open the safe, take the money out, and hold it for him. Lou did so. The sheriffs appeared, and so did the *Las Vegas Sun*, whose reporter took a picture of Lou standing inside the whorehouse. Greenspun's headline the following day was: "Famous Local Attorney Tends Bar at Local Whorehouse." This was a continuation of the Wiener-Greenspun personal feud.

There's another funny story about Roxie's Four Mile. Roxie's owner, Clippinger, was determined to eliminate the competition and be a local monopoly. A second whorehouse was opened on Tropicana; the new owner didn't have the sense to stay out of competition with Roxie's. The establishment had a circular driveway. At Louie's suggestion, Clippinger stationed a car at each of the entrances with an occupant who wrote down the license plate numbers of every visitor. The wives of those visitors were sent the information. That business closed down soon thereafter. Lou's advice was instrumental in destroying the competition.

The 20 year battle between Greenspun and Wiener remained at full strength even until Lou's death, which followed Hank Greenspun's death by many years. Lou told me one day that for his funeral, he wanted to make sure his body was put in the coffin face down, so that during the ceremony people would walk by the coffin and could see Lou face down. I asked him why he thought that was a reasonable request. He told me that this way, if the Greenspuns walked by his casket, they'd have an opportunity to "kiss [his] ass." Obviously I refused to do this, but when Lou died I did call his children and tell them about Lou's request. The children said the open coffin would not be acceptable.

As an aside, Lou made a fortune in business investments in southern Nevada. At no time in his 55 years of practice did he ever make more than $100,000 a year from his law practice. He gave away more than half of his services and did so because he had the wherewithal to do it and because he always helped people who were unable to afford first class legal help. Lou's relationship with the southern Nevada judiciary was unique in that every one of the judges had been a law clerk to Lou at one time or another. Lou always treated them as though they were still his law clerks. In one instance, Lou was representing the wife of a local attorney who had two small children. Lou was seeking child support. At the end of the hearing the judge awarded the mother what Lou felt an inadequate amount. Lou asked if he could approach the bench. He did so and said to the judge: "Your honor, you son of a bitch. How can you in good conscience award this lady such a pittance? You ought to be ashamed of yourself." The judge responded: "Lou everyone doesn't have your money. If you want to assure her greater child support, you should pay her." Lou did.

> One of Dad's greatest peeves involved fathers who tried to squirm out of adequate child support. He would make a long list of things the child would need . . . clothes, food, medical, school supplies, etc. . . . then show the dads that the kids' mothers wouldn't get enough money to cover children's expenses, even if they got the maximum allowed by law. Dad would often say, with great frustration, "It's amazing how

many of these dads all of a sudden believed in Immaculate Conception when it came to *their own* kids."

Valerie Wiener, Lou Wiener's Daughter,
Former State Senator

*

I first got to know Lou when I was in high school. I had gone to high school with one of his nephews, and everybody in town knew Lou. When we moved to Las Vegas in 1951-1952 the population was 21,000 people, but when Lou moved here in 1931 the population was about 4,000. Everybody knew everybody. Lou was almost exactly my father's age, and over a period of time they got to be good friends. My first real discussion with Lou was a little advice that he gave me when I started to practice law; he said, "You know Jim, I see your father all the time and you know your father is a clothes horse. He wears beautiful clothes, believes that a businessman should look professional and wear a coat and tie. I wear a coat and tie. Your father is embarrassed by the way you look, because you're known for going to the courthouse or meeting with important people and never having a coat or a tie on. I'm telling you this even though he won't tell you. You had better be wearing a coat and a tie every time I see you." I said, "Well, Uncle Lou (everyone called him Uncle Lou), I appreciate what you are saying and I will see to it that I do." From then on, every time I went to the courthouse – and there were many times – I put on my coat and tie. When I walked out of the courtroom I took it off, but if I saw Lou walking down the hall toward me, I hustled into the bathroom to put my coat and tie back on.

Senator Richard Bryan, who was the Governor of Nevada for six years before entering the Senate, and Harry Reid, now the Senate majority leader, and I had all grown up at the same time in southern Nevada. Senator Reid went to Basic High School in Henderson, and Richard Bryan and I went to Las Vegas High School. I graduated in 1956, Richard graduated in 1955 (I think he was the president of the senior class), and of course Harry had been one of the outstanding students out of Basic High. The three of us sat for the bar together in

1963, and I'm pleased to say I came in second. I just found out that Harry Reid was number one.

Richard Bryan had just finished college when he met Louie Wiener on the street in Las Vegas. Lou asked him, "Richard, what are you going to do?" and Richard said, "I'm going to go to law school, but I don't have enough money yet." Lou advanced Richard sufficient funds to go through law school at Hastings, a very fine school. Richard might not have become an attorney had he not had the financial support of Louie. Richard paid every dime back to Louie. Louie remained his mentor when he began the practice of law.

> Lou Wiener was one of the ablest southern Nevada lawyers of his generation. He had an impressive client list and a presence in the legal community that made him one of the most prominent men in Las Vegas for seven decades. I first met Louie when I was in grade school. He was a friend of my father, who was also a lawyer, but more importantly he was the Waldman boys' uncle. They were my contemporaries and before Louie married and had children of his own, they were the beneficiaries of his extraordinary generosity.
>
> Richard Bryan, Attorney and Former Nevada Governor

Lou was also Harry Reid's financial advisor. Each of us knew Louie very well. In effect, we were his children.

> I had a wonderful relationship with Lou Wiener. When I was a brand-new lawyer, it was fairly traditional at that time for people to take a coffee break and go out somewhere on Fremont Street, because all the law offices at that time were on Fremont Street. I was working for Rex Jimmerson at the time. We always went to Dennison's BBQ, and Louie Wiener held court there. He was very, very talkative, a real storyteller. Lou did a lot to help me plan my life. One day he came in and said, "Let me give you a little advice, young man. I have invested money in multiple things, and I've lost money in almost every one of them. Here's what I want to tell you: Las Vegas is growing, and the only thing you should invest money in is raw land. People can do anything to it, drive over it, piss on it – but they can't hurt it. All you have to do is pay the

taxes." So that's what I did. I made a lot of money on that land.

Harry Reid, U.S. Senator

Lou had his eccentricities, one of which was the love of women. He married several times. I remember asking him about the alimony he paid. Although he was only obligated to pay alimony to one lady for a period of five years, he'd paid it for 25 years. He said, "Well, Jim, she was really a nice lady and we didn't get along entirely, but she was a good woman and she really didn't have the funds after the alimony was to have ended, so I just kept paying the money until she died." Louie always did what he deemed the "right" thing.

One other short story about Louie: Louie was 80 years old and he came to my office one New Year's Eve. He said, "I've got a little problem, Jim. I have two dates tonight and I don't know what I'm going to do." I replied, "Well, Lou, you're the one who's stupid enough to ask two women out. What are you going to do?" and he said, "Well, I'll think of something." The next morning he came in and I said, "Well, I see you're still alive. You must have handled it alright," and he said, "Well, you know I'm 80 years old, so I convinced the first woman that I simply couldn't stay out until midnight, that I had to go home and go to bed, and I took her home early. Then I went by and picked up the second lady and we went out and had a hell of a time."

I knew Lou was brilliant. He could do financial computations faster than a court reporter or a mathematician could calculate interest rates, payment schedules, or determine how much money had to be paid on a monthly basis. If the payment included interest of six percent and the total bill was $3 million dollars, Lou could compute that in his head. He was one of the best businessmen in Las Vegas. I think at one time or another he owned a bit of every piece of property in Las Vegas. Lou and I became very close. In the year after we got the license for the television station, Lou was retained by the other 15 stockholders to take a look at what I was doing. They didn't believe that I was competent, and thought that I should be removed as the chairman of the television station.

Lou came to see me, and to make a long story short, eventually Lou and I bought everyone else out of the television station. We remained partners and co-shareholders for a period of about 15 years. We'd entered into a buy/sell agreement for Lou's stock and I bought his stock when he passed on. He had moved into the station in 1986 and died in 1996. He and I saw each other every day for ten years. He was sound, smart, and fair beyond belief, and he took care of people like no one I have ever known.

When I got divorced the first time, I needed cash to buy a house. I went to Lou and told him that I needed some money. The next morning I found $50,000 cash in my drawer. I went in and asked Lou if he wanted a note from me and he said, "Well, you intend to pay it back, don't you?" I said "Yes." He asked: "Why would I need a note?" Money meant nothing to Lou. He made a lot of it and spent a lot of it. I would guess that in Lou's 55 years of practice, he gave away over $10 million dollars. I'm not sure if anyone could ever track the money he gave away because he kept no records. He never wrote checks, and only dealt in cash.

Lou came into my office on a daily basis and would sit down and say, "You know, Jim, you and I have been far luckier than we are talented or smart; we've made a lot of money and this town has been good to us and our educations have served us well. Without education, neither one of us would have anything. We owe it to our community and to our fellow man to take care of them." Lou and I did, together, take care of people. He would say he wanted his last check when he died to bring his bank balance to zero. He would often talk about wanting to give money away with a warm hand rather than a cold, dead hand.

In all the years I knew Lou, he never gave less than 10 percent of his income to local charities. That would have been more than $100,000 per year. Lou also never gave less than another 10 percent – more often 15 percent – to needy individuals. That's another $150,000. I would bet that no one in this community gave away as much money as Lou did through the time he died.

Before he died, Dad established a charitable remainder trust naming 10 nonprofits as beneficiaries, e.g., Wiener Elementary, WestCare, University of Nevada Medical School, UNLV Soccer Program, and others. The sums he left each recipient would allow each to receive enough interest income each year to equal his giving while he was alive. He wanted them to receive, in perpetuity, what he gave to them while he was living. However, he didn't make it a condition that they could not go into the principle, so while some of the nonprofits honored his wishes to use only the interest, others dipped into the principle and have diminished the corpus.

Valerie Wiener, Lou Wiener's Daughter,
Former State Senator

Lou didn't watch the store. Strangely enough, he trusted everyone and assumed those who worked for him would take care of him as he took care of them above and beyond their salaries. One morning I arrived at the station to find that agents from the IRS were sitting in Lou's office demanding that he pay $125,000 immediately to cover withholding taxes. The IRS claimed the accounting staff that handled his contract with the county for providing slot machine service at the airport hadn't forwarded the appropriate taxes. The way the airport contract worked was that a private individual or company would bid against others for the contractual rights to provide slot machines at the airport. The winnings were divided between the county and the providers. My recollection is that with respect to Lou's contract, he got 9 percent of the winnings and the county got 91 percent. The slot machine mechanics and other related workers were on Lou's payroll. I went into Lou's office and needless to say, he was more than angry. As it happened, I had the $125,000, which I gave to Lou. Once more there was no documentation of the transaction because I knew that as soon as possible Lou would repay me. There's no telling how much money Lou's employees took off the top. If it bothered him, it didn't bother him very much.

Dad also had the gift shops [at the airport]. And, probably when all of this was going on – or this is what was going on – the airport was undergoing substantial expansion and renovations, which shut out access to most of the slots and gift shops. The County Commission was livid that revenues had dropped (as I recall, as much as half or more), and commissioners decided to pull Dad's franchise and award the slots (and probably gift shops, too) to someone else (I believe this was Jackie Gaughan). They also wanted Dad to pay the county what they considered the lost revenue, which they asserted he owed (the difference between what the slots actually earned and what the commissioners expected them to earn).

Dad offered to "catch up on what he owed, plus interest" if they would allow him to pay over a period of time. To him, the math whiz, this would have actually generated substantially more money for the county because of the interest percentage he offered. However, the commissioners denied him. Even with that, he wrote a personal thank-you note to each commissioner – in long hand – because he believed thank-you notes should be written. The twist on this: Gaughan couldn't get an expedited license to run the slots and it was expected to take several months for a license to be granted. So even after not granting him a franchise renewal, they came back with a request that he continue to operate the slots till Gaughan's license went through. I don't know if he agreed to do this or not.

Valerie Wiener, Lou Wiener's Daughter,
Former State Senator

Lou had a habit of lending people money to get them out of scrapes. When they paid him back, he wouldn't cash the checks because he figured they needed the money more than he did. When Lou died, we opened the trunk of his car and there were over $35,000 in uncashed checks. Some were very old, from the times he'd loaned money to people so they could feed their families. Often Lou would say, "Please don't pay me back" but they would insist, so Lou's answer was, "Well, I won't cash the check," and he never did. I'd been in London the morning he died and I flew back to Las Vegas to try to handle things. Lou had simply dropped dead walking out to get the newspaper. There had been no indication it was going to happen; his health was not bad, but he was, after all, 80 years old.

Louie died February 6, 1996. He told me prior to his death, in order to emphasize his belief that people should give their money away during their lifetimes, that at his funeral he wanted a Brinks truck to follow his hearse with a sign on the side saying: "I've changed my mind. I've decided to take it with me." Louie Wiener had an enormous impact on the Las Vegas community. We knew the funeral would draw many people. Rather than have it at a funeral home, we decided to have it in the auditorium at Las Vegas High School, which seats over 1,000 people. When the funeral started, the place was packed and every one of those 1,000 seats was occupied. The morning of the funeral I called Brinks Truck Company and said I needed a truck. The manager asked me why and I told him. He thought it was the funniest thing he'd ever heard, but he didn't have one he could release because they were all scheduled to be at specific places at specific times. The man I spoke to recommended I call another truck company to see if it had a truck available. We got the truck, put it behind the hearse, and put a sign on the side which read: "I've changed my mind. I've decided to take it with me."

> At my dad's funeral on February 12, 1996, the four main speakers were: Jim Rogers, Senator Richard Bryan, Senator Harry Reid, and me. About 300 people attended the visitation on February 11th; 1,100 people attended the funeral services at the old Las Vegas High School Auditorium (Dad was a 1932 graduate of Las Vegas High School); and 500 attended the post-funeral gathering. Jim remembered Dad's wishes to have an armored car at the funeral. On the side of the parked vehicle, which remained outside during the funeral service, hung a banner that read: "I changed my mind. I decided to take it with me."
>
> Valerie Wiener, Lou Wiener's Daughter,
> Former State Senator

My former wife, Cheryl, came to the funeral. She walked by me and asked, "Who thought that up? I think that's the most obnoxious thing I've ever seen. I can't believe you would have the nerve to put that on the side of a truck and put it behind the hearse. I said to her, "Cheryl, you have to understand, this is what Louie wanted and that's why we've done it. When the eulogies are finished you'll understand." At the funeral, Dick Bryan and Harry Reid and I each spoke for 15-20 minutes. Lou was a character in every sense of the word. There was more laughter at this funeral than you'd have heard at a Shecky Green performance. Everyone in that room knew of Louie's peculiarities, and the fun he had during his life.

The receptionist stopped me as I went into the office the day after Louie's funeral and said, "Jim, I have a problem. Last week the transmission blew up on my car and I didn't have the money to get it fixed and I asked Uncle Lou what to do. He said to take it over to the Ford agency to get it fixed and have them send him the bill." She said, "The bill is almost $1,700 and I don't have the money." I said, "Give me the bill and we'll pay it because I know Lou and I know Lou told you he'd take care of it." He never bragged about his generosity because he didn't want thanks from all the people he helped. He took care of anyone who had need, and he was fortunate enough to have been able to generate enough income and develop extensive assets. No one ever got a greater joy out of living than Lou Wiener.

Lou had had quite a few lady friends up until the end of his life. He took care of them. Several months after Lou died a young lady came into my office. She said, "Mr. Rogers, my name is Annie. I assume you have heard about me," and I said, "No I really haven't." She started to cry. I said, "Oh yes, yes, yes, I have heard of you, Lou spoke very highly of you." I had no idea who she was. She said, "I have a problem. I have two checks that I got from Lou, each for $25,000 when I had some problems, and it says on the bottom of the checks that these are loans, but Lou always promised me that if he died I wouldn't have to pay him back. I don't know what to do, because I don't have anything in writing from Louie, but I assume you'll honor his promise." I said, "I didn't know anything about the $50,000, but if you tell me that's what Lou told you, I can assure you my knowledge of Louie Wiener over these last years would make me believe that was absolutely true. Forget the $50,000." That was somewhat typical of Louie. He didn't give out $50,000 to every young lady he met, but I think he was very generous with his lady friends.

Lou had a profound effect on me. His business acumen was unparalleled. He supported me and helped me achieve the ambitions most people considered reckless. His philosophy of supporting community efforts shaped my understanding of the importance of philanthropy, particularly education. I revered him as a man, a partner, and a mentor.

*

Louie Weiner and I had a reputation for fair dealing because of our long-standing involvement in Nevada business. Lou was always open and fair-minded. He never tried to overpower anyone; he never felt he had to wring the last cent out of a deal. He used to say, "Leave something for the next guy. It doesn't do you any good to get every nickel." Louie would come into my office, which was about 30 feet from his. He would either tell a joke that made him laugh so hard he'd actually cry, or he'd talk to me about our responsibility to our community. He always said we had been very fortunate, far more than our talent or brains deserved. It had been sheer luck for us that Las Vegas had grown as it did, making us wealthy.

We spent hours discussing our plans for the disposal of our wealth. We discussed medical care and other public needs and causes, but ultimately decided that because the education system was falling apart and because students could no longer afford to go to school without borrowing tremendous amounts of money, we would concentrate our efforts on education. Because our own educations had served us so well, we wanted to provide others the same opportunities. It wasn't long before we learned how to do that.

Louie had given large sums to various charities in Las Vegas. He had substantial income not only from the television station, but from properties he owned throughout the valley. Lou lived very simply. He wore suits he'd had for 20 years. He lived in a moderately priced condominium and drove a small car. His living expenses were minimal. He was a major donor to Boalt Hall at Berkeley and his history at that school taught me the value of my legal education.

I went to the University of Arizona in the summer of 1989 as the dean of the law school. One of the very first people I met during my getting out and about with alumni and donors was Jim. My predecessor had suggested that I meet with Jim early, so I flew to Las Vegas to have lunch with him. I had to wait a bit, a half hour or something like that, because he was actually down in court. In those days, even though he was running the station, he was doing a little practicing of law, and court kept him over a bit, so I had a chance to talk with his partner, Lou Wiener. He was a graduate of the Berkeley law school (UC), and I think was a big supporter (of them). And he said to me, "Tom, when you meet Jim, you've got to get him involved in University of Arizona, because it's been one of the most important things in my life to be involved with my alma mater." I really had a great conversation with him while waiting for Jim.

Tom Sullivan, President, University of Vermont

The first gift made to the University of Arizona was an accident. My son was in law school at Arizona. He called to tell me how beat up and worn out the furniture was – students couldn't study comfortably. I came to Tucson, saw how poorly equipped the law college was, and I decided to buy some furniture for them.

The whole story about him getting involved here is kind of folklore. Perry called him and told him that he thought the law school could use his help. He came down, not specifically for that, and there was this dumpy old furniture in the lobby. So, he bought a new couch. A 54-foot, "S" shaped couch that ran the length of the lobby. When I started to work here that couch was already an iconic fixture. When people look back on their law school years they remember sitting on the old blue couch – that became the red couch – that became the multi-colored couch – pieces of it are still over in that [the old law school] building. That was his first engagement with the college since he had graduated.

Nancy Stanley, Assistant Dean for Advancement,
James E. Rogers College of Law, University of Arizona

The couch purchase introduced me to a number of people, who then, of course, saw the potential for future donations. Working with them was an interesting process. I learned how university fundraising worked. I also did my best to make sure that whatever donations I gave them went to the best uses possible. Most universities absorb large donations for administrative costs. I didn't want that. I wanted to see everything I gave go directly to benefit the students, to hire faculty, or to construct buildings that were urgently needed. This involved close eyeballing and tight control in the gift contracts, which I did to ensure the money got to where it would help most.

> There was a particular concern that Jim expressed from the very beginning, which was entirely legitimate. When you give money to a public institution that is also receiving money from the state, there is a fear that the state will say, "Well, you've got Jim's money, so you don't need state money. And particularly for the law schools at U of A and ASU, there is a danger that the state – which is miserly and frankly not supportive of higher education and its manifestations – will turn around and say, "Oh, you can run that on your own. You don't need us."
>
> Jim did not want his gifts to be undercut by a corresponding reduction of funds. If I had ever said, "Jim's given the college of law all this money, but these poor folks in philosophy need it more," that would have been a violation of my commitment to him. Jim put money into philosophy, too, incidentally, because philosophy and law have a natural nexus. We have a very, very good philosophy department here at the University of Arizona.
>
> Pete Likins, Former President, University of Arizona

Many donors believe if they give a little money that gives them the privileges of an owner or chief executive of the institution. A gift of $5,000 brings them rights of a dictatorship. Most donors have no idea of the costs in running a college or even a simple program – their idea of a lot of money is just a drop in the bucket. I tried to learn how the university viewed donors. Many donors believe they have a say in faculty hires, or ways in which the college should or shouldn't interact with the public, or other branches of the system. I always tried to trust the people running the university to do their jobs. I've worked with many brilliant people, and I think they've done wonderful things because I didn't get in their way.

> [Donors] tend to think that their donation should give them access. I don't know if it should or not, but it usually does. And people think that if they give inordinate amounts of money to an institution they get special privileges. I have never known [Jim] to do that. All the things you hear about donors – he doesn't do. Yes, he's referred people to us, but he has never suggested they should get extra consideration – and here is the important part: he doesn't really expect it.

> I've always thought that was a really ethical position for a man who could throw his weight around. Because who among us might not try to throw our weight around a little bit more? He has never said, "I want a faculty member hired" or "I want a faculty member fired;" he's never said, "You need to name this after me." In fact, one time he was looking at his sign and said to me, "You know, I've often thought that these naming rights should only be sold for thirty years or so at a time."

> He understands the public franchise he's coupled with here and he doesn't mess with it. I think that's pretty amazing for a man who has given as much as he has here.

> > Nancy Stanley, Assistant Dean for Advancement,
> > James E. Rogers College of Law, University of Arizona

/

Jim's heart was in a different place than the usual types of university benefactors. I don't mean to characterize that very wide and diverse population of university benefactors, but for many it really is about "their building" with their name on it. For Jim, it's about a passion for what we do here – in the law college, certainly, but also elsewhere in the university.

I told Toni Massaro, the dean Jim developed a strong relationship with: "Jim will respect strength. He knows the rules. Benefactors do not design curricula. He understands that as the principal benefactor of the college of law that he is not the corporate owner; he is not in charge – the dean is in charge." He had an unusual recognition and respect for the academic process, and not every benefactor understands that.

Many donors can't clearly draw the line between being a benefactor and being a manager. And it's natural, I suppose, in a business organization, when you put the money behind the business – you're in charge, right? You get to call the shots. But Jim puts the money behind the enterprise and then trusts the dean or the president to do right. That's rare. Not many benefactors have that deep understanding of the academic process.

Pete Likins, Former President, University of Arizona

*

Pete Likins

I've dealt with some outstanding university presidents. All of them are intellectual giants. In all of my dealings with college presidents, the most outstanding has been Pete Likins. Pete had been the provost at Columbia, the president at Lehigh, and then he came to the University of Arizona, where he served as president for nine years. All the progress at the University of Arizona before Pete became president did not equal the progress made during his nine-year tenure. Because of a speech he made at his inauguration – I was sitting in the audience – I realized the school had a world-class future. With his kind of leadership it couldn't fail. I had already decided to give the school $5 to $6 million dollars. Because of his speech about the future of the University of Arizona, what he thought it capable of doing and how he planned on reaching its potential, Beverly and I decided to increase our pledge to over $100 million dollars.

At the time I think Jim's gift was the largest gift ever made to a law school, and we were all stunned. I also remember people saying that they were very pleased with the way the contract/donor papers had been written up because it specified that if the state gave us less money, the gift would be reduced. In other words, we were to get this gift on top of what we got from the state, not in place of. It was really good thinking; but anyone who knows Jim knows that he would have thought of that.

Jane Korn, Dean, Gonzaga University School of Law

Pete and I developed a very close relationship. He is not only smart; he is wise and his judgment is flawless. A lot of smart people have no ability to judge what needs to be done and how to get it done. They have great capacity to learn, but no capacity to do. Pete is the most productive and effective person I have ever known. Although he is now retired from the presidency of the University of Arizona, he continues to be very active.

> I know a lot of lawyers; I know a lot of businesspeople. Very, very few among them could do what Jim did. Very, very few of them have their passion so completely dedicated to higher education – to public higher education. It's really unusual – and then to have the aptitude to actually try to make things better personally, opposed to making them better just through benefactors. He's unique – unlike anybody I've ever known in my life. And of course, living all the years of my life in higher education and much of that in private universities, I've known a lot of benefactors and have had wonderful relationships with a lot of folks who have helped me accomplish my mission in the university – but I've never met anybody like Jim Rogers.

> Pete Likins, Former President, University of Arizona

/

Jim was wonderful. He was more than a donor; he became a friend. It was a friendship I valued. I arrived to become dean of University of Arizona's law school [1995-1999] in July 1995, and I had never fundraised in my life. The first potential supporter of the University of Arizona law school that I spoke to was Jim. Jim was extraordinarily gracious. We had a two-hour luncheon, and he told these wonderful stories about, among other things, Channel 3 and his early career. We had a little bit of overlap (father worked for KNPB in Los Angeles many years earlier). I knew because of conversations he had had with my predecessor, Tom Sullivan, that he contributed some support to the law school before, and potentially wanted the main building at the law school named after him.

Jim and I got to the point where I would never ask him for money. He would basically say he wanted to support more. We got to a point (maybe the spring of 1998) when he announced that he was going to make one of the largest gifts imaginable to a very small school of law – about a $20 million commitment. We must have negotiated this agreement, which was just a few pages long, through 20 or 30 drafts, sending it back and forth. Jim was very cognizant that he wanted to be really supportive to the university but he didn't want the state to take any support away, so we focused on how to phrase that. I think we focused on a challenge, which is when you create an endowed gift, you're never quite sure what will be most important in the future. At this point, I thought, Jim has been the best friend of the school of law, a good friend to me, but I didn't expect that there would ever be another gift.

A few months later, he flew down for the inauguration of Pete Likins as president. We attended the event together, and he said, "When you've got a minute, there's something I want to talk to you about." We had lunch and he looked at me and said, "I've been thinking of increasing my gift to $30 or $50 million dollars." And Jim claims, and I'm sure he's right, that my jaw dropped at this point. Every gift he made after the first one, I never asked for anything. It was always Jim wanting to provide more support in his incredibly generous way. And I think I was – I certainly hope I was – incredibly grateful, and tried to imagine aloud how transformative that kind of support would be.

Ultimately, his gifts exceeded $130 million. He wanted to contribute not just to the school of law, but other parts of campus. We wanted some support for the central university so they wouldn't be jealous of the support the law school was getting. It's still the largest gift in the history of legal education; and this was all Jim. I was his friend, I tried to give him a vision of where the college of law could go; I tried to show him how much his support had already meant: new faculty, a cap on tuition, physical expansion, new programs. It was just astonishing what a difference his support meant.

Joel Seligman, President, University of Rochester

*

Indigenous Peoples Law and Policy Program

As a donor, I wanted so see some measurable way to help set my alma mater apart from other law schools. I visited with or called people we knew who were deans of other law schools. I asked their advice on how we could make a significant improvement in the development of the University of Arizona's law school. Some of the best advice we received was from the dean of the Yale Law School, who said we should look at an area in which the school was naturally strong, and develop that area into a program that could become a national leader. Based on that advice we started the Indigenous Peoples Law and Policy Program. Arizona Law has long been renowned for its expertise in Indigenous Peoples law. One of my gifts went to help the IPLP Program build upon that foundation, and now the University of Arizona law school is the only law school offering all three law degrees (JD, LL.M, and SJD) with a concentration in Indigenous Peoples law. These outstanding scholars provide the world's most advanced education in the field, and the reputation and the work of IPLP faculty, staff, alumni, and students reaches out to populations around the globe.

> Jim is the ultimate education philanthropist, because what motivates him is the ideas going on with the faculty members, and how they convey that to their students and the world at large. I had the privilege of joining Jim and other faculty members and hearing about various work they were doing. I remember one in particular when Jim Rogers met with Jim Anaya, who was a faculty member in the Indigenous Peoples program at the law school at U of A. And as Jim listened to Jim Anaya talk about his work, you could see his eyes light up with interest.
>
> Jim Rogers asked, "What is it going to take to competitively differentiate us from other schools?" – particularly from ASU, which has a similar program. He and Dean Massaro crafted great opportunities for our faculty and got their work out there, and give them the resources they needed to make that program successful. And Jim understood that the

resources he could provide would be used in ways that would competitively differentiate our program, and at the same time, promote the ideas that the faculty had, and basically do good in the world.

People don't traditionally make the size gift that Jim was making, period, but certainly the large gift would be in the top at any institution. Very often they are endowments, because people want to make sure their gift remains indefinitely to benefit the program. Jim understood that a large infusion of cash in a short term is what could really change the program. Jim's gift, because it wasn't endowed, allowed for new faculty, for support of administration, new programs, and the resulting media – if you look at the ranks now, they continue to move up. And benefit long term from the investment that Jim made back in the 1990s. It's rare to find someone who's giving, like $5 million a year, versus a planned gift. It really allowed us to hire people; there are several members of faculty and administration who, but for Jim's annual commitment, couldn't have been hired. So the students had incredible faculty that we wouldn't have been able to keep, otherwise, and student services to help with job placement, new programs – it just was transformative.

> Vicki Fleischer, Assistant Dean of Seton Hall Law School,
> Former Sr. Director of Development, University of Arizona
> Eller College of Management

This program needed its own space in which to expand on campus. There was a sorority house next to the law school. We decided to ask its member if they were interested in moving. We said we'd pay for everything, and they agreed. We renovated the entire building, which now houses the Indigenous Peoples Program.

Jim was an early supporter of [the Indigenous Peoples Program]. So, they were renovating this building and they wanted to simultaneously create a culture of philanthropy in students early on, so they convinced us to do a few annual events. One was a first year [1L] luncheon, giving students the chance to hear from the law college's big supporters. The idea was to give them a little bit of comfort, hearing from graduates who had been successful, but also to challenge them to think about how they would give back. And we also started the 3L lunch, for students who were graduating. We have a class gift program and we ask them to chip in and pledge over a period of years – maybe stretch a little to make their pledge. It was extremely successful and this law school was probably more successful than any other state law school, with between 90 percent to 95 percent participation.

Nancy Stanley, Assistant Dean for Advancement,
James E. Rogers College of Law, University of Arizona

*

Branching Out

Once I began donating to the University of Arizona, I was included on every education donor list at every university. I began receiving phone calls from people I'd never heard of who just loved me and wanted me to become a part of their school. I joined many law school boards. Being on all of these boards was costly. I had to practice what I preached. If I were going to be very active in a school and solicit funds from others, I had to show my own financial support. Support can come in a variety of ways. Institutions always need money to hire big-name faculty and construct buildings. I want tangible results from my donations. Anyone who receives money from me knows I want two things: I want my money spent, not saved for a rainy day, and I want it spent on students.

One of my first involvements was based on my love of music. My father had a very fine baritone solo voice, and my mother was in the top five percent of non-professional pianists. My father won every singing contest he ever entered and was good enough to sing with the Jan Garber orchestra in the 1940s, but neither parent was ever good enough to earn a living. The love of music must be an inherited trait because at age seven, I was listening to Chopin and Tchaikovsky, Mozart, Beethoven and the others in that group. In 1945, Jose Iturbi recorded Chopin's Polonaise in A, which I believe sold more records that year than any other single record regardless of content. Jose Iturbi was one of Kathryn Grayson's closest friends. Kathryn had been the leading singing star of MGM from the late 1940s through the middle 1950s. She had the voice of an angel – a four-octave range. It was

Kathryn who discovered Mario Lanza, one of the ten greatest tenor voices of all time. At age 14 I went to see *Showboat* 15 times to listen to Kathryn. She, Ava Gardner, Howard Keel, and Marge and Gower Champion created a movie that would come to be of the top ten musicals of all time. I fell in love with Kathryn.

In 1995 I called Kathryn and talked about establishing the Kathryn Grayson Music Department at Idaho State. She and I went to Idaho State, established the program, and for several years she taught there. Her tremendous talent and her desire to teach students encouraged us to establish the Kathryn Grayson School of Voice at Idaho State University. When Louie and I bought the station in Pocatello in 1995, our first act was to go to the local university (ISU) and donate $75,000 for a general scholarship fund to be used as they saw fit. They were in shock; they'd never had that much donated at one time, and they never had anyone donate without first being solicited. They couldn't imagine someone coming in from out of state and having such an interest in local education.

We developed the Mass Communications Department at ISU as well. We brought people to teach, including executives from NBC, media lawyers from Washington, and a cadre of experts. The students learned what rules and regulations were, what they could and couldn't do, and what their responsibilities were as a holder of a federally granted license to broadcast. Those programs have had a solid impact on the students and the community – a good example of the positive and vital interaction between business and education that can improve any community.

> One day, out of the blue, Jim Rogers and Louie Weiner came into the university conference room and to meet the president [Dick Bowen] and me. Jim and Louie announced that they had just purchased the television station and [they only looked to expand] in cities where there were universities, and in those cities their first priority was to support – in a significant way – the university in that town. They brought us a check that very day – for something like $13,000. To us – to this institution – then and even now, that is a significant gift. They gave us that gift for music. I think they bought some pianos, as I recall.

And that began my relationship and this institution's relationship with Jim Rogers.

Kent Tingey, Vice President of University Advancement,
Idaho State University

*

Capital Campaigns

In the 1940s and '50s, universities received 80 percent or more of their funding from the state. The remaining 20 percent came from student tuition. The tuition students paid was generally very small. As colleges found their state funding dwindling, they started running capital campaigns – large-scale, multi-year fundraising drives to help continue to build and operate programs. Universities soon learned that research institutions were profit centers.

Higher education funding is changing radically and swiftly. For example, in the past few years, some state universities have seen their state support decrease to four percent. The other 96 percent of its revenue might come from other sources. Those other sources have been very profitable. Even with limited state revenue, some major universities remained the top 10 public institutions by raising money privately – from donors or research grants funded by governments or private industry.

The future of public higher education is only viable if it moves away from dependence on state funding. The world-class programs at our major universities will be driven by the demand of private industries. Universities must provide research to support the projects of private industry. Too often the public believes research centers mean the school has a lunatic in a basement developing an H-bomb. The expertise and knowledge the universities have developed from the sciences and other related areas are focal points for creativity. Businesses bring scientific projects to the universities so the universities can get government and private industry contracts to do research. As state funding continues to diminish, research funding will become even more important.

Even with research grants, capital campaigns are necessary to fund universities to keep them competitive. Capital campaigns have become very popular and have the additional purpose of getting the alums back into the university. Colleges and universities attempt to convince financially successful graduates that they have not paid the full cost of their education while there – much of their education had been subsidized by state taxes. Enlisting the aid of donors also keeps those donors close to their school. The donors begin to understand very profitable potential projects, especially in scientific research, and that universities can make substantial financial contributions to their communities.

I am surprised at the naivety of many of those in education about money. They don't think as businessmen do. A university or college's finances must be operated like any business – a concept that has been fought by academics since the beginning of time. Money spent must create a return. Colleges and universities must plan for the development of new products. If they don't, then they will fail to be competitive with those institutions that do. One of the major problems I've seen is that universities, eager to have buildings or colleges named after individuals, seek an initial gift that is too small. Assume $10 million is raised for the naming of the Agriculture College. Once the $10 million is donated, the naming of every other college at the university cannot and will not be more than $10 million. The initial gift sets a benchmark for what other donors will give. It's very important, as schools are thinking of naming a building or college after donors, that they understand they may be limiting future donations.

The second problem in raising money for a university is that if you're going to have just one capital campaign, 20 years after it ends when you need additional money, you'll find it difficult to raise more because you have nothing to sell. I've suggested that naming opportunities only last for a period of time. For example, the law school at the University of Arizona is named after me. I would have no problem if, 20 or 30 years from now when my family is no longer directly involved in the school, the university wanted to sell the law school building name again. Families don't need their names to last in perpetuity. Universities should think about term limits in order to be able to rename buildings, schools and colleges in the future.

Another danger in fundraising is making poor selections for the institution's board. The dean of a school will appoint a board – to support the school and shape its future – composed of alums or other business people in the community who don't know anything about education. I think there is a general misconception on the part of the business community that a university is a group of people teaching courses with no value, like English 101, the classics, and so forth, courses that will never be useful to the community at large. Having very little knowledge about how institutions are supported financially, deans tend to get their friends and community social leaders to serve. Frankly, they don't know how to use the universities' funds. They don't understand operating costs, sources of revenue, and other money that make a university tick.

On one occasion I spoke to the governing board of a law school. I was talking to the committee in charge of raising funds. When I looked around the room, I discovered that about one-third of the board were judges. The judges had been chosen because they had great credibility and stature in the community. Their cache as graduates of that law school could be converted into funds for the school – or so the board thought. No one considered that these appointments had a major problem: judges are not allowed to solicit money for anything. If a judge calls someone and asks for money, the potential donor is afraid not to give it for fear of future courtroom retribution. I suggested to the board (and I know I offended every one of them) that they all go home that night and type up their letters of resignation because there wasn't one person on that board who could actually solicit money for that school.

Eventually, most of this country's universities realized how much money could be raised by private campaigns, which are now fairly standard practice. Several asked me to advise them about fundraising because many had never done it. Development officers, whose job is primarily to secure donors and handle fundraising, are not, in my opinion, the best way to secure funding. I have strong feelings about full-time university employees being hired as "development officers." These people usually come up through the ranks; they have no understanding of money, have never given a nickel to any organization, and have nothing in common with major donors. I have always refused to deal with fundraisers from a university. I've always found it takes money to raise money. If my money is not important enough to have the president of the school call me directly, I don't feel that the school is important enough for me to donate to. I have always functioned under the assumption that presidents talk to presidents and donors talk to presidents, but donors don't talk to fundraisers. I've stayed away from those people as much as I can other than for record keeping. They're a type of shepherd and not real producers of funds.

> I'm in charge of (USC's ongoing) capital campaign, as president, but in the previous (campaign), Jim was really very helpful in the sense of giving me advice for some people or potential donors, or people who would be good to connect with the university, who could be very helpful one day. And that's what I really appreciated; I found that his advice was very valuable. I can give you one specific example. I just called to thank him about that recently. A number of years ago he called to my attention the Fertitta family in Las Vegas; Frank Fertitta is a graduate of the USC business school. He said, "This family could be very important to you one day." That's all he said. Just a month ago we announced a large gift from that family, to construct a new building for our business school. It took so many years, but the Fertittas have been wonderful. Frank is now on our Board of Trustees. I called Jim out of the blue and said, "I want to thank you for the advice you gave me about fundraising 6-7 years ago."
>
> Max Nikias, President, University of Southern California

*

Idaho

In 1995, I determined it would be best for the overall political strength of the stations that we expand into the intermountain west states, specifically Montana, Wyoming, Idaho and Arizona. My partner

Lou was not in favor because he saw the financial strength of stations in those small states as insufficient to justify the investment. However, Lou gave way to my position and we began to expand. Having built the Yuma station in 1989 and purchased the Reno station shortly thereafter, our next acquisition was in Pocatello, Idaho.

Lou and I had determined that our participation in the local higher education system would be important to us and the community. In the fall of 1995, Lou and I made arrangements for a meeting with the president of Idaho State University, Dick Bowen and his first vice president, Kent Tingey, to provide scholarships for students at Idaho State. Idaho State at that time had been converted from a community college to a four-year university only recently and was attempting to develop the broad range of four year college degree courses. Lou and I called President Bowen and told him we would like to meet with him and Dr. Tingey. At that meeting we expressed our desire to support higher education in southeast Idaho and we made a pledge to fund scholarships for $75,000. They were shocked that someone from out of town would contribute funds to the school. That initial investment by Lou and me continued after his death on February 6, 1996, and eventually our pledge to the school exceeded $4 million.

I was surprised to find I had become the local hero because donor support of Idaho State had been next to nothing. As I continued to support Idaho State, my role at Idaho State continued to grow. Idaho State seemed to me to have little understanding of the need for outside support from the community. The board of trustees and the president decided to have a capital campaign. I had been elected to the board of trustees because of my fundraising history at other schools. There were about 23 or 24 other people on the board. I have found that boards designed to advise universities are ineffective. They know very little about the university. They don't ever learn about the underpinnings of the school; they don't know what the problems are or what the solutions are because they don't have the time, background, interest or experience to understand education funding. My experience at the University of Arizona raising money, especially at the law school, was considered critical to the Idaho State campaign – I was made the chairman.

> Quite simply, in a word, what Jim brings to any organization is raw, fearless leadership. He is able to, in a very forceful and business-like way, but in the same time in a very optimistic way to say to everyone that we're shooting too low, we're thinking too small. Here's not only what we should do, but what we are very capable of doing, and he does that in a way that is so confident that when you're in that room and you're hearing him speak you just don't feel like you can fail. That's what he brought to the initial phase of the campaign – and then his leadership continued by being the largest donor and by being willing to step forward and go ask others to contribute.
>
> People who don't know him look at him as unapproachable, but as soon as you are involved in a project with him you realize that not only is he at the front of the pack, but he's also in the trenches and willing to work on things in a hands-on way.
>
> Pauline Thiros, Director of Planned Giving,
> Idaho State University

The initial meeting to discuss the goal of the campaign was heated. We asked everyone what they thought we should try to raise over a period of three to five years. The figure that stuck in everybody's mind was $25-30 million dollars. When it was my turn, I said my experience led me to believe there was a lot more money available, and if the school were to run a $30 million dollar campaign, that would be very shortsighted. I suggested a capital campaign goal of $102 million dollars. Two of the members resigned from the committee, saying they did not want to be embarrassed by attempting to raise $102 million dollars because that would fail. They said goodbye and good luck. The rest of the committee was shocked as well, but asked me how I came up with a goal of $102 million. I said, "Well, I picked $102 million because an odd figure like $102 million indicates we have an actual budget for what the departments and programs need. If we had simply picked a $100 million goal, people would think it an arbitrary figure and not realistic." The committee was cooperative and supportive, and adopted the $102 million goal.

I remember this university had never had a capital campaign when we first got to know Jim. We were new in the fund-raising business and Jim is an extraordinary fund-raiser for those causes that are important to him – and obviously higher education is critically important to him. We wanted to invite Jim to be on the Idaho State University Board of Directors – we had been talking about doing the university's first-time ever capital campaign. Jim guided us in that effort and became the president of the Idaho State University Foundation.

We struggled as a board to determine what that figure should be [the amount to raise in the campaign]. The only other capital campaign in the history of the state of Idaho had been a capital campaign by the University of Idaho, which was about twenty-five years older than our institution. Their goal was to raise $50 million dollars and I think they failed – although they got close to it, as I recall.

We were struggling to know what our goal should be. Some people said, let's try to raise $10 million and others said let's try to raise $20 million. People were saying that we could never hope to raise as much as the University of Idaho did, because they had been in the business much longer. I remember Jim saying, "I will not settle for that kind of fundraising effort. If you're going to think that small, then I am not going to involve myself in the fundraising at Idaho State University." So we started talking about $25 million - $50 million – and some people were aghast. I recall we were at a meeting, I believe it was in Sun Valley – in those days we had a meeting every six months – and as I recall, Jim said, "We're going to set a goal of $102 million dollars." That was beyond our comprehension; it wasn't even thinkable at the time and it upset a couple of our board members so badly that they walked out of the meeting and didn't return. They thought we were grasping at straws.

The foundation voted and approved a $102 million dollar campaign entitled "Creating Legacies at ISU." It was for three things: scholarships for students; academic enhancement – which could be anything that could help a teacher teach better or a student learn better; the final thing was a dream that we had – a beautiful performing arts center.

Kent Tingey, Vice President of University Advancement,
Idaho State University

At that same time Pocatello, Idaho, which has been a community interested in good schools, talked about building a special events center. They developed a plan, and the projected cost was between $30 and $35 million dollars. We undertook the raising of that money. Strangely enough, although the goal was projected over a five-year period, the goal was reached in three years. The final amount raised was about $165 million dollars. That was more than anyone ever dreamed possible. The performing arts center was built for $30 to $35 million. It now stands as a tribute to the people of eastern Idaho. It is a world-class performing arts center and has brought in leading orchestras, and world-class performances. If one really wants to see what a small town performing arts center can be, the one in Pocatello, Idaho, is a shining example.

> [Jim] brought up Louie Weiner and they had bought the TV station in Pocatello and they made an appointment to see me. They came in together and it was just a friendly meeting. They said they wanted to get acquainted with me and the university. One of the big things that they wanted to talk about was their philosophy of education and philanthropy. I got the impression that Louie had pretty much trained Jim in the philosophy of higher Ed and Jim expressed it. If I recall, Jim carried the burden of the conversation and Louie was supportive, but not as talkative. Still, I had the feeling that Louie was the senior member.
>
> The next thing I specifically remember is after Louie died, Jim was interested in building a journalism dept. We had a meeting, I think we were talking about a redesign of the liberal arts building or something, but it had something to do with building that communications/journalism major. Jim got up – and you could have knocked me over when he said that he intended to donate $20 million dollars to the school. Such things were unheard of – there was a lady from Arizona who had committed $10 million and we had named a building after her. Jim told me I sold the name of that building too cheap!

So, it just went on from there. When he came to town he liked to relate to the institution.

Dick Bowen, President, Idaho State University

If you look at education as a business, then all the institutions are going to have similar problems, even if they're on different scales. Sometimes a solution will work at one university or in one system, but doesn't have a chance in another. There's always something to learn. By being aware of what challenges universities face and how to deal with them – success comes relatively easily.

I'm not one who likes to visit my businesses and stay in hotels and motels. In each city where we have a station, we purchased a home and we spend an appreciable amount of time at that home. I purchased a home in Yuma, Arizona, which we eventually sold; a home in Reno, Nevada, which I kept for more than 15 years; a home in Helena, Montana, which we still have; and a property with several houses in Pocatello, Idaho. In January of 1996, we purchased a home in Pocatello that was on five acres of land immediately adjacent to the local golf course. The home was one quarter of a mile off the main highway and in an area that was sparsely populated; most of the home sites were two to ten acres. Being acquisitive as I am and one who has a neurotic need for more and more real estate, I began to buy the surrounding homes as they became available. From 1995 through 2011 we purchased approximately 48 acres, on which there were six homes. In each case we remodeled the homes. Because I intended to spend a great deal of my time there, we constructed facilities to store 30 of my classic automobiles. At the same time, having grown up in a family that owned and rode horses, and having owned ponies and horses since I was seven years old, I began purchasing Tennessee Walking horses. The horses grew in number to 28. We did not raise the horses for sale. They remain pets to this day. My grandchildren have been raised around horses, and during the summer they visit and ride the Walkers.

Eventually we built the main house, which houses more than $2 million in Western art. We built the main house to entertain and provide Idaho State with a venue for courting politicians and potential donors. Although only three bedrooms, the living room is by itself nearly 3,000 square feet, and along with the dining and television rooms easily holds 150 people. Idaho State which has used it on numerous occasions for fundraising.

*

The University of Arizona Capital Campaign

The University of Arizona decided to have a capital campaign. This campaign followed major capital campaigns at other schools in the Pacific 10. The Pac-10 schools are UCLA, USC, Stanford, Berkeley, the two Oregon schools, the two Washington schools, and of course the University of Arizona. Arizona State has also become a part of the Pacific 10. The University of Southern California initially adopted a $500 million dollar capital campaign goal. The campaign soon raised the $500 million. The goal was increased. Eventually the USC capital campaign raised $3 billion dollars. All of the other Pac-10 schools had capital campaigns and each raised hundreds of millions of dollars. Arizona decided to have its own capital campaign.

The campaign committee was formed; Karl Eller, for whom the business school is named (he gave over $20 million dollars), and I were appointed the co-chairs of the committee. We had an initial meeting and talked about the figure to be raised. The figure, as I recall, was in the area of $600 to $700 million dollars. I told the group I would not be a party to such a low goal. I thought the members of the Pacific 10 looked down on the University of Arizona as a stepchild that couldn't really compete with the big boys. If we picked a modest capital campaign figure, it would confirm this feeling. We picked the figure of $1.2 billion dollars to be raised over a 5-year period. As I recall, $1.3 billion was raised in less than the 5-year period established.

*

The William S. Boyd College of Law

Although I didn't go to college or law school in Nevada, it's my home state, and I've gotten involved in many Nevada higher education projects. Some have been very successful, and others haven't. You never know how something is going to work out until you get deep into it. I don't believe in doing things in half measures, and I never ask someone for money if I haven't got my own skin in the game. When I was approached about helping corral donors for a law school in Las Vegas, I immediately committed a substantial amount of money. As more and more local donors got involved, and the real possibility took shape to construct a solid, competitive college of law, I got more and more involved.

> What Jim did with the law school was just a miracle; I thought we'd never have a law school here, and but for him we probably wouldn't, to tell you the truth. So God bless him for — we were one of two states (with Alaska) to not have a law school, and it was really a strain on the legal community to not have a law school here. It was an embarrassment for a state this size to not have a law school; and he made sure we had one that's in the top 100 already, and it's incredible that such a new school is already ranked so highly, as ours is. That's mainly due to Jim Rogers. He promoted the school, made sure we had great professors, excellent admission standards His hands are all over the creation of that law school and that's top notch in his philanthropy as far as I'm concerned. I know he's a very generous man.
>
> Mike Cherry, Justice, Nevada Supreme Court

The first step — even before the building was finished — was to find a dean capable of taking a new school and putting it on the map. Dick Morgan was the perfect person to be the first dean of the law school at UNLV. When the law school opened its doors, its first ranking was in the 70s — really a fantastic start.

One of the reasons I wanted to become dean of a new law school rather than an established law school was because I figured there'd be less resistance to doing things differently. Most established law schools are hesitant about making changes too rapidly and have a conservative bent. One of my goals (in becoming dean of a new law school) was to try to be able to create a vision of a law school that would be based on community service; the law school ought to be seen as a resource that makes the community in which it's situated better. It shouldn't be just about training lawyers or producing arcane legal scholarship. There are many ways in which the law school can tangibly make the community a better place. So I wanted there to be a strong community component to the mission and vision of the school. As part of that, it was my desire to have students, right from the start of their legal education, participate in legal issues in the community, not only to make a tangible contribution to the community and the underserved population, but also to give the students exposure right from the start about the huge legal needs that people in the community have.

I hadn't quite figured out how to do this, but on the second day I was on the job as newly appointed dean of the School of Law, Barbara Buckley came to see me and explained to me that she was the director of what's now called the Legal Aid Center of Nevada (it was then called Clark County Legal Services) and said that she wanted to have connections with the law school. She hadn't quite figured out how to do that, but she knew that with a new law school, the Legal Aid Center should be connected. We agreed that having the first year law students participate in helping to educate low-income people about various areas of the law would be a good way to connect our students to Legal Aid and to connect Legal Aid to our law school.

Every first-year student (in groups), under supervision of real lawyers, prepares a workshop which they offer to the low income community to explain to them how things work in divorce court or small claims court, or the basic requirements of bankruptcy law. These are just informational sessions; it's not students giving legal advice, [as] they're not qualified to give legal advice, but they are providing a sort of self-help informational center for people in need. And Legal Aid uses those sessions as a precondition to getting services from them. Over the years, some 50,000 people have been helped by UNLV law students.

Dick Morgan, Former Dean, UNLV School of Law

Dick Morgan did a world-class job of building the UNLV law school. He poached faculty from other schools. You could block out UNLV's name from the top of the list of UNLV's law faculty and distribute it among the 180 law schools in the country – not one of them would disagree with the statement that it's a top ten faculty.

It's not difficult to put together a good school – but you have to specialize in the areas you can offer that your competition can't offer. There are only about eight law schools in the U.S. that offer a Doctorate in Judicial Science, called the JSD. Arizona offers two, and the University of Arizona brings people from all over the world to those programs. UNLV therefore got into areas where it wouldn't have competition. Gaming Law, for example, is an area that not many other law schools offer, even though there's gaming everywhere.

People have often noted that I'm very specific with my financial gifts, and that's true. I don't like endowments, which is when large donations are squirreled away in the bank and the university or college tries to live on the interest. That doesn't make a big enough impact for me. I want to see buildings go up, students funded, faculty hired. I don't want my donations molding away in a bank account somewhere. I make sure that institutions I'm giving money to use it immediately.

The only express restriction that Jim put on the money he gave to the [William S. Boyd] law school over the years was that it could not be used as an endowment. Endowment, of course, connotes a gift of which the principle amount is invested, and the earnings off of the principle are then spent for the benefit of the program (with the endowment itself being inviolate – it can't be spent). Jim's condition for us (and for most of his gifts at the University of Arizona as well) was that they *NOT* be endowment gifts – that they be spent.

He started out by giving us $250,000 a year for ten years, and then for the following ten years his commitment was to give $500,000 a year, and then for the third decade was to give $750,000 a year. The terms for those gifts, however, was that we had to spend the money. The whole amount was to be spent. And so we did, on things like scholarships for students, supplementing faculty salaries so that we could hire faculty from top institutions at competitive salary packages. We'd take whatever the state could provide for salary and then added on a chunk on top of that of private money. We called a number of those people James E. Rogers professors.

We spent money on building improvements; when the law school was started, we had to design and construct different facilities. The first was a temporary facility over in the old Paradise Elementary School on Tropicana, right across from campus, where Jim's mother had taught for 35 years. We turned that into a temporary law school, which required a fair amount of monetary investment, and after that we turned the old library in the center of the UNLV campus into the permanent law school, which required a good deal of funding. And while the legislature put up most of the money for both of those facilities, we used private funds – some from Jim, some from other donors – to do that work as well. Mostly the donation money was for scholarships for students or salaries for faculty, or facilities.

Jim's only input for us as a donor was that he wanted the law school to be first rate. And he didn't want us to do things in a cheap way or to cut corners, and his money was there as the augmentation or the resource that could really help us to do things in an excellent way. But he never stepped in to say things like, "I want you to hire faculty members who are interested in this subject," or "I don't want you to hire faculty interested in this subject."

Our funding didn't grow [in the down years] as much as we would have liked, but the legislature treated us very fairly throughout. Jim had a role in that too – he included (in all of his gifts to us and the University of Arizona) a provision in the gift arrangement that said his gift was conditioned upon the legislature providing reasonable support and that if he found out that his money was being used to replace legislative money that was being withdrawn, that he would cancel the gift. Because he was fully aware, when there was a lot of publicity about his putting in major gifts, that there would be people in public office who would say, "Those must be rich law schools now, which means the legislature doesn't have to support them as much." So he put these provisions in his gifts saying that the legislature *DOES* have to continue steady support. I think the clause said was that the law school couldn't be disproportionately funded – it didn't prevent the legislature from cutting budgets, but just said they couldn't be singled out for cuts based on their donations.

Dick Morgan, Former Dean, UNLV School of Law

UNLV recruited some really first class faculty, many of whom teach at night in addition to their full-time law practices in town. It's important for students to learn from people who actually *DO* – if they're not good at winning cases in the area they're teaching, what can they offer? Having successful, practicing lawyers makes the UNLV program really good, and a bit different from some of its competitors.

> UNLV recruited first class faculty. Jim is the rare business person/donor who really understands higher education very, very well. Jim understands the importance of excellence. Everyone wants greatness, but when the rubber hits the road their notion of greatness is ceded to other ideas that they think are important. But I think the most substantial thing, particularly in the context of the law school – and law schools are very, very competitive amongst one another – is that having an excellent faculty is key to having an excellent program. In the long term, having a great faculty with a great reputation will pay dividends years down the line as the reputation of the school continues to grow.

John White, Executive Vice President and Provost, UNLV

Another really important aspect of UNLV's program is that it really requires students to become engaged in the local community. I believe in the importance of knowing about problems around you. Everything in a community is connected, from the top to the bottom. You can't live in a bubble and hope the city's economy and education miraculously improves on its own. It takes teamwork. I was able to help introduce a few people around town that really made this idea of community service a part of UNLV's law school, and I couldn't be happier about the success they've had, and the quality of experience this brings to UNLV's law students.

I can't even begin to tell you what a difference the law school has made on Legal Aid. Prior to the law school coming, we would have thousands of people coming to us with the same question. It's a matter of figuring out how you funnel your limited resources to help as many people as you can.

And the law school, from year one, embarked on a partnership with us, through which all the law students are required to do community service as a condition of graduation. Most of the students take a crash course in the law with us, watch us teach classes, and then the next week they teach the classes. So every week, we have over 150 people attending classes on divorce, custody, bankruptcy, small claims, guardianship, foreclosure, how to represent yourself in small claims court – and since the beginning of the law school, 60,000 people have gone through these classes, and so instead of us explaining one at a time, "Okay this is what you have to do for guardianship," we do it en masse, and then give people applications for our services, so that when people come in they have the application complete. We would never have been able to perform that innovation without the law school. We would have never gotten the law school without Jim Rogers.

Barbara Buckley, Former Nevada State Assemblywoman

Overall, I think UNLV's law school has really done well, and I'm happy to have been an instrumental part of its early growth. I've moved on to other projects since, but the William S. Boyd School of Law is really first rate, and it's been a wonderful addition to education in Nevada, and the city of Las Vegas itself.

*

Desert Research Institute (DRI)

I discovered the Desert Research Institute was an education entity unto itself separate from the other institutions of the Nevada System of Higher Education. It has faculty without tenure. It does not have students. It performs research and has developed an international reputation for environmental research. As I learned a year ago, the Desert Research Institute is a profitable entity. Every nickel the state gives it is matched by $4 of outside investment. DRI is a shining example of how research institutions must operate outside with external funding to stay alive.

I got involved with DRI for personal reasons. In 1951, it was decided the Nevada Test Site would be developed for experimentation of atomic devices. My father was the chief operating officer at the Nevada Test Site, and came to Las Vegas in 1951 to establish what was to become the Nevada Test Site, and to determine where the primary support system for the atomic testing would be constructed. A town called Mercury, Nevada, was constructed. The company my father worked for got the construction contract in late 1951. In June of 1953 my mother and I moved from Los Alamos to Las Vegas. I had just finished my freshman year in high school.

When the initial devices were detonated, they were dropped from an airplane and exploded at 500 to 1,000 feet above ground. The explosion occurred between eight a.m. and ten a.m. The air pressure was such that the explosion caused windows on Fremont Street in Las Vegas to be blown out. Later detonations were set off from three a.m. to four a.m. because the air pressure was different, and did not cause destruction in downtown Las Vegas. During the first ten years of its existence, the Nevada Test Site employed between 500 to 10,000 workers at one time based upon the level of activity. When there was no testing, the population dropped to 500. When there was testing, the population went as high as 10,000. Las Vegas, in the early 50s, had a population of approximately 20,000. That made the test site the largest employer in the state and the most significant driver of the economy. I spent summers working and living at the test site.

Approximately eight years ago, Troy Wade and other test site workers who had been involved in the above-ground and below ground testing came to see me about constructing an Atomic Museum at the DRI on the UNLV Campus. They suggested that the museum be named for my father. They also suggested that it would be helpful if I donated $ 3 million for the project.

Our (DRI) major involvement came with Jim before he was chancellor. We were looking to build the new building on our campus (now called the Frank Rogers building in honor of Jim's father), and in that building is a significant component of the history of the Nevada test site, for which both Jim and his father worked. That was where the atomic testing was done. The records are held on the second floor of that museum. At the time a museum was being planned to honor all of that work.

Troy Wade, from the Atomic Historical Testing Society, and I thought that it might be appropriate to see if Jim would be interested in providing support. Jim became captivated by this building, by the program that DRI has run now for almost 40 years, providing environmental science studies to the test site area, and stepped up and made a commitment of $3 Million, which he's fulfilling as we speak. There's a center at DRI for environmental remediation that's named after his father, The Frank Rogers Center.

When I was talking to him about making a gift to the DRI, he said, "I want to give to something that has meaning to southern Nevada that has an impact, something that has given DRI and southern Nevada an oomph to it." That's why we have this center, and we do a lot of work through the test site. He was so captivated with our history, and the fact that we had scientists who had worked out there when his father was there. His only requirement was to put it towards something that makes a difference and has an impact on southern Nevada. So I was really touched by that. The building recognizes his father's role in the test site; in fact, his father's desk sits in the Atomic Testing Museum. He was extremely excited when the historical society and DRI worked together to get the Smithsonian affiliation with that museum. That really made a difference for him, knowing that within the building is a Smithsonian affiliated museum.

Steve Wells, President, Desert Research Institute

The museum was built and opened and has been very successful. It explains the effects of the development of the atomic bomb on the entire world. It shows the planning and the eventual detonation of the two atomic bombs in Nagasaki and Hiroshima, Japan. Those two explosions killed substantially more than 200,000 people. Knowing that two bombs could do that much destruction, one would think that

the atomic bomb era would have long been abandoned. Obviously
that is not the case. During the last 60 years, from the first detonation
at the Test Site to the present day, every single year is filled with
threats from new nations to build atomic weapons.

As you tour the museum, you will note a small metal desk that is
approximately 4 feet wide and 3 feet deep. On that desk is a nameplate
with my father's name on it. That desk is his original desk from 1951.
It was found at the test site in a remote warehouse in the year the
museum was opened.

My summers at the test site are still clear in my mind. The
museum is a great snapshot of history and a substantive lesson in
human relationships.

*

I've had a lot of opportunities to meet many dynamic people who
have helped me contribute to the development of education, not only
in Arizona and Nevada, but other states in the intermountain west
region. I'm happy to see so many of the programs and projects I
helped shape or get started are doing so well today, although they
continue to face funding and legislative challenges. If everyone took an
interest in and did what they could for their local universities, there
would be a correlating development in the engagement and
achievements of the communities themselves. I really believe this –
everyone must get involved to make their cities and universities a
success.

I've ruffled some feathers by rescinding donations – in fact, I've
gotten some pretty bad press, particularly in Nevada, for changing my
mind about a donation. I want my money to go directly to helping
students via scholarships, faculty, buildings, and other tangible and
immediately helpful ways. If I give money with the intention of
helping a particular group or college, and the administration decides it
is going to use it for something else – they will never get another
nickel from me. I know some donors don't care where their money is
actually spent. They may be concerned about their name on a building
– but they *should* be wary of having their funds sucked up by

administrative salaries and university operating costs. I like to see immediate results and development – I love building, but I also love scholarships. I want to see results, numbers, and projects completed with my money.

Chapter VI

HIGHER EDUCATION

From the history of the United States, following the Depression of 1929 and through the end of World War II and then the Korean War, I have formed an opinion of what may have led to the slow death of America's education system in the 1980s, 1990s and 2000s. I'm not a historian, a sociologist, an expert in education, a financial wizard, or knowledgeable in international relations, but I still have a few views of my own.

Prior to the Depression, society believed the key to success was education. Unfortunately, less than ten percent of high school graduates then had the opportunity to go to college. Going to college was generally a central goal in the lives of all families. The Depression of 1929 made the U.S. population begin to understand that the U.S. economy was so complex and the business environment so filled with flaws, that the only way to solve our problems was to develop an educated work force from the top to the bottom of the economic strata so that every citizen could help develop and sustain the U.S. economy.

The Second World War began in the late 1930s, although the U.S. wasn't directly involved until late 1941. The first half of the 1940s certainly took its toll, not only on American lives, but on the American economy. The American economy then shifted to provide for the needs of the war effort and produce goods and services needed by the army. The Second World War ended in 1945. When Americans looked around, the rest of the world appeared destroyed. Germany had been leveled, England had been buried, Russia had lost 18 million of its citizens, Japan had literally been blown to pieces, and China was not a force in any way. America had no competition and was in a position to build an economy that could sustain itself and not be affected by the economies of any other nation.

Without competition from outsiders, every American got a piece of the pie. But unobserved by most Americans, the economies of Europe began to grow. The Japanese economy exploded, and even the Chinese finally began to understand economics and competition and how they could become a real world competitor. While every other economy was growing, the United States' economy exploded. Americans began to believe that they were "entitled" to a living – that the world owed them a living and they didn't have any responsibility. The concept of "entitlement" ruled every conscious thought of the great majority of Americans.

Once the entitlement concept penetrated the American mind and soul, Americans began to believe they had no responsibility to participate in and support their own society and their own economy. That's when education began to fail. The average American's attitude was, "Why should I work hard, go to college and waste four to eight years of my life when I can live off an economy which is self-sustaining, highly productive and capable of sustaining itself forever? The machinery, technology and inventiveness of the American mind has created an economic utopia that will support me the rest of my life."

Education was the primary victim of this new thought process. Few people sought an education purely for the sake of improving their minds. They only did so because they wanted to increase the weight of their pocketbooks. If the pocketbook is full, why go to college? What the working man didn't learn was that while he thought the economy didn't need him to remain strong, the economy learned that it didn't need the worker at all. That began the increase in the division between the rich and the poor. The rich found they could develop technology that would produce everything previously made by the hands-on labor of the working man, and if the economy was strong enough to fully support the richer half, that half could sustain and support itself without the participation of the bottom half.

The 50 percent of Americans who quit high school before graduation constitute a great segment of the U.S. population that is lost forever. It has no way to recover from its present condition.

Although that segment has now found itself outside the American economy, the economy continues to grow and move even farther and farther away from this lost generation. I'm not so sure the generation of students in the education system in the next 20 years will have developed sufficient knowledge to be able to escape the effects the present generation has had on education, but my belief is that we had better start preparing for that next generation. We need to make sure that this generation is aware of the benefits of an education – not only to deal with the everyday problems in life, but to be able to participate in the American economy.

One thing is certain: the rich will continue to get richer, the middle class will shrink, and the lower class will find itself totally isolated from an economy that neither needs nor wants them.

The average American might have had two or three issues in the 1950s that affected his life; now he has 100 issues preventing him from making a living, saving enough money to retire, and taking care of himself in his later years. In 1938, the year I was born, the life expectancy of an American was 59 years. Now it's almost 20 years longer. People retire when they're 65 because the economy no longer has a need for them. Unfortunately they can't live on what they've saved. I remember my parents talking about retiring. There was no Social Security – people didn't need a Social Security System because life was so short. They didn't anticipate living 20 years after they retired. Today, an education and a good paying job are necessary to provide funds to support yourself after retirement.

America trains an embarrassingly low number of highly educated professionals – especially engineers and mathematicians. America's road to success can only be built by a population that starts pushing its children in the first grade and pushing them to graduate from college and take jobs that are productive for the American economy.

Twenty years ago I believed that our education problems could be solved. I now believe they cannot be solved. The failure of the American education system has been festering for at least the last few decades. Americans have decided that culture is not important; being able to read is not very important; listening to good music is not important; being able to go to a lecture and understand the speaker is not important. What is important to Americans is how little they can do to get as much as they can to live the good life.

I have examined the education system carefully and thoroughly the last 25 years. When I was in college 50 years ago, the public believed those who went to college produced a product that benefited everyone. An educated population improved the standard of living and quality of life for everyone. Those who were highly educated developed products that created a healthier public and enhanced lives. That belief is gone. Those without education believe those with an education could and should pay for that education because it only benefits those who are educated.

> Historically, before WWII, higher education was largely reserved to people of high income or certain socio-economic backgrounds. The GI Bill opened up education to a huge sector of our society. That has been a very positive thing and one of the great accomplishments of our country. But, over time, because of economic and social pressures and changes in demographics, that opportunity is beginning to fade. Whether it is because of economic reasons or social reasons or cultural reasons . . . people are beginning to lose that opportunity. I am a product of a public education system and the concern I have is that over time we are going to become a multi-tiered society in which only the few, the wealthy, and the connected will have access to the best institutions. A lot of opportunities are limited to those who have access to the opportunities those institutions provide.
>
> Michael Wixom, Nevada Board of Regents

Not only is an education necessary for financial success; to have a society of substance, its members must have the ability to understand life, to participate in the community and to understand political and economic problems. Seven billion people presently populate the earth. That population will grow to 14 billion people in our lifetimes. How do we feed them, clothe them? How will they get from point A to point B? The complications of today's life are infinitely greater than those 50 years ago. If education 50 years ago was critical to the success of the United States, how can it be anything less today?

The failure of the American education system is the fault of every American. The financial and moral support of our teachers is a disgrace. There is a direct relationship between what you pay and what you get. You can attempt to fool yourselves by saying those who want to teach should be devoted and want to teach for minimum wage because they love children, regardless of what they're paid. That is an illogical thought process contrary to every concept in the human mind. Everyone wants to be paid what he or she is worth. When you tell a teacher that his or her work is not worth a living wage, you can't expect enthusiasm or good results.

Society only seems to react to disasters. We do well in fighting wars. We are able to mobilize to fight an Adolph Hitler, a Stalin, or the Iranians. We recover from disasters because disasters require us to come together. We focus on the problem and then the solution. When we are repairing the results of a disaster, Americans focus on the problems and their solutions until such time as the problem is solved. Over a period of years, as the level of education began to fall, that fall was exacerbated because the uneducated could no longer support a higher education system to produce produce engineers, accountants, lawyers and doctors. When the entire population does not assume the responsibility of the costs of higher education, and the cost are thrust upon the college student, those who don't want an education won't get it, and those who want an education won't be able to afford it.

Legislators across this country have misunderstood the difference between education and training. State legislators are unsophisticated. They often ask ignorant questions. Why should we teach history? Why should we teach economics and music and advanced mathematics when more than 50 percent of our students will never graduate from high school? For the 50 percent who do graduate, the more sophisticated courses that have been taught in high school will have no use. Trade schools teach skills related to manual labor and give the impression that a trade school education is more than adequate to allow its graduates to fully participate in their communities. Nothing could be farther from the truth. Those who have simple answers and solutions to this country's problems have no idea what this country's problems really are. Given their lack of education and flawed understanding of how this country functions, they believe that our problems are simple and have simple solutions. That is the foundation of the Tea Party and that simplistic approach has created the series of actions that have no connection with the country's problems. Sarah Palin, Sharron Angle, Mike Huckabee, Rick Santorum, Michele Bachmann and Eric Cantor have solutions to problems that don't exist, and no solutions to problems that do exist. Their lack of understanding is proof positive that this country's education system is failing because its population is failing.

*

The Cost of Higher Education

I have become more and more concerned about the exclusion of so many from the economy because of the ever-increasing costs of obtaining a college education. The cost of education is the largest single economic problem facing the United States. No other problem goes to the core of the American worker's ability to succeed intellectually and financially. Financial support for a college education has either disappeared or has become so expensive that students can't afford it. I went to college for eight years, and my entire tuition bill was below $5,000. Tuition now runs an average of $25,000 to $30,000 per year at many schools. The great majority of students cannot generate enough money to pay the $30,000 tuition plus food and other living expenses. A student who does graduate from college often does so with debts he or she will never be able to pay. We've always called the United States "the land of opportunity." In the past 50 years, the growth of technology has transformed the economy into one few ever thought possible. Every American ought to be able to participate in that success. I believe that view prevailed until the last ten years. The new economic philosophy of America is that free enterprise, unrestricted competition, and greed are standards by which we get ahead. The thought of helping others become successful seems to have disappeared.

The present inadequacy of the higher education system to respond to the needs of the public and the inadequacy and inability of the public to know what its own needs are creates larger problems. An education system should satisfy those needs. Over the last 20 years, we've put ourselves into a position of not being able to get from point A to point B.

> Jim is right – I've never known his assessment to be wrong – I've known his solutions to be wrong. He doesn't have the patience for the entanglements that govern us. But he was right about what was wrong. Right now I categorize UNLV as a fairly average, moderately large state institution, with – like any other fairly average, moderately large state institution – some terrific programs and some okay programs. We are incredibly efficient, as a result of being starved, and we have produced some stunningly successful students and some students who are okay. We're challenged by a first-generation population, a population in which only 20 percent hold higher ed degrees.
>
> Those are the passions that drive Jim. How do you take a first generation population and build a highly educated population? How do you take a city of immigrants and turn it into a knowledge center? How do you respect the diversity and global nature of our population and educate them?
>
> Neal Smatresk, Former President,
> University of Nevada, Las Vegas

*

Education in Nevada

Louie was 24 years older than I was. At age 60, he wasn't very interested in the expansion of the company. One of the projects we were both interested in was bringing the state together; the north and the south at that time might just as well have been in two different states. Neither the north nor the south understood the other, and there was a constant bitter and destructive battle between them. The Nevada legislature was always split and ill prepared to govern; it did a very poor job of planning. The north took advantage of the south's naïveté, and pushed legislation through the system that favored the north and cheated the south. Bill Raggio had so much power that, for all intents and purposes, he was king of the state – not just head of the Republican party and the majority leader in the Senate. He had more, infinitely more, power than the governor – and he used and abused it. That caused all sorts of problems. There were terrible discrepancies in state funding between northern Nevada schools and southern Nevada schools. Southern Nevada had 75 percent of the population and produced 75 percent of the state's tax income, but received only 50 percent of the state's funds. This caused all of southern Nevada's governmental functions to fail, especially education.

Louie and I felt if we broadcast news in the north related to the south and vice versa, we could do something to encourage joint efforts between the two. We purchased the NBC station in Reno and later bought the construction permit for Channel 10 in northeast Nevada and built a station on the Great Basin Campus in Elko. We were not very successful in bringing the state together. In fact, we were not very successful in getting our three NBC stations to cooperate. Their viewpoints were different. I'm not sure exactly how to describe it, but none of the stations had much use or respect for the others. The stations in the south thought northerners phonies, an arrogant and empty-headed group that hadn't had a creative thought in 100 years. The northerners thought the southerners were gambling bums who ran whorehouses and never read books or listened to good music. The misconception that there is nothing to talk about with northern Nevadans continues today.

Louie and I tried to do our best to support both universities in Reno and Las Vegas. We gave $750,000 to one of the scientific projects at UNR. We also gave money to the medical school in Reno with the hope that by participating in the northern education system, they would be more amenable to joint ventures with UNLV. Unfortunately, that didn't prove to be true. UNR looked down its nose at UNLV, and thought UNLV was a junior college with a university's name. UNR seemed to think that UNLV would never catch up to it in size or influence. In some aspects that was true and remains true today because northern legislators made sure that money coming from southern Nevada wasn't equitably distributed throughout the higher education institutions. Another problem we encountered while trying to encourage cooperation was that the very nature of Las Vegas did not support a university. The inability or refusal of faculty and staff to sell themselves to the public by participating in community activities also made it impossible for the university to grow. While southern Nevadans knew very little about UNLV, northern Nevadans knew more about UNR and enthusiastically supported their local institution.

The College of Southern Nevada, for example, is the third largest community college in the country today. Nevada has several other institutions, each serving distinct and often specialized populations around the state. Most Nevadans have not heard of Great Basin College, Western Nevada College, and Nevada State College, yet each excels at what it does. The only education institutions within their regions, they get little or no local support. They have to fight for every dollar they get.

> We are a small institution, so it's easy for us to fall through the cracks. Today, the institutions about whom the state is most concerned are the two universities and the largest community college (CSN). The other institutions have two problems: they're small, especially Great Basin College and Western Nevada College; and secondly, we're community colleges. Community colleges in this state don't get enough respect. The principle reason you have community colleges is not well understood. I don't really think many of the regents understand the importance of the community colleges to the social and economic welfare of the state.

> The fact is, if you really want to build a middle class, if you really want to improve education long term, you really have to start at the grassroots level. And that's what good community colleges do. My focus is on getting kids either trained in occupations, or to get them ready to go to college and teach them how to succeed in college. These are not remedial issues in our part of the state, as much as they are developmental issues. Our students are first generation and

first in family students who need help adjusting to the various challenges of succeeding.

Carol Lucey, Former President, Western Nevada College

This inequity has dominated the state's history. The Nevada legislature, even though structured to have given UNLV adequate funding during the early development of UNLV, gave unfair and excessive funding to the north even though the south held a majority in both the House and the Senate. Legislators in the south knew very little about the higher education system in Nevada, and did not seem to be interested in learning its importance. Southern Nevada's legislators made little effort to examine the Nevada system of higher education because their careers outside the legislature required their full-time attention.

The Bill Raggio power regime began to grow in the early 1970s. That regime supported northern Nevada's education system and gave little support to the higher education system in southern Nevada. During all those years, when southern Nevada supplied 75 percent of the tax revenue of the state and enrolled 75 percent of the state's higher education students, the north managed to ensure an even split of tax revenues allocated for education. The inequitable distribution of state funding shouldered UNLV with additional burdens. As time went by, and UNLV rapidly expanded in step with the growth of the city of Las Vegas, the fiscal hardships for southern Nevada schools became even worse.

> We talked about the NSHE system, and that the monies weren't distributed properly (and they haven't been since 1973 when I came here); we talked about the bureaucracy of it all and discussed the fact that education is probably the most inflexible bureaucracy in the country today. A lot of people become entrenched, and rather than looking at new ideas or ways to share leadership, they try to throw up roadblocks. And Jim of course was on the cutting edge of things, and he's a blunt person who will tell you what he thinks. He felt very strongly that we should try some new things, but the system wasn't ready for those new things. And in bureaucracy we play a lot of games and Jim wasn't one for

playing games, either. Now, I don't always agree with Jim;
there have been times we've differed – not very many – but
even when I didn't agree, he always had some good reasoning
behind his opinions.

Lois Tarkanian, Las Vegas City Councilwoman

It's easy to blame the presidents of the system for not
cooperating and acting as one institution. The underlying structure of
the system was flawed from the start and that problem was
exacerbated because the legislature did not equitably distribute funds.
The confrontations caused by this inequitable distribution of money
were explosive. The presidents didn't speak to each other and did
everything they could to undo what the others were doing. The
presidents would lobby the legislature at five a.m. on the last day of the
session to plead for more than their fair share of tax funds. The two
universities were bitter enemies. There was no chance the two
institutions could work together and combine their strengths to build a
good system.

Fortunately for the Nevada system, which is different from many
other state systems, there is a single Board of Regents that oversees the
higher education system. Arizona has two types of Boards of Regents
– one board governs the three state universities, and boards in each
county govern their community colleges. In many states, even though
there is a Board of Regents overseeing all three or four or five of that
state's universities, there is no administrator to coordinate the efforts
of those universities. In Idaho, the Board of Regents administers the
state's education system from K through 16. However, the three
universities – The University of Idaho, Boise State, and Idaho State –
do not have anyone coordinating efforts among them. They tend to
duplicate projects. There is no way to coordinate and control the
efforts of the schools, whose competition hurts all three. The schools
have separate goals, openly criticize each other's programs, and
complain about each other to the legislature. The legislature tends to
believe all the negative reports about the inefficiencies of the
institutions.

This structure is fundamentally flawed. Nevada's system is a superior way to administer the operations of a university system. While each institution wants its own professional schools and programs, a smaller state the size of Idaho or Nevada cannot have two or three universities each with its own medical school, dental school, and law school. It's just not a fiscal reality.

> Jim's vision – and I certainly support and agree with that vision – holds that higher education has a two-pronged responsibility here in Nevada. The first is that every qualified, prepared student has an opportunity to attend an institution of higher education and pursue whatever goals or dreams he or she has. That is an inherent obligation in our state constitution. Nevada is the only state that has four branches of government: the executive, the legislative, the judicial – and higher education. The Board of Regents here is the only one of its kind in the U.S. The other side of this is that institutions have to provide a quality education, and the access must be meaningful. There has to be an opportunity to move vertically.
>
> Jim's vision was not just to improve access, but to pull quality along. In that regard he was very frank, and said some things that were not politically correct, but they were accurate and they are still what we need to do to improve quality. Sometimes feathers need to be ruffled.
>
> Michael Wixom, Nevada Board of Regents

*

Other Problems with the Nevada System of Higher Education

There are a lot of problems with the system. I don't know if they're all fixable, but certainly some of them that are impeding the growth of the state and the communities around the universities can be fixed.

> UNLV is in a unique position – and not necessarily a good one. When most schools grew dramatically, in the 60s and 70s, there was a lot of money around and elected officials deferred – to a great degree – about how the money should be spent. UNLV grew at a time when the money wasn't quite

as available and wasn't really able to catch up with its growth. We struggled to catch up. We're kind of an island – we have to recruit faculty from far-away places, with the attendant difficulties of trailing spouses and our inability to be able to place a spouse in outside industry because we lack economic diversity. So, we made inordinate use of part-time instructors and never got our faculty as big as it should be . . . and then we were walloped with massive cuts.

The second difficulty for UNLV is that because the town has grown so rapidly, a lot of pressure has been put on us to serve the town – on the one hand – and yet the people who moved here came for economic opportunities rather than because this was their dream place to live. There is a tremendous disconnect with UNLV as an institution. There is also the problem that most of our growth has taken place since we won the national championship, so most people's view of UNLV is frozen in time, 20+ years ago when we had 13,000 students and we were a little tiny college town here. I can't tell you how many times I have been with folk who were students here and came on campus and couldn't believe how much it has grown. You'd think they would know.

If you put all those pieces together, you have a community that has a certain view of UNLV that is not consistent with what we currently are. They have a diminished view, relative to schools that they remember from their original towns, and last, we have a press here that for whatever reason isn't really invested in supporting us. So, yes, if you put it all together, we do have some substantial need to try and convey who we are, the accomplishments of our faculty, the excellence we have achieved – even the pedigree of our faculty.

John White, Executive Vice President and Provost, UNLV

The system of higher education in Nevada has many overwhelming problems – all large systems do. Nevada, however, has a special set of problems. There is a total disconnect between the community and its educators. Nevada's educators don't see a need to promote what they do. The refusal of faculty members to market the university's products is a major problem. The public does not know what UNLV does to earn its keep. If universities are in the business of teaching students, those teachers ought to expand their actions to teach the public at large. They should help the public understand the importance of the university system, what it adds to the culture and economy of a community. The University of California, Berkeley, Stanford University, MIT, and Harvard understand the importance of a university system and what it does for the local culture and economy. Those institutions all reach out to the public for help and support while simultaneously keeping the public informed of what it is getting for its money. Nevada's education system has done little to sell itself to the community. Every time the state cuts funding, the public either doesn't notice or doesn't care. The public's feeling seems to be that education has more funds than necessary, and that college professors don't work very hard – college professors teach two or three courses a week and don't participate in the community. Because of this misperception, the public does not see the need to support education financially.

> I was always struck with Jim's passion for higher education. He wants quality higher education in the state of Nevada. He is willing to champion it and he was willing to sacrifice for it; he was willing to contribute to it and I always found that to be a real tribute to him because his passion for higher education means he is passionate for the next generation and the next generation's success.
>
> He has also been one to challenge the quality of what we do. It's not enough that we do it; we need to want to do it well. In all my dealings with him he has stressed quality and educational standards. That's what we try to do here and we now have thirty programs that have specialized accreditation, where it is available, and that says something about the quality of those programs. As the word gets out to the public, it can rely on the fact that these are programs of national quality. Jim set the tone for that and so I give him a lot of credit for that as well.
>
> Mike Richards, President, College of Southern Nevada

I was positively shocked by many professors throughout the Nevada system who believe that their function is solely to do research or to teach, and they are not in the job of community relations. This arrogance and ignorance has resulted in many state legislatures across the country concluding that public education is grossly inefficient: higher education is arrogant and does not pay its community rent. The recent gutting of the higher education system budget reflects not only a lack of money, but an attitude of disinterest by the public – even if there were money available for education, the public would still not fund it. As bright as academics are, their ability to understand their relationship with the community is shockingly absent. Some day they may discover they don't have a university because the public never understood its value and finally just closed it down.

> One problem with faculty is that they are not good marketers. UNLV is a really good school, but not consistent. The programs that are good are really good, and the programs that are crappy are crappy. In the past that didn't matter because of Nevada's growth, but the downturn has changed that. When we went through, as a system, and cut programs, we'd discover some XYZ program that had 10 kids in it and nobody had ever graduated from it, but it was still around. If you have good programs, you have to let people know about them, and if you have programs that are weak, you shouldn't, for example, be pushing a mediocre Ph.D program.

> UNLV has an advantage. It's the only university in town. It should be able to get people to help, but sometimes it seems like they just don't. They seem very insular. They have a bit of group-think going on. They have had some people, like the Brookings Institute, who have come in – but they need more people who want to help. People like Jim.

> Kevin Page, Nevada Board of Regents

The problems grow and the educators make them worse. Their position is: "We are here to teach. We are not here to play in politics, not here to get money from the legislature. That is someone else's job." That position won't continue to fly. No one has a greater interest and more knowledge about the problems, costs, and value of education than the professors. But until they start to pitch their product, the public will not stop reducing funding for higher education.

Because Jim's interest in education kind of runs the gamut, I'll often run across him and we'll talk about different topics that I know he's pretty much an expert on. I really respect his opinion – although I might not always agree with it. Jim and I probably wouldn't agree on all of the solutions to education. That certainly doesn't make me right; we just come at it from a different perspective. What I admire most about him is that he is passionate about it – and I don't think anyone can question that. My experience has been, whenever anyone reaches out to him on education issues, he's there.

John Guedry, President, Bank of Nevada

*

Tenure

Another major problem with the education system is the concept of tenure. I have always had a dislike of tenure. It's an inefficient system that is outdated and prevents universities from maintaining a highly producing faculty. Tenure was originally developed to protect the free speech and research interests of faculty. Professors apply for tenure after six years. They must show they've published, served the campus community, and excelled in the classroom. Most new or young faculty do all these things. Once tenure is awarded, however, it becomes nearly impossible for a university to terminate that professor – even if that professor is no longer fulfilling his or her commitments. Tenure is viewed as the holy grail of job security. While there are many long-time tenured faculty who produce quality teaching and resources for the university, many just stop working. There's no compelling reason for them to continue to work as hard as they did to get tenure – and many of them don't. The university is left with a large contingent of former academic rock stars just coasting on minimum power until retirement. Tenure slows down the efficiency and productivity of universities all across the country.

This concept would bankrupt a business venture. As a CEO, if I looked at the bottom 10 percent of my company's employees and found them to be unproductive, I would terminate that 10 percent and replace the staff with those who would produce. If this type of "performance evaluation" is done on a regular basis, and one replaces the bottom 10 percent of employees every year, the quality of employees and therefore the quality of the product will improve. This doesn't mean younger is better. Experienced employees are able to perform with skills that can only be developed after years of trial-and-error and personal development. But too often employees get comfortable and no longer go through evaluation checkpoints to make sure they're performing well. They get lazy. It's human nature. Providing regular assessments – setting goals and performance requirements – and performance bonuses – ensures that employees and companies are functioning at their optimum.

If a college has 100 tenured professors and the bottom 10 are incompetent, and don't produce a damn thing, they keep their jobs. If they use the same notes for teaching they used 35 years before, never seem to be on campus, and don't have any relationship with the students, it doesn't matter because tenure will protect them. If the institution wants to unload that professor and get a new, young professor to teach those courses, one who will relate to the students and who will take them under his or her wing to develop top graduates, it can't be done. Without the ability to upgrade, the system is condemned to mediocrity. That bottom 10 percent lacks ability, lacks enthusiasm, and lacks productivity, all of which will infect the institution itself. As the group gets older, productivity and enthusiasm diminish. Without new blood, colleges not only can't compete – their productivity will deteriorate.

> At the Cleveland Clinic, which Jim is a big supporter and fan of, every doctor is on a one-year letter of engagement. When I had the opportunity to go around to different universities and different places [finding a partner for the Ruvo Center], I chose the Cleveland Clinic in part because of those one-year appointments. There is no tenure; employees have to constantly prove themselves to be part of the system.
>
> Larry Ruvo, Vice President and General Manager,
> Southern Nevada Wine and Spirits

Let me give you another example of the shortcomings of tenure. The various presidents who were hired by the NSHE while I was the chancellor all received contracts for a period of three or four years with renewal clauses after the first or second year. Even though there were two or three years left on the contract, it would automatically be extended each year, so that there were always several years left on the contract regardless of how long the president had been there. When each of the presidents was hired, even though each had been in academia for many, many years, and had moved up from assistant to associate professor to full professor, then department chair, and then dean of the college, many lost most of the understanding of the day-to-day obligations of a professor on the front line of teaching. As each president moved up the administrative ladder, he or she retained tenure so if terminated as president, he or she would return to the classroom although they hadn't performed for 20 years.

If the institution hired a president and that president had been an engineer or scientist 20 years before going up through the ranks of management, that president was very likely completely out of touch with the current status of that profession. Yet most presidents are given tenure when hired, and if terminated for any cause (other than criminal), tenure allows them to be transferred to the department in which they had taught 20 years earlier and keep their jobs. The problem with this system is that even though the president is given at least one year to adjust to the new position, having been out of that profession for 10, 20 or 30 years, they are not eager to return to teaching. The university has bought itself a dead horse and may be feeding that dead horse for many years.

> Frankly, tenure can, in some universities, protect incompetent faculty from losing their job. On the other hand, if you're in the right kind of university – and many corporate executives don't know this – the tenure award process is a very severe screening process. In my early faculty life, I watched my colleagues drop around me – only half of us survived the tenure process. And getting tenure doesn't mean you relax, because you're not capable of relaxing – your whole life is about earning your spurs, earning your recognition in the

national research community that you are part of, so tenure does not have the consequence that many corporate executives fear.

On the other hand, tenure doesn't work for a second-class or third-class university. Because if the screening is not as rigorous, then faculty may not be driven to the kind of intellectual aspirations that are an essential part of a research university, so I understand the criticism. I do believe that lawyers should be the last ones to criticize, however. Making partner has many of the same characteristics [of tenure] and they make mistakes there, too. There are lots of arenas other than the academy in which you are obliged to go through the challenging test of your long-term competence. And if you pass that test then you are relatively secure in your employment, but psychologically unable to stop striving.

This is a counterpoint, but it's not exactly a contradiction. I think in some ways that tenure for administrators, even if it is faculty tenure for administrators, is probably not such a healthy idea. An administrator is much more like a corporate executive; if you're a university president you are rewarded in a way that is consistent with risk and you should – in my opinion – be prepared to do that job without tenure.

I demonstrated that for fifteen years, and when I came [to University of Arizona] they gave me a faculty appointment that had tenure – that means nothing to me as president. I would never leave a presidency to hang onto a faculty tenure – but some do and I don't think that's a healthy thing.

Pete Likins, Former President, University of Arizona

I know not everyone in academia agrees with me on my objections to tenure. I've had some lively conversations about this. I did a series of Tweets, trying to expose the problems that this archaic system helps promote and I got varying responses, some of which slightly changed my mind. Everything gets stale – if universities want to be on the cutting edge of research and business, they need a constant supply of fresh, motivated faculty.

*

Visibility Via Sports – The Value of College Sports Programs

I'm a huge sports fan – no question. But there are a lot of
distorted perceptions about the value of athletic teams to a university.
I think, first and foremost, that a university's most effective
connection to its community – not its most important connection, but
its most effective – is its sports teams. Residents of any decent sized
town, as well as alumni, flock to college athletic games. They're a
significant part of helping the community feel a connection to their
local university.

> When I went to UNLV and Jackie Robinson was there, in
> 1975, when the community was basically 500,000 - 600,000
> people, it was basically all about hotels and gambling. The
> community wanted their university and the city of Las Vegas
> to get more than just from gambling. Those days, the
> philosophy was that the more national news and national
> publicity the university got because of basketball, the more
> publicity Las Vegas got outside of gaming. It gave the city a
> much broader perspective nationally. In those days Las Vegas
> was fighting a battle with Atlantic City (for tourist business),
> and the basketball team, because of the national exposure,
> helped propel Vegas into the national limelight. We were on
> the sports channels and the team was being talked about (and
> they were mentioned in the same stories with Frank Sinatra).
> It was entertainment; it was fun. People who live in Vegas
> understand the importance of entertainment. They knew the
> importance of that program to Las Vegas.

> I played for UNLV, and Jim was a big supporter of athletics
> at UNLV. I was at the Final Four; I used to work at the
> University of Louisville and they won the national
> championship this year. I met Jim really probably when I was
> 17 years old. Obviously he's a pillar in the Las Vegas
> community and a supporter of UNLV Basketball and UNLV
> in general.

> Jim and I got closer because he was one of the main reasons
> that I actually started coaching basketball. It was Jim's idea;
> he put the thought in my head in the beginning that I could
> start coaching. He thought that I would make a great coach

for UNLV basketball, and he knew that I would have to go back to school to get my degree. He was tremendously encouraging and supportive about pursuing further education. His advice started a whole new career for me.

Reggie Theus, Head Coach, California State Northridge

There's a lot of talk right now in Nevada about building a larger stadium. UNLV's football stadium is the farthest off campus of any school in the southwest. It's not convenient for anyone. It doesn't create a sense of community between the town and the school. But UNLV has had numerous problems with the local casinos, who agree that the city needs a bigger stadium – but would prefer to build it themselves. There's been some squabbling over land, issues with the airport approach path, and debates about how large a stadium should be. These discussions are still going around in circles, but I hope the city does support a large university stadium. I think it would go a long way to creating that sense of community that UNLV has always struggled with.

We have talked about that [the importance of a university's program to its image and attractiveness to potential students and its community] very candidly. Jim sees it not unlike other presidents that I have worked for – I was not here at the time that he was chancellor – but I really believe, and I think this is what Jim would say, he sees athletics as tied to the front porch. A lot of times your athletic programs are never going to be, nor should they be, more important than what you're doing academically, there's no question about that, but [athletics] are another way to get people interested, another way through marketing, publicity, television, and other kinds of things, to actually have people know more about what you're doing – one might see the Rebels play North Carolina and watch the game and say "I'd like to find out more about UNLV" just because of a game (through that experience).

Jim Livengood, Former Athletic Director, UNLV, Retired

Ultimately, athletics are good for universities. Athletic scholarships provide an avenue for an affordable education to those who might not otherwise be able to go. Cities and communities view their teams – when they win – as a source of local pride. They give a tangible cohesion to the community. It's important to remember that student athletes graduate and move on – whether it's into the pros (which has less than a 1 percent chance of success) or into the business/professional community. Athletics give the university a public face – and schools need to be more effective in connecting that face to education and the community.

College is a challenge for even the best and the brightest high school graduates. I was always a fairly good student, but I never took one course in my eight years of college and law school that didn't require hours of studying every day. If these are the requirements of every student, how can a college athlete possibly ever learn anything of value in college when every waking hour is spent conditioning himself or herself to mentally and physically participate in a college sport to earn a scholarship to pay for his or her education? The answer is, he or she can't, period.

The financial exploitation of the student athlete is the most blatant, immoral and unethical activity of our society. It is in every sense of the word modern-day slavery. In order to satisfy the need for one's school to defeat another school in a collegiate sport, a student athlete's entire life is spent achieving a totally meaningless goal. One difference between our university athletic program and slavery in the 1700s is that our modern-day slaves are free to some extent to choose this life, gambling that one in every 1,000 student athletes will become a pro and earn millions of dollars. I am not sure the argument is ethically sustainable.

So what does this education system do to rid itself of the unethical stigma that has no justification? The only answer I see is to let the student athletes form athletic unions to bargain collectively on behalf of the student athletes, to ensure they are adequately compensated for providing their school with such a valuable economic asset. The university system has fought this from the get-go – how dare a student request, much less demand, that athletes be compensated for entertaining the college fan?

I am sickened that our society, especially those who claim to be the best educated, who dictate the moral and ethical tone of society, seem to have no understanding of the fundamental ethical conflict in the way the U.S. higher education system enslaves its athletic population to earn millions for the university while giving nothing in return. To the National College Athletics Association I say – You ought to be ashamed. You have stolen the lives of hundreds of thousands of student athletes in order to satisfy the meaningless athletic revenue you earn every Saturday afternoon on every college athletic field or court in this country.

Chapter VII

In the Chancellor's Office of Nevada's Higher Education System

By 2004, I understood the destructive competition between UNLV and UNR. The schools spent too much effort in criticizing each other. The legislature was unable to deal with the issue. The Board of Regents could not decide which proposals from the various institutions should be approved because every proposal by every school was criticized and sandbagged by all the others.

> When Jim decided to offer his services as chancellor, I encouraged him to do it, and I lobbied the regents for him. I called them, told them all the reasons he'd be good for the university system: he had independence because he had the financial independence to do what was right; he had the passion for education; and he brought his business prowess to the table. And that's what the chancellor's job should be all about. You know, a businessperson who understands that it's not just academics – you need a place to teach, and need things called classrooms and university growth, and Nevada needed some synergy between the north and south.
>
> Sig Rogich, President, Rogich Communications Group

Jane Nichols had decided to retire because of health problems. The Board thought it would do a search for her replacement. She had been the eighth chancellor. For the most part, the chancellor had been a figurehead – the position had little power. It had no authority to terminate presidents in the event they didn't carry out Board policies. Most of the time the chancellor shuffled papers from one side of the desk to the other.

One day, when I was flying from Las Vegas to Pocatello, Idaho, I changed flights in Salt Lake City. I ran into two members of the Board of Regents and while chatting with them I said, "When you're looking for a new chancellor, I would be pleased if you would consider me as an interim chancellor." Both regents thought my offer was a good idea, especially since I mentioned I would serve without pay. They suggested I apply for the job. They set an appointment on the agenda at the next board meeting. I appeared at the next meeting of the Board of Regents, volunteering to serve as the interim chancellor for one year. I said I didn't want any salary, and I would both supply and pay for my own staff. This way, there would be no financial burden on the system.

> When Jim became chancellor, we started working very closely together and developed a great relationship. I have great respect for him, and he is very passionate about higher education. That is his big deal.
>
> And he came in with kind of the attitude that higher education in Nevada, both on university or college level – was unacceptable. He believed the universities had to get better, become more research oriented. He started going a hundred miles an hour. Jim is a man of action. That's why I liked him. Our meetings were 10 minutes at the most and I liked it that way. We'd get right down to business – get the right people on top of a problem and then he'd move things along.
>
> He put a lot of time into the job of chancellor, and I think he did a great job.
>
> Stavros Anthony, Mayor Pro Tem, City of Las Vegas

My business was operating very profitably and it allowed me to devote the required attention to the chancellorship. I believed my business management philosophy could help the system.

At ten a.m. the morning of the regents' meeting, Regent Steve Sisolak asked me, "When can you go to work?" I looked at my watch and told him I could start at ten thirty a.m. Thirty minutes after the Board heard my proposal, Jane Nichols stepped down and I took her place.

> Jim came from a background that was both political and professional, where he really effectively used public communication and relationships with the press and elected officials to benefit the system, and I think he did a masterful

job of doing that. He had more savvy, if you will, about doing that than prior chancellors probably had.

Jim was absolutely dedicated to improving the quality of education in Nevada. It was devastating to him personally to see his state, and his community, to be at the bottom in terms of performance measures that were used nationally to talk about education, and he set out as chancellor (and later applied for the superintendent's job) because he felt that he could change that, and he did a number of wonderful things to address them.

He changed the conversation, so that people were talking about national rankings; people were talking about the national measures; people were willing to consider that perhaps the universities particularly – and he always cared deeply about the two universities – could be world class; There was no room in his vision for mediocrity or to be just "good;" he wanted the universities to be world class.

Jane Nichols, Vice Chancellor,
Academic and Student Affairs, Nevada Board of Regents

Academics tend to be isolationists. They live in a world apart from their communities and so they fail to teach those communities the importance of higher education. Most people in Las Vegas have little or no knowledge about the system. Although UNLV's enrollment has grown to about 30,000 students, its surrounding population really knows nothing about UNLV – other than its basketball team. It doesn't understand how it fits into the Las Vegas community, and how important it is to the development of Las Vegas' economy. Because academics tend to stay on their university island, their product – student education – has little visibility in the community. Professors teach, do their research, and write with the idea that their world ends at the campus border. Most professors have little to no relationship with their communities. The lack of public relations between the system and its communities has always been a major problem. This lack of connection made it impossible to obtain financial support from Nevada communities. The level of higher education among Las Vegans is less than 20 percent. The majority of southern Nevadans consider the university a luxury no one really needed. A common question was, "Why do you need to go to college when you can go park cars on the strip and make $100,000 a year?" The schools did little or nothing to convince the public of the value of higher education.

> One of Jim's strengths in the chancellor's office was his ability to get the public's attention on the education system in Nevada. He got their attention. I think his background in the news was absolutely wonderful. He was up to date, very firm. Nobody questioned him. During the time he was in office, he made progress. There are still areas out there where he obtained property and set it aside for university development. His ability to speak to professors and administration on a level that got them to pay attention made a difference. He had a good understanding of the education system.
>
> Thalia Dondero, Clark County Commissioner, Retired

Before I became the interim chancellor, if you'd asked 1,000 people in southern Nevada or in the entire state who the chancellor was, not one of them would have known. One reason for the system being mysterious was because it functioned as a secret organization. It published as little information about itself as possible. I took the position that the public had the right to know everything about the institutions. If one of the newspapers asked for information, I made sure they got that information. Part of this new openness included talking with people throughout the community. It became my habit to speak to as many groups as possible each week. Once a year on my own television stations, during the six p.m. news, I gave a State of the System Address, which reached every household in Nevada. I was pleased to learn that people actually watched and listened to it. The public began to understand the importance of education in general, higher education specifically, the cost of education, and why the eight Nevada institutions had to work together to deliver a quality, low cost product.

I think he was probably one of the best chancellors we could have ever had because of what he brought to the table. The integrity – one thing I have never questioned is his integrity and his fairness.

Jack Schofield, Nevada Board of Regents

*

I was the first chancellor of the Nevada System of Higher Education who was not an educator. I had been closely associated with education for 20 years, but did not consider this experience to qualify me as an educator. I am an administrator, though, and I'd learned in other jobs that management principles apply to every operation, including higher education. That was verified on a weekly basis during my time in the chancellor's office.

> When Jim called me to tell me that the Governor had asked him to take this responsibility as chancellor of the entire state system of higher education, he was very excited. After a long pause, I said, "Jim, you're not a patient man." He went on enthusiastically, telling me about all the wonderful things he was going to do, and after another long pause, I repeated, "Jim, you're not a patient man."
>
> He loves to tell that story, but in fact he adapted to the extraordinary demands for patience in higher education. He had been a guy that had run a company he created. He's the boss, no ambiguity about that, in his corporate life, and then he stepped into this very different arena of higher education with constraints at every turn, and government to work with, and faculty to work with, and he managed to somehow navigate those treacherous shoals as well as he had previously with his broadcast business.

Pete Likins, Former President, University of Arizona

When I became the chancellor, I told the presidents I would run the system exactly as I ran every other entity I have been involved in over the years. I told them the principles of management are transferrable from one type of institution to another. I don't know whether they believed that initially, but I felt that the strength of my own personality was such that I could force feed them, at least long enough for them to conclude I knew what I was talking about. A CEO's responsibilities and actions are similar to those of a symphony conductor. Every time a CEO begins to perform tasks members of the board don't like, the first accusation made is that he or she is micromanaging the company. Micromanagement is one of the all-encompassing faults that can cost a CEO the job. That is not an unsound principle, but there must be a distinction made between micromanaging and fact gathering. It is the CEO's job to understand the activities in the layers of management below him. I dislike using the word "below," but that is the term generally recognized.

The problem created by a micromanaging CEO is comparable to the conductor of a symphony orchestra telling the first violin to move over because the conductor is going to be playing first violin. Obviously that can't happen. The conductor is there to conduct, not to play any specific instrument. His job is to coordinate the efforts of the musicians to make sure the music is in balance and that each instrument is coordinated with all the other instruments.

If a corporate CEO claims he or she is working a 15-hour day, that CEO doesn't know how to manage. Effective CEOs understand the principles of management: they are coordinators of the efforts of other people. Many CEOs say they work five to seven-hour days, never a 10-hour or 12-hour day, unless they're called on to entertain potential customers. They should not be painting the walls or scrubbing the bathrooms. They should be coordinating the efforts of those who do.

> Jim agreed to take on the role of chancellor at an extremely difficult time in the history of the Board of Regents and the presidents of the universities. I think it was a crossroads for higher education in Nevada. The pot was boiling over, so to speak, and Jim really got things quickly under control in a very professional, reasonable way. It didn't make everybody happy, but he got a handle on it and reined things in. Were it not for that, I don't know where higher education would be today. I really don't. He was the stabilizing force and brought instant credibility to the system by his stature.

There was a lot of in-fighting between the presidents at the time. It's difficult when you hire presidents and tell them, "Your job is to strongly advocate for your institution – but get along with everybody else." It took someone of Jim's caliber to sit down and say: This is how we're going to do this. His expertise allowed him to bring it together at a time when I don't think anyone else could. Originally, Jim was only going to take the job on an interim basis, but I think he saw he had made some progress and decided to stay.

Steve Sisolak, Clark County Commissioner

*

My appointment was a shock to academics, most of whom believed they alone understood how to manage higher education. They believed that regardless of how the outside world, especially the business community, operated, those management policies would not work in the education system. Academics generally believe the governance policies of a university are totally different from those of General Motors or Albertson's or the NBC network. They are wrong. One of the major problems I had when I started was one of the schools' presidents telling me, "You don't understand how academics work. We are not a General Electric. We are not a division of light bulbs or refrigerators or jet engines. The principles of operating those three entities are totally different from operating a university." I explained to that president that the Chairman of the Board of Boeing Aircraft had recently become the Chairman of the Board of Ford, and as far as I knew Ford had never made any airplanes nor had Boeing ever produced any cars. I also pointed out that the new president of Albertson's markets had been Vice President of General Electric, and as far as I knew General Electric had never grown any lettuce. From the beginning, it was apparent that at least one of the presidents did not, and would not, believe an outside businessperson could begin to understand and solve the problems of the education system.

[When Jim took over as chancellor], the Board of Regents had been getting kind of crazy and some issues had totally spun out of control; Jim was the fireman. He put out the fire, he got things calmed down. He got the board organized and he

made it very clear – and this comes from his business
background – that he was running a CEO type operation and
he was the CEO. He brought the presidents into line, so they
knew they were reporting to him and through him to the
board. He was the perfect person for the job at the time he
took over.

Dan Klaich, Chancellor, Nevada Board of Regents

The inefficiencies were compounded by the inability of the
presidents to cooperate with each other. I informed the board that if I
were to be effective as chancellor, I must be given the right to
terminate a president if that president refused to follow board policy.
The board was reluctant to give me that authority, but eventually did
so with the understanding if I fired one of the presidents, the president
would have the right of appeal. I certainly had no problem with that. I
didn't need absolute and final authority – the board should retain this.
It was important for the chancellor's office to have meaningful
authority over the presidents, in order to make substantive changes to
the system.

Jim didn't care about the fall-out. The regents did. They are
elected and the political fall-out and reactions of powerful
donors was important to them. Jim didn't care. He made the
decision that was best for the institution and the students, not
some powerful casino owner. He was right. You can't put
somebody in that position without giving him the authority
to fire a president if the president ignores the rules in place to
improve the entire system. But the presidents would ignore
those rules, or go to the regents to get around the rules they
didn't like. It was completely dysfunctional.

[Giving the chancellor the power to fire presidents] worked
well for Jim, but I'm not sure how well it would work for
other chancellors. They don't command the respect he did –
and they also want to keep their job. I don't know if this
power has continued with the current chancellor, as a matter
of fact.

Jim was a strong personality and could rise above the protectiveness that the presidents have for their institutions. That's unusual.

Steve Sisolak, Clark County Commissioner

*

I moved into the chancellor's office with my staff and began to examine the way the system functioned. There was a variety of problems I was able to resolve immediately. The seemingly endless meetings caught my interest. The presidents and all administrators loved to hold meetings that seemed never to reach any conclusion beyond appointing a committee and subcommittee to analyze problems that could have been solved with little thought and effort. When I became chancellor, each and every time I called one of the presidents, I was told that president was in a meeting. I had never heard of so many meetings. As slow as academia moves, I couldn't imagine what was discussed. I don't believe in meetings that last more than a half hour. I don't believe in committees, and I don't believe in subcommittees. There isn't any issue I can't decide in very short order. I instituted a rule on meetings – 30 minutes maximum. This saved the institution from funding pointless, lengthy meetings, and increased the time available to move projects forward without delays.

My next order of business was to convince the college presidents, who had never been in any structure outside education, and didn't understand how the business and financial worlds functioned, that my experience could help them. It was an uphill climb. The Board of Regents also didn't understand how to manage projects because not one of them had ever operated any entity of any size. The board was made up of lawyers, doctors and small businessman who were sole practitioners. Not one person on that board had ever employed more than 10 people, or had an operating budget exceeding a half a million dollars. No one on the board, other than Steve Sisolak and later Dorothy Gallagher, had ever had significant financial training, experience or responsibility. They didn't understand the various aspects of operating a large organization, or what their roles in governing that entity should be. The presidents believed they lived in a superior intellectual world that required a special type of administration different from management principles outside of education.

> I thought we had good leadership in the office before Jim, but I believe he was a vital person to come in at that particular time to address not just the situation with the board and the institutions – which some perceived as running amuck – but also with a number of other things. He very quickly became the well-known voice of higher education: a very strong voice. He got higher education a seat at the table in the community, in the legislature, and in the state. Those were really important steps for the system to take and I have no doubt that the system is in better shape today – or conversely it would be in a worse state today if he had not stepped in and provided that strong voice and leadership. It came at a time when, initially times were still good economically, but not long after they started to really turn down. He carried the system through some very bad years.
>
> Bart Patterson, President, Nevada State College

An initial discussion I had with several of the system's presidents led me to believe that university presidents have unrealistic views of the importance of their positions and their powers. The concept of shared governance provides faculty with a strong voice in the system. A university's faculty is certainly more qualified, better trained, and better educated than workers in nearly any other large-scale organization. Because of their expertise, and because they know their subjects of instruction far better than any president, dean, or department head, they have tremendous input into the system. That doesn't mean faculty get to run the system – it means that the administrators must look to them for advice and be able to recognize what the system needs.

When it is necessary to make a change in personnel at a high level in an academic system, it is damn near impossible to do. As the chancellor, it was my obligation to determine whether all those who reported to me were performing their duties satisfactory. I made several high-level personnel changes. I dislike having such a serious effect on the lives of people and their families, but those decisions must be made regardless of the immediate cost. Lingering personnel problems cripple the heart of an organization. Actions to solve them must be quick, thorough and fair.

I told each of the presidents they would report to me and I would coordinate their efforts to maximize the system's efficiency. I warned them that if I found they were politicking the regents behind my back, there would be hell to pay. I suggested the presidents begin speaking with each other and begin working together. Because the negative feelings between the president at UNLV and the president at UNR were so severe, the fundamental operations of each school suffered. It was apparent that a change in leadership at both schools was necessary. We implemented this change and new presidents were hired with the understanding each would cooperate with the other and act as a team before the legislature. I wanted them to produce joint programs. Competition should be restricted to the football and basketball courts.

> Jim cared about all the institutions. There are some people who would say that universities are much more important than community colleges. Or, Nevada State College is brand-new and it's struggling so maybe it's not worth investing in . . . but Jim cared about all of them and wanted them all to be successful. He was very in tune to the presidents of each institution and whether or not they were doing a good job. And he was good at knowing if it was time for some of them to move on, or whether some should be there for the rest of their lives. Over time there were quite a few changes. He removed two presidents that people thought were going to be there for the rest of their lives — and they thought that, too. But he did it in a way because he has this personal power, not as chancellor, but as Jim Rogers. If they didn't want to go he gave them a nice way out and out they went.
>
> Suzanne Ernst, Public Relations, Retired

My examination of the hierarchy of the system only dealt with the presidents. Those below that position were the responsibility of the president. I examined the relationship among all eight system presidents, how they functioned together, how they functioned separately, who couldn't be a team player, who was pushing forward, and how each affected the system. I believed that my position as chancellor required me to be involved with those only in the level immediately below me – the presidents. I had no input in governing the provosts, the deans, or the professors. The candidates for president of one of the institutions were interviewed by a committee appointed by the regents. The hiring decisions were made by the Board of Regents. I had some input on who would be chosen, which never caused a problem for me because, in every instance, I agreed with the choice the Board of Regents made. The first evaluations I made of the presidents convinced me that all of them were very competent, very cooperative, and interested in building a better system.

> I do think that one of the failures of NSHE is that the presidents aren't accountable. Under the Jim Rogers regime, he really pushed hard to both hold them accountable and to be more aggressive about fund-raising. His view is a top down management; if you have the right leader and you pay them the right amount of money, then the institution will benefit as a whole.
>
> Sylvia Lazos, Professor of Law, UNLV

Occasionally I was at loggerheads with presidents. I'll share a few of those stories here. The hiring of David Ashley as the president of UNLV came after the top candidate decided not to take the job. Ashley would have been my second choice and initially I found him to be very easy to deal with and extremely bright. He had good ideas about where the school could go. He had been the dean of engineering at Ohio State, one of the largest engineering colleges in the United States. He'd recently been made the provost of the startup at the University of California in Merced. I found Ashley easy to work with. Little did I know about a personal issue that would make it impossible for him to succeed – his wife. I won't go into the problems with Dr. Ashley's wife; she eventually cost him the UNLV presidency and future presidential jobs.

During my tenure, I had several face-to-face confrontations with the president of UNR, Dr. John Lilley. Dr. Lilley believed UNR was the only school in the system and no other school was important. Lilley sequestered the UNR medical school for years by insisting the dean, previously stationed in Las Vegas, move to Reno. That was a further indication that the medical school would never serve the needs of southern Nevada. Lilley was arrogant, distant and inflexible. He and I had very confrontational discussions, after which he left to become the president of Baylor University.

*

When I became chancellor, the system was embroiled in litigation, much of which had been going on for years and had cost the system a fortune. Even more important than the financial cost was the loss of time spent in dealing with them. Every time anybody accused the system of doing something wrong, the system used a "circle the wagons" response. Refusing to produce information about the system's actions initiated extensive litigation. I changed that. I gave instructions that anyone – media, employees, citizens – requesting information about the university would get it – that day. A public institution, supported by state funds, is accountable to everyone. The policy of refusing to give the public information about the system was ridiculous. Becoming responsive to questions about the system and to questions from the regents for information on how the system worked did much to improve the system's credibility.

I was shocked at how much litigation the system had. I deemed it a priority to settle these cases when I took office.

> Shortly after Jim became chancellor, he reorganized the legal offices. We had all the lawyers at that point in either Las Vegas or in Reno. Jim believed that we should have attorneys at the campuses, so they could participate and provide more direct legal advice to the presidents. That decision was precipitated by events at CSN – the Remington affair. It was a good move and it is still the standard today. So, I was the first general counsel at CSN and NSC back in 2004.
>
> Bart Patterson, President, Nevada State College

I called one of my friends, who represented a gentleman who had filed a suit, and suggested we get together. When we went to the meeting to settle the case, there were 14 people there. I asked, "Who are all of you and what you doing here?" They replied, "We're the committee that is going to decide how this case is going to be settled." I said, "No, you're not. Your committee is now disbanded. I'll settle this case myself." My attorney friend told me she'd spent $125,000 trying to resolve this case; the system had stonewalled her at every opportunity. I knew when the case went to court it would cost the system at least $150,000 in legal fees. It took us two hours to settle that case; everybody went away satisfied. There were four or five other cases similar to this one. For each of those cases I called the lawyer on the other side, sat there with him/her alone, and worked out a settlement acceptable to everyone. The resolution of all outstanding litigation was very important because it had long detracted from what the institution was meant to do. Universities are not in the business of litigating; they are in the business of educating students to become active members of society.

> There were multiple cases I was working on that involved faculty rights. The main issue then was the math department at UNLV. Usually we went outside for legal counsel if it came to litigation. [Jim] was very accommodating, very interested in doing things that would improve the university, so I went to see him in his office. He was also very aware that you can change rules, but you can't change practices if you don't change the people involved. He understood that sometimes people are difficult. That was a result of him being from outside academia. In academia, folks just kind of wait things out. He wanted to get things done, and that's what I admire about him the most, is that sometimes he knew that there was bad leadership and that leadership has to change.
>
> I took the whole math department to his office. My take as a litigator is to not be afraid of the sunshine; we had nothing to hide. I really believed my side was right. We tried mediation. Then we tried meeting and talking; over time, the result was the math department has become the most content and productive they've ever been. The rivalries were solved. Jim put them in a position where they could discuss the selection

of their leadership and make some productive changes. I think they now work together very well.

Robert Correales, Professor of Law, UNLV

*

When I accepted the position of chancellor, I had the advantage of not needing the salary. The state bylaws dictate that the chancellor must accept a minimum salary, which was $80,000 a year. I'd promised not to draw a salary, though, so we found a way to turn those mandated funds back into the system.

> Jim wanted to be chancellor for a dollar a year, but the state law requires employees to work for minimum wage. When he was appointed, his contract was the minimum salary dictated by the state – and when he got paid every two weeks, he gave that money back to the schools, creating a student emergency fund, so if there were any students who needed to get home due to a family emergency and couldn't afford it, those funds were available to them.
>
> JoAnn Prevetti, Director of Operations, GCG, Nevada

I attempted to give the chancellor's office the prestige, power, and authority it needed to coordinate the eight institutions. Without a coordination of effort, and the ability to eliminate duplicative programs, the system would not be able to sustain itself financially. It was my intention to create consistent operating policies across the eight institutions. These policies stayed within the very broad policies of the Board of Regents. I found that during the five years I served as chancellor, the board and I never had a misunderstanding or a difference over what we felt the system should be doing. The principles I outlined for moving the system forward were the principles adopted by the board. I believed there were several major problems in the Nevada system beyond financing. The inability of the eight institutions to work together was the major obstacle to the system's progress. Eighty percent of my efforts were spent getting the eight institutions to work together so that the system could work more efficiently, using the very limited money it had.

Cooperative efforts had to be developed to compensate for the extreme shortfalls of funding. Seven of the state institutions had their own nursing programs. These nursing programs didn't speak to each other, and their equipment frequently sat idle because each institution had purchased a full array of equipment, even though there was a lack of full-time demand. The programs should have been coordinated long before to maximize use of the equipment and academic talent. Several of the nursing school deans had never actually spoken to each other, even though they'd been in their respective offices for more than 15 years. We did a survey to list all the programs that related to medical education. There were over 150 medical programs operated separately throughout the institutions. In many cases they were redundant and could have been eliminated had one system been developed. I suggested to the Board of Regents that it develop a Health Sciences System to encompass all medical programs, including the dental school and the medical school.

When the Board of Regents began developing the Health Sciences System, UNLV owned a 60,000 square foot building near UMC. UNLV refused to allow UNR to use it. UNR had its own feeling about that building. UNR's position on this space was, "We don't want it because we don't want to be involved in any projects operated by UNLV." That problem has now been solved. The medical school, the dental school and the nursing programs have been combined under the Health Sciences System and share a new, state of the art skills lab. This program continued to be developed after I left office and has been very successful.

During my five years as chancellor, only moderate successes were achieved. The Health Sciences System, one of my pet projects, continues to grow. I'm not sure it is necessary for the medical school to remain in Reno when it continues to refuse to serve southern Nevada. I'm not sure that UNLV and UNR had to be "experts" in every academic area. The system would have been far more efficient if UNR had specialized in one field and UNLV had specialized in a separate and unrelated field. There was no reason for many of the programs at UNR to be duplicated at UNLV. It would have been less costly to have students go to the schools, rather than the schools come to the students. The inefficiencies and duplications of programs seemed so great that the legislature and public had a legitimate complaint about the inefficient use of funds.

> I worked with Jim when he was chancellor, starting as external relations officer for the new Health Sciences System. In 2007, I became the interim vice chancellor for the HSS. The Health Sciences System is part of NSHE, and represents the two research universities, one state college, four community colleges, and the Desert Research Institute.
>
> Early on, what we discovered is that at any one time, about 14 percent of the total student body is studying to enter the health science profession. Jim realized that was a pretty high percentage of students and a pretty significant amount of resources being dedicated to one industry. So, he started to look at how to coordinate the different institutions – to make them more inter-disciplinary. NSHE has a medical school at UNR and a dental school at UNLV, seven different nursing programs spread across the system – over 150 different health science programs in total.
>
> Jim wanted to make the system more effective by coordinating all these programs, as well as to make sure that the health sciences were serving enough students to make it efficient and offer a high quality of education. He wanted to meet the needs of students, the state, and the people of Nevada.
>
> One of the big projects that he instituted was a building project. There were three different buildings proposed to improve the training and education of health science students. A dedicated building for medicine and nursing at UNR opened in the fall of 2011 and is completely state of the art, with a clinical simulation lab as well as classrooms and it is big enough to grow with the student population.
>
> One of the fun projects was a clinical simulation center here in Las Vegas, at the Shadow Lane campus. The HSS Clinical Simulation Center of Las Vegas is a mock hospital with five simulation rooms with high-tech mannequins that cover a wide range of circumstances – from a woman in labor to a child. These mannequins are able to simulate a variety of

conditions; they can cry and through a speaker inside the head; they can "speak." They allow students to experience a really realistic training experience.

This 31,000 square foot building serves UNLV and NSC schools of nursing and the University of Nevada School of Medicine. In addition to the simulation rooms, it also has a whole ward for bedside training and doctors' offices that look just like real offices. These rooms have cameras set up to record what goes on inside them. We get actors to come in and pretend to be patients – they are taught to exhibit symptoms of disease or whatever – and the students interact with them. The reason it is taped is so the professors' don't have to be in the room, which can impact the way the student thinks and behaves. It is very realistic and useful and a real point of pride for the system.

The third building planned was for the UNLV School of Nursing because that school is split between UNLV and Shadow Lane. It would be built on the Shadow Lane campus. It's shovel ready – we have all the architectural and engineering plans ready to go – but we need more funding before it can be built.

Another thing we're doing is trying to help RNs become BSNs – to both work and complete their bachelor's degrees. This is called the RN to BSN Degree Completion Program and it is working through UNLV, UNR, NSC, and Great Basin CC. It is almost completely online to assist working nurses in achieving these goals.

Jim had to fight really hard to get people to work together in the system, but it's starting to look up. By creating a Health Sciences System, he started to break down the barriers that had stopped institutions from working with each other.

I used to work for UMC and I understand both organizations [UMC and HSS]. UMC is a great resource and it provides fantastic care. It has the only level one trauma center in the south of the state, and the doctors in the med school help to run that.

The Health Science System is the coordinating body between NSHE and UMC. One of the things that Jim accomplished was to facilitate an improved relationship between Clark County and NSHE. UMC is a county hospital and the primary teaching center for the School of Medicine and it's a great place. But it could be better – stronger and more robust. That hurts everybody, from patients to students to educators and staff.

Jim worked – we all worked – to develop a memorandum of understanding between the county and the system and NSHE to enhance the partnerships that operate at UMC. UMC is more than a hospital – it is a health center, and there are so many different students studying different fields getting their clinical experience there. So far that is working out pretty well and we're getting a lot of support from the county commissioners.

Marcia Turner, Vice Chancellor of Health Sciences,
Nevada System of Higher Education

The lack of power in the chancellor's office encouraged the universities to go their own way when lobbying the state legislature, contracting with outside vendors, communicating with newspapers and media, and dealing with the public. In fact, it was not a system. It acted like eight competitors rather than like eight partners. The most obvious example of competition between UNR and UNLV is the medical school, which had been started in the late 1960s at UNR in Reno. The medical school should have been housed and developed in southern Nevada because southern Nevada had the larger population. As the budget was developed for higher education, Bill Raggio very conveniently arranged that the medical school not be funded as part of the regular higher education system. The medical school was given a separate budget, which allowed it to get the first shot at an unfair portion of tax revenue. What remained of state education funds – after the medical school got the first helping – was then divided among the eight institutions.

The medical school had been formed about the same time as the medical schools at Arizona, New Mexico and Utah. However, the Reno medical school had never seen fit to serve any area other than Reno. Its leadership actually refused to believe that southern Nevada had any medical needs. Initially the school only enrolled 20 students, and then 40, and eventually 50. At the same time, Arizona, New

Mexico, and Utah increased their graduates to 150 per year. The deans of the medical school believed they were bullet proof – and, in fact, they were. Each believed Bill Raggio's protection made it impossible for any president, provost or chancellor to affect what that dean was doing.

> We discovered pretty quickly that the UNR medical school
> […] just does not serve southern Nevada well at all. It's too
> small, and it doesn't have the sense of community that it has
> with Reno. They haven't yet found a dean who gets this – or
> they had with Bob Miller and then he left. He had a real sense
> of what we needed, and he lived in Las Vegas, which drove
> them crazy in Reno. It's a tough job anyway to do, but the
> very fact that the UNR medical school has existed for some
> time and gets $31 million state dollars for 60 students per year
> was just aggravating to everyone else.
>
> And then we created a law school here in Las Vegas, which
> by the way should've been there. We should have had it
> reversed – the law school should have been in Reno, right
> next to the state capital, and the medical school should have
> been in Las Vegas, where the larger population was. But to
> make UNLV a major university you had to have professional
> schools here. And that's why during my time as president of
> UNLV, the law school, the dental school, and the
> architectural school were established.
>
> Carol Harter, Executive Director,
> UNLV Black Mountain Institute

There have been efforts in Las Vegas to develop a medical school separate from the school in Reno, but that has not come to fruition. The state cannot afford one medical school, let alone two. Despite receiving an unfair share of the state's funds, Reno's medical school has been allowed to stagnate and has lagged decades behind the medical schools in Utah, Arizona and New Mexico.

In addition to trying to eliminate the duplication and waste, there were other fires that kept popping up.

> It seems like from the moment I became Chair of the Board
> of Regents, we had one crisis after another to address. The
> first crisis was my very first day in office on July 1, 2007. I

opened up the RJ that morning and there was a large article about the apprenticeship program at CSN disintegrating – which involved about 6,000 students. It was about the horrific relationships that the unions had with CSN and the previous president and the interim president.

Jim and I worked very closely on that over the next few months, and I quickly understood Jim's method of problem-solving. First, Jim doesn't put up with much nonsense, and I appreciated that. We focused on the issues, and I appreciated Jim's thought process because it's very similar to mine – focus on what needs to be accomplished and figure out how to get from here to there.

I had taken over at a time when the board was relatively fractured and there had been a lot of issues between regents. Jim was enormously valuable in helping develop relationships with key regents that continue today. Those relationships have become invaluable. Jim could see what needed to be done, and I appreciated his thoughts and advice.

Jim and I spent the bulk of our time (while I was Chair) dealing with budget problems. On Oct 7, 2007, I received a phone call saying that Governor Gibbons had announced that the NSHE system had to reduce its budget by five percent. Jim and I spent virtually all of our time together over the next nearly two years focused on these issues. I really saw how deeply he cares for higher education in Nevada. We spent our time figuring out budgets and holding rallies and giving informational statements and planning how we would address the shortfall. Jim was available 24 hours a day and we talked a lot – three or four times a week, sometimes three or four times a day. We didn't always agree, and I think that is the sign of a healthy relationship. We had some really strenuous conversations about certain issues, but we always ended up in a happy place – and he helped me to understand issues in a way that I never would have understood them without his insight and commitment.

I don't think it's a small thing at all, that period of time – I can honestly say it was a pivotal time in the history of higher education in Nevada. Had we not succeeded in keeping the wheels on the bus (to use a metaphor Jim uses quite often) higher education could have been permanently damaged. Instead, we established a framework for the future that otherwise we never would have had, and kept the basic structure. Yes, there were cuts and they hurt and there was damage done – but the way we went about our budget cutting process and the way we went about addressing the issues that we faced allowed us to move forward. Right now – and this is a fact that is not really appreciated – higher education in Nevada is in much better shape than education in its sister states, in connection with the way we are positioned now because we took – with Jim's input – a proactive approach. Our institutions have made enormous progress – and in ways that are not always evident, so people don't always appreciate them.

These are things in which Jim should take great pride and I was happy to work with him during that process. I have a great admiration and affection for him and his commitment to the state and higher education. I think Jim is appreciated now in ways that are very meaningful – and he deserves that. I wish there were ways we could appreciate him more, but I suspect time will tell a lot of stories.

Michael Wixom, Nevada Board of Regents

During the time I was chancellor I had the misfortune of dealing with a doctor by the name of James McDonald. McDonald was a genius. I don't know how high his IQ is, but I might not be able to count that high. He also got a Ph.D in science before he went to medical school. He had a world-class education. He also had the problem of believing that his position was bullet proof because standing in front of any attack against him or the medical school was Senator Raggio, who would have destroyed the political career or any career of any individual who went after the medical school. In spite of repeated requests by me for financials and for documents describing the medical school's operation, I never got a return phone call from Dr. McDonald. On several occasions he had acted in a manner that exposed the system to extensive liability, but in each case he managed to avoid any serious consequences.

In 2008, I went to the hospital for cancer surgery. I called the president of UNR, Milt Glick, and told Dr. Glick that when I got out of the hospital, I wanted Dr. McDonald gone. McDonald had created serious problems between the medical school and the Ruvo Center. McDonald did not tend to business and many of his actions in public had become an embarrassment to the system. Glick promised me when I got out of the hospital, McDonald would be gone. When I got out of the hospital, Milt had promoted him to a position superior to the dean of the medical school. While the system was absorbing his $500,000 a year salary for a position that was not necessary, it was compelled to seek a new dean for the medical school.

That search produced a super star, Tom Schwenk, a doctor from the faculty and administration of the University of Michigan School of Medicine, certainly one of the top medical schools in the United States. For the five or six years that McDonald was the dean, the medical school made no movement. It failed to raise money, and it did not modernize its techniques or offerings. It continued to refuse to meet its obligation to support medicine in southern Nevada.

> The Cleveland Clinic's involvement in Las Vegas is huge, thanks to Jim Rogers. In his usual way, Jim called me out of the blue and said, "That god damned McDonald just told me that the University of Nevada is responsible for staffing and operating the new brain center they are building here. We can't do that. We need to get someplace like the Cleveland Clinic to come out here and run that thing." I said to him, "Jim, I'm just a soldier here in the trenches (at the Cleveland Clinic in OH), but I do know Cosgrove, and I'll be glad to pass that along to him and to his head of operations." The next day I passed it along at the clinic, and they got in touch with Jim, and long story short, it got done. Jim's always been good about getting things rolling and getting people from different entities to talk to each other.
>
> Bob Savage, M.D., Family Physician, Cleveland Clinic

*

My Battle with Governor Jim Gibbons

The election of Jim Gibbons as Governor of Nevada proved that anything can happen regardless of the statistical proof that an event is extremely unlikely. Jim Gibbons defied all statistics when he was elected Governor of the State of Nevada. He was the most incompetent human being I have ever known. As chancellor, I sought a meeting with him to discuss the system's problems. His secretary said that Gibbons didn't have an hour and a half to see me but I could get one half hour. The vice chancellor, Dan Klaich, and I went to see the governor. I talked for one half hour and he didn't say a word. He continued to look down at his lap and didn't seem to be listening. When we left the governor's office, Dan asked if I had noticed the governor didn't look at me in that entire half hour. As Dan explained, Gibbons was texting that entire half hour and didn't hear a word I said. Enough was enough; when I was asked by the Carson City newspaper to write an op-ed about education in Nevada, I wrote the following:

By Jim Rogers

Nevada Higher Education System Chancellor

Special to the Nevada Appeal

Sunday, February 22, 2009

How many slogans can greed hide behind? How many disguises can greed use to cover its motives and actions?

I grew up with grandparents and parents whose core values all related to helping other people. My relatives never tried to get an advantage. They never overcharged so that the other guy got shorted.

They were astute business people who were successful because they were talented in producing goods that benefitted everyone, rather than being people who became successful by taking unfair advantage of those with whom they dealt.

For 40 years, I was a registered Republican. Which party was my party really was of little importance because I viewed my country, then my state, then my local governments as the institutions of importance. The party was simply an organized mechanism for supporting government.

I also never thought of my own success being more important than the success of various governments I supported. Was I naïve, really ignorant or was it that I had no real understanding of how society functioned? Was the "help thy neighbor" concept merely camouflage for life's real purpose – cheat, lie and steal all you can for he who dies with the most money wins life's race?

I am constantly confused by Jim Gibbons having become the governor of Nevada. What strange set of facts could possibly have come together to elect this man whose every characteristic supports one cause – Jim Gibbons. The man has absolutely no regard for the welfare of any other human being.

Rather than a governor, Nevadans elected an executioner. Did he snooker us all? Was he able to camouflage himself to such an extent, and hide behind so many empty slogans that a majority of Nevada would vote for this man in the empty suit, for an ideology that has three simple words: "No new taxes?"

These words from Gibbons' mouth represent a total lack of understanding of the purpose of government. His words also evidence no understanding of the devastation these three little words can cause.

If implanted, the political and economic policy of this man in the empty suit will shut down Nevada's programs to provide health care for children and care for the elderly who have no way to care for themselves.

His policies will permanently injure students who hope to grab a part of what used to be the American dream – to get a college education. Without support from the state, that dream will be denied.

Gibbons calls himself a conservative Republican. I am told his political and economic policies may be more closely aligned to the Libertarians. My own feeling is that Gibbons is neither a conservative Republican nor a Libertarian. He is simply a greedy, uninterested, unengaged human being whose only, and I mean only, goal is to see what Gibbons can do for himself and his greedy friends.

Fortunately for all Nevadans, he has revealed himself to be what he is, and the public, sometimes a little slow to catch on, has caught on. Several people have suggested a recall of Gibbons is in order. I disagree. It is not worth the time, effort and money because Gibbons has already held his own recall. The public is done with Gibbons. He is no longer a governor – even a former governor.

Fortunately Nevada has a legislature that has the power, the ability and the apparent willingness to prevent Gibbons' bent for destruction. I have faith that Bill Raggio, Warren Hardy, Steve Horsford and Barbara Buckley, along with the other 59 legislators, will put Nevada back on the right track.

*Jim Rogers is Chancellor of the Nevada System of Higher Education.

As you can see from the above, I held back nothing of my opinion of Gibbons. I did not call any of the regents before I published the editorial because I didn't want to put any of them in the position of having approve or object to the document. To say that state Republicans went crazy would be an understatement. If lynching had still been a method of punishment, I would have been lynched.

I never met with anyone who disagreed with what I said about Gibbons – but I've also never talked with anyone who told me they would have been able to write the editorial. Not once since it was published have I been sorry I wrote it. I'm only sorry that no one else ever stood up to Gibbons and his empty-headed friends to say that Nevada should never again elect such an incompetent ass. As long as we continue to elect and appoint non-entities like Gibbons, we don't have a shot at success.

*

Another major issue I tried to tackle was to facilitate communication between the higher education system and the K-12 system in Nevada. Clark County graduates have a hard time getting into the colleges in Nevada for a variety of reasons. I tried to help introduce people working on the problem, to get them to talk about where the problems were and how to fix them. We'd have meetings at restaurants, and I'd invite people from different parts of the community and from different sectors of business, to try to facilitate some sort of coordinated effort to benefit students.

There was a group of Asian community leaders that was brought together, and at that time he was the chancellor [...] There were a variety of people from the community there and some of the people were in education, and Jim used to be there and I think he was the one who was calling the meetings. And I think he was the one trying to bring in what the needs of the community were.

After that meeting (about the Asian community) I was asked to attend these other meetings. The emphasis at that time was on the fact that a lot of Clark County graduates were not – they were spending a lot of remedial time in college to get into college. There was some effort, and I think Jim was working with the superintendent (Brian Cram) because the preponderance of the students in the CCSD [Clark County School District] were Hispanic, and many of them were not English speaking, and their graduation rate was not that great, and those who wanted to go to college were having a hard time getting into UNLV. I don't recall how that turned out, but I think Jim was just trying to get people together to talk about how to help that population.

Buck Wong, Entrepreneur, Retired

/

Jim had these monthly lunch meetings called roundtables. I think from his perspective, there were the equivalent to a real time Twitter account. He had these policy initiatives that he thought were necessary to bring education and higher ed forward. One of them was that CCSD and higher ed should not be competing with each other; the system should be K through 16. [At] one time he was also very concerned about high school drop-out rates – why we can't agree on a number, what is wrong with that particular number, etc.

Sylvia Lazos, Professor of Law, UNLV

/

One thing I respected about Jim was that resistance never bothered him – it didn't stand in the way of some of the changes that he was trying to make. To that end, when Jim was chancellor, we had a VP of diversity in our institutions. Since Jim left as chancellor, little by little, one by one, that initiative has fallen off – and once that happens the whole program becomes nil. I do quite a bit of volunteering with the higher education institutions in Las Vegas, and one of the colleges had maybe three different people in the last year and a half, two years, to fill the position ineffectively – because obviously with that much turnover you never get much stability. Then one of the colleges has just pretty much abandoned the program, for many reasons, but it is easy to abandon a program when your heart is not in it anyway. [...] But a lot of the issue with diversity is that if it isn't in your heart, it just isn't important to you.

Hannah Brown, Community Developer

*

Before I became chancellor, I'd tried to help make connections between the university and the Clark County School District, unsuccessfully. I had more luck as chancellor. I could never get the previous superintendent to take my phone calls. When Walt Rulffes became superintendent, that changed. He understood, as I did, that separate systems – especially in a state in which the majority of matriculating university students is locals – makes no sense. The macro-picture, for the good of the state, and the education systems, is a picture that views all education together.

We found we both had the same burning passion to improve education and neither of us needed to work; it was purely a labor of love and a commitment to education. That, I think, was a bond between us because neither one of us was worried about where we're going to get our next meal; we were able to pursue that common goal of trying to improve education – and really, it is very poor in Nevada. We recognized that.

Because of our relationship we were able to collaborate on all sorts of things. We brought together the key players in higher education and K-12 education. It wasn't just me, even though my district represented 70 percent of the enrollment; he reached out to all 17 superintendents in the state. It was the first time, to my knowledge, that all of higher ed's top staff came together with the 17 CCSD superintendents. We actually had routine meetings to talk about joint issues and that was productive, but we kind of had to move it down to the more hands-on level.

Jim and I developed a pact to work together to improve K-12 and Higher Ed in a seamless manner. Here are some examples:

- Conducted joint meetings with higher Ed officials and all NV superintendents.

- We developed statewide "State of Education" messages to Economic Development and broadcast statewide via the Intermountain West stations.

- We made a pact to work together with legislative funding and NV education issues.

- We did joint editorial staff meetings on educational issues, NV week, etc.

- I spoke to Higher Ed forums; Jim spoke to K-12 forums.

So, although Jim wasn't personally active all the time himself, through his encouragement we brought together the players of the universities with me. It included people like David Ashley and Fred Maryanski, who has since passed and Milt Glick, who has since passed, Mike Richards and Dan Klaich. Then, of course, Neal Smatresk came on and I worked closely with him and enjoyed that because he had a lot of interest in K-12 students being prepared for college and being knowledgeable about UNLV.

Walt Rulffes, Former Superintendent Clark
County School District

Walt did a wonderful job while he was superintendent. Any problems with the CCSD today are a result of the inefficient and underqualified board of directors who continue to mismanage education in this state.

The university system is only as good as the students it gets from the K-12 system. Because we have such a high percentage of our students who stay here – 86 percent of UNLV's students are local – the university system serves the needs of the people of this state. Jim was reaching down and working with the people from K-12, and I thought "How marvelous is that? That's exactly what we need to be doing." We need to be K-16. If we're not, all we're doing is graduating people who can only wait tables. The education was good that I got at the time. Now it's obsolete. Jim knows all that. He tried to educate everyone about it, and he used his own resources to do it.

Shelley Berkley, Former U.S. Congresswoman

/

There have been some improvements in the system, but I'm not sure the connections and programs we've established have survived in the successive administrations. We tried, though, to take a larger, more comprehensive approach to the state's approach to education. I think Jim will be remembered for his ability to link the north and south of our state and the university systems, and the articulation of the importance of K-16 education, which had never been done before. His range of impact and influence is so much greater than we know, and people who have had the privilege of working with him recognize it.

Judy Steele, President, Public Education Foundation

*

The Nevada System Budget Crisis

When the budget crisis hit, the system was faced with many tough choices. Getting the campuses to talk to the public, to explain what they did and what they needed to do it, became more important than ever. Many people worked with me to get the legislature to pay attention to the needs of education in the state. Their comments on the budget crisis tell the story better than I can.

We got along very well because I always felt that he told me exactly what was going on and exactly what he wanted. He doesn't suffer fools gladly. I appreciate that. He would always say exactly what's on his mind. We don't see that very often in the legislature. I remember arguing with him, telling him that they were great ideas but we were nowhere near funding something on that scale. I just knew it wasn't going to happen;

I tried to get him to think about if he couldn't get all of it funded — what would make sense to get done first. And he found it very hard to downscale his vision to fit reality. But he was unabashed about his support for higher education. I don't think I've ever met anyone who was that committed to higher education and I appreciated that.

Sheila Leslie, Former Nevada State Senator

/

I remember sitting around talking about working with the legislature, saying, "Hey, we should get a couple of letters of support from legislators instead of us sending them letters of support." He said, "I want 63," [note: that's the entire legislature – 21 in the Senate, 42 in the Assembly] "and I'm going to get 63. I'm not going to tell them what to say, but every one of them should support higher education in their own way."

He said, "It would be great if we didn't have to wait for [the legislature] to give us our acorns. Let's establish in writing the reality that all of those legislators, in some aspect or in all aspects, support what we, NSHE, are doing. Let's actually make our relationship preceding that election the other way – let's have them write us letters telling us what we do well – in a community, in local outreach, or a large business that benefits from higher ed." What we did completely changed the way we lobby for a public entity. Rather than going with our hand out, it was "Tell us what you like and tell us what you think we're doing wrong." It created some level of ownership for those 63 legislators.

We got 63 letters. Jim got business leaders to write letters, too. That was one of those things that started off in a fun way and became an obsessive one. The result transformed the way people like me lobby for a public entity. It was hard to do. It was work – and one of the best professional experiences I've ever gone through. Jim's enthusiasm is contagious.

We got some great letters. My job as the system's lobbyist was to go ask speakers and senators and committee chairs to write these letters. I thought it would be really hard to get them to do it, but after the first five or six people really liked it – even his critics did it. His most conservative critics who criticized him on all his policies did it. He got members of the teachers' union to do it. Robert Reich did it! He flew next to him on an airplane and got a memo out of him.

I believe this was done before the 2009 session and we did very well in the legislature. We did well in 2005 and 2007, but 2009 was when the economy started going, and I attribute it to those memos. Everyone knew we had those letters of support. It wasn't a trick; everyone knew we had them; it was an incredibly difficult, time-consuming process that yielded incredible results for NSHE in a very tough year. If I were running things in a public entity, I would do the same thing. I would try to get those letters of support. Things can look bleak, but those letters give you a real sense of how important your job is – I think those should be dusted off and made public.

Josh Griffin, Lobbyist

/

Jim was right there, out in front, saying "these are the consequences – this is a horrible situation." He would write regular memos to the legislature, the governor, and the public to let them know that higher education just could not suffer these things. I think that helped a lot to explain to people that this was not just a reduction in numbers, this affected people's lives and it impacted students and our ability to serve students. Towards the end, as that great recession got worse, we were predicting losing 5,000 students from this institution – and we did. It was a horrible situation and it's probably going to take a decade for us to recover from it.

I give Jim credit for explaining the consequences of this to the public, because otherwise they would not have understood that. Not only did he explain consequences, though, he also advocated for it with the public. He made time available on his station for interviews with presidents, with public service ads – to let people know that there are very positive things occurring in higher education in Nevada. People need to know and appreciate it. He is still making that time available.

Jim got people involved. He got students involved. He put a human face on those cuts and used the station to put together some very powerful stories. A lot of legislators were kind of looking at the budget as a check box and he made them see the ramifications of what they were deciding.

John Kuhlman, Public Information,
Nevada System of Higher Education

/

When the economic forum met, we started realizing that the budget numbers were not going to be good and they might have to take back merit pay and they were talking about raising tuition. And so, pretty quickly, I started needing to meet with the regents and meet with the chancellor because we were getting ready to go into a legislative session. I needed to know what our strategy was going to be. When I got to know Jim that way – and it was clear that higher ed was going to come under fire in the legislative session – that is when I got to know another side of Jim Rogers.

When he saw that we were going to be vulnerable and threatened, he really stepped up to the plate and starting doing things to protect us. I came to really respect Jim and wanted to work with him during the legislative session because he seemed to be somebody who was going to go to bat for us. During the legislative session, as we worked through budget numbers and committees – and NSHE was always the last budget that they closed because they are constitutionally required to do K-12 first, Jim really wanted faculty and students to stand up and fight for higher ed.

Jim started calling me regularly and I always knew it was him because I would hear, "Hey, kiddo" – he wanted to come to the faculty senate meetings to talk to faculty and encourage them to stand up and call the legislature and call the governor . . . he did the same thing with the student government. As things went on, it became more and more apparent that things were not going to be good for our budget. That's when he started calling and saying, "We need to start having rallies – we need busloads of people going up to Carson City." He'd say, "I'm going to pay for buses, you fill them up," or "I'm going to have the sound equipment set up at UNLV or at the government center, and you need to call your people and have them show up."

Sandra Cosgrove, History Professor,
College of Southern Nevada

/

I've had a very good relationship with Jim over the years. We're both very passionate about the idea that there need to be improvements in the state of education in Nevada. We need to put the right resources into it. Especially when he became chancellor, and he was more focused on higher education; during my tenure, we increased the budget for higher education more than any governor before or after my term. We had a common bond too. We had somewhat of a personal relationship.

Bob Miller, Former Nevada Governor

*

Student Government Participation

We worked real closely on the budget rallies. He loaned us his yellow Dodge van; he offered that – we didn't ask him. He very much wanted to get the students involved. He wasn't above talking to students, mixing it up with us, telling us what he thought. If he thought we were full of it on something, he would tell us. He's the only person I can think of at this meeting (a regents meeting) that was not upset about having 250 or so students at this meeting. I think he knew it was going to be kind of raucous. He said that he was glad we had all finally gotten involved.

At that point, I knew that he didn't want to see the tuition increases that were a manifestation of the budget climate we were in. The students were maybe more docile and asleep than they should have been.

Adam Cronis, Former UNLV CSUN President

/

Historically, the chancellor has always worked with the presidents of student government. We were trying to figure out what to do about the impending budget cuts. We were throwing ideas back and forth. Jim Rogers came into the CSUN senate meeting and got a fire going under us. He wasn't happy with us as students because we were just sitting back and taking it. He said, "You guys need to do something big to get people's attention because sitting around waiting isn't going to help." Ideas started generating, we began reaching out to other bodies on campus and at the other institutions, and it snowballed from that point.

We didn't want to use student funds to shuttle students back and forth to Reno for meetings, so we decided to carpool. We called Jim once when there was a major vote we wanted to make a showing at. He said call Mike and he'll give you a van: and it was a Twinkie yellow van with streamers painted on the side in neon colors. We drove it 600 miles to Carson City and parked it outside the legislative building. Everyone was really funny; they appreciated the humiliation we went through to get there.

We were there to provide the faces of the programs that were being cut. Legislators were making incorrect assumptions about liberal arts, where the money was going, how many different programs there are. We were there to let them know exactly what the cuts were going to do to students. Legislators wanted to clump everything together instead of see individual programs and their benefits. We helped the public see exactly what the effects of the proposed cuts would do to the science program, to engineering, to English. We met everybody on both sides, friends and foes.

Vik Sehdev, Former UNLV CSUN Vice President

/

We did press releases for the rallies; he asked us all to write in for the memos so he could publish them. He lets people use him as a mouthpiece to help get the word out. I think he's a huge advocate for education and that always worked really well for us, the students. Jim would frequently step forward and say, "Here – I want you to write this," mentoring us and showing us how things got done. I learned a lot from him about that – writing things and making available to the public information about what the university is doing. I think now

things are changing a bit and Jim had a lot to do with that
transparency.

Jessica Lucero, Former President, Graduate Student and
Professional Association, UNLV

*

The Nevada Board of Regents

The competition for state money to support the operation of a
university is complicated. The fundamental structure of the state
education system may have been adequate in 1864 when Nevada first
became a state, but those days are long gone. As Nevada grew, the
differences between the north and the south widened and their
respective institutions became destructively competitive. Attempts at
cooperation stood little chance. The education system in the state of
Nevada has a very peculiar structure – it is supposed to be a separate
branch of government. Nevada has judicial, legislative, and executive
branches, but it also elects its regents to manage the system of higher
education.

> There are only two-three states that elect their regents, and
> we're one of them. In other states, regents are appointed by
> the governor and answer to him/her. Nevada's Board of
> Regents is independent, a fourth branch of government,
> answerable to everybody, but nevertheless the governing
> body for education throughout the state. At the time I was
> serving on the Board of Regents, I think I was the only regent
> who had actually graduated from UNLV. Regional
> differences or loyalties cropped up a lot. There were a lot of
> UNR alumni regents on the board. Time is going to change
> that. But for those of us who are very supportive of UNLV,
> that time is not soon enough.

Shelley Berkley, Former U.S. Congresswoman

The Nevada Constitution created a Board of Regents. The Board
today is made up of 13 members, nine of whom are from southern
Nevada and four of whom are from northern Nevada. With very few
exceptions, the Board of Regents has not had educators as members.
Its members are lawyers, doctors, businessmen, and those who aspire

to political office in Nevada. Becoming a board member is not very costly, and the burden placed on a person who wins does not require that person to give up his or her personal or professional life. Doctors could continue to practice medicine full time and only spend a few days a year governing the higher education system. The problem I've seen with the Board of Regents, other than it has no power because it has no taxing authority, is that it is a position that carries some prestige (although there is little reason for that prestige). Very few people seek the position – it pays absolutely nothing (less than $1,000 a year). The Board of Regents meets four times a year for two days. During that limited time, it is supposed to develop all of the policies for the system.

> The Board of Regents doesn't have its own independent revenue stream; it's dependent on not only the governor to present a good budget to the legislature, but at the mercy of the legislature, too. I like having an elected board; I think it's very democratic. But in the 21st century, nobody in this state would agree to pay for a full time legislature with a staff that could work throughout the year. That's not our history and that's not our culture. But you get what you pay for, and we're doing this on the cheap.
>
> And also, we expect our legislators to work miracles. These are good, average citizens with full time jobs. They don't have staffs or researchers. They just don't have the ability when the legislature is out of session to really do much. And yet, the needs of the state continue to grow. So we make a choice: do we want a first rate education system? You've got to pay for it. If you don't want it – then underfund it. Don't meet your funding goals. If you've got two-thirds of the formula, you're going to get two-thirds of the success. I recognize that money doesn't solve every problem, but it goes a long way to helping the problem.
>
> Shelley Berkley, Former U.S. Congresswoman

The Board of Regents was originally designed in 1865 to govern the one-room schoolhouses that administered all education in the state, K-16. At that time, the thought of a higher education system was remote. When the board was formed, the concept was to create a governing board from people in the communities who would take on their roles as a part-time job. At that time, the Board of Regents met six times a year for two days each time, and most of those meetings were to rubber stamp the policies the universities themselves had developed. The Board of Regents was not staffed with educators. While I believe it probably would not have been effective if it were made up of educators, those who were on the board were not as smart as the academics over whom they governed. Whenever an academic wanted to slide something from the regents, it was easy to do so. There were mountains of paperwork that accompanied requests, which prohibited the board from fully examining any issue in depth. The presidents of the higher education schools constantly played games with the regents. The regents didn't have the information or the background to understand the issues that came before them.

> I think Jim's frustration with the Board of Regents is that they're not all that smart and they're not very diligent in preparing for the meetings. There were a lot of regents that didn't take the job seriously or they were peacocking because they had their own agenda. I don't know that they are particularly effective in supervising the chancellor. I think that rubbed Jim to his core.
>
> Sylvia Lazos, Professor of Law, UNLV

The Board of Regents was originally established as a separate governmental entity. It didn't report to the governor or the legislature. That should have created some independence, but unfortunately it didn't because they had no taxing authority. Not having taxing authority left them totally dependent on the legislature and the governor to make sure the higher education system got the funds it needed. Because of the lack of interest in education in general, especially higher education in Nevada, the funding of education has always been inadequate.

> I think if our funding structure had been reasonably fair to begin with, there wouldn't have been, almost by necessity, the kind of competition inside the system that there was. As president of UNLV, I saw it as my job to try to get some

equity with UNR in terms of funding. [...] When Governor
Raggio was running the whole system of education in Nevada
– and he was an absolutely brilliant politician – as a UNR
graduate there was no way he was going to let a little upstart
campus down in Las Vegas in some way threaten, from his
perspective, UNR. I kept saying, we can bring some equity to
UNLV by simply increasing the funding levels as you go
forward, like 2:1 or 3:1 compared to Reno; eventually you
would get parity. You don't have to cut funding to UNR to
give to UNLV.

I was never able to convince a politician or chancellor to take
this issue seriously and see that a more equitable distribution
of funding was possible without taking from someone else. I
think that whole funding disparity was at the root of problems
within the system of getting along. Jim did inherit that
problem; there's no question about that. All the presidents felt
we had an issue and were going to press for our institutions
as much as possible. It's much less of a problem today.
Decisions have since been made that brought more equity to
the system, and the new funding formula that's going forward
now will further rectify that imbalance.

Carol Harter, Executive Director,
UNLV Black Mountain Institute

The growth of southern Nevada was incompatible with the
original structure of the Board of Regents. No one foresaw that
southern Nevada would grow as quickly it did, and that it would need
to develop a higher education system separate from the northern
Nevada system. As southern Nevada grew, the legislature finally
determined that southern Nevada needed a higher education system of
its own. UNLV was established not as a separate institution, but as a
branch of UNR. Putting both schools together under one governing
board made UNLV's success impossible, regardless of what was done
to support that system.

I understand that there's a lot of history and a lot of misery
and a lot of politics involved in the Nevada school system,
but I still think we can run a state-wide school with two full
campuses that would take advantage of the resources of the
entire state, and take advantage of all of the complementary

nature of both the campuses, but we've got to build these campuses up. People don't seem to realize that for all the attention on Las Vegas and building a facility, which is what they mostly focus on (the UMC campus), I have a whole set of issues in Reno; a whole different set of problems including clinical teaching capacity, clinical practice development, specialty teaching in Reno, it's a whole different marketplace. There's a huge private practice community that's not connected to the school. So if I had one (problem) or the other, that would be a full time job, but I've got both.

Tom Schwenk, Dean,
University of Nevada School of Medicine

The tremendous difference between northern and southern Nevada, between the motivation and goals of the two communities, is mind-boggling. Reno was only interested in sustaining its own system, while Las Vegas wanted to do everything possible to make its new university grow and prosper, and establish itself in the community. These self-interested philosophies made it impossible for a single board to govern a state-wide higher education system with consistent and compatible policies. UNR and UNLV do not share institutional goals and never will. It took me a long time to realize the system has no future.

*

The Regents

Many state leaders we've had started out as regents, and go forward on one of two paths. First are those who are genuinely interested in education and have some background in it (even though it may be remote); then there are those who want to use the position as a stepping stone for another, more ambitious political position. I can distinguish, within 15 minutes into a conversation, a regent who has political aspirations in Nevada from one who truly cares about education. The problem with those who try to use the position as a stepping-stone is that they tend to sell out at some point – they forget what's right or wrong on an education issue, and instead consider how they are going to be viewed in their future political career. This makes them essentially useless to the health and well-being of the higher education system.

If someone is elected regent, that regent should forever be barred from running for any other office in the state. The reason is simple: education should not be involved in the political activities of the state because it prevents the system from functioning independently. Some regents seek office for the sole purpose of giving themselves public exposure, and then they move on to a political position in the state. Political aspirations compromise the ability of a regent to set policy for the university system. My first encounter with this political problem was a minor war I got into 20 years ago with then regent Shelley Berkley. When Shelley ran for the Board of Regents, I wrote her a letter and told her I couldn't support her because I believed she wanted to use that position as a stepping-stone to other political offices. Whatever she did as a regent for the higher education system in Nevada would be politically motivated, and education as education would take a backseat. She called me and assured me she had no intention of running for any political office; she said all she wanted was to be a member of the Board of Regents. I supported her. As you know, this isn't the way things developed. To this day Shelley swears she never intended to run for Congress. She claims she believed she would be politically satisfied as a member of the Board of Regents.

Let me give you some other examples. James Dean won an election for regent when his competitor, who actually won the higher number of votes, was declared ineligible because he didn't actually live in the district. Dean had an enormous ego, and believed he was destined to enter politics from his position as a regent. He thought about being a judge, mayor, congressman or U.S. senator. Obviously those were delusions. I was – and am always – pretty clear about what I think of people who use this position for self-gain. I've got no patience with people who aren't in education to make it better. Unfortunately, there are always people like Dean who are looking out for number one. At one point, Dean and another member of the board, Bret Whipple, decided they would force me out because they didn't like being held accountable for their decisions. They did about everything they could to force me out – unsuccessfully.

Those political conspiracies have a habit of coming to the front and being exposed. Unfortunately they overshadow the real job, and slow down the progress of the job. Dean was not shy about his efforts to "bring Jim Rogers down." On one occasion at a restaurant, he spoke to the wife of a friend of mine (not knowing that she and her husband were my friends), and introduced himself by saying, "I'm James Dean, a member of the Board of Regents, and I am the one who will be responsible for bringing Jim Rogers down." My friend's wife was not impressed, and somewhat surprised that Dean would openly discuss such a topic with a stranger. The next day the husband came to my office to tell me about the bizarre event. Shortly thereafter, I wrote a note to Bret Whipple, chairman of the board, which I assumed would be confidential as its contents were intended for him and him alone. It said that if James Dean was elected chairman during the next term, I would resign as chancellor. I was surprised to learn that the following week Whipple and Dean called a press conference to announce that they could no longer support me as chancellor and that I should resign. They suggested I was trying to determine the appointment of the next chairman and that I was overstepping my position. I viewed this incident as absurd, childish, and politically amateurish. I've never objected to criticism, but this sort of child's play to try to force my resignation was too much – it was a giant waste of everyone's time. I quit, and notified the board. Several days later, after a conference with several regents, I returned to my job – one difficult enough without juvenile grandstanding.

I tell this story because it illustrates what happens when a person is elected to the Board of Regents and develops (or comes in with) political ambitions. Dean really believed he was going to become strong enough as a regent to run against Harry Reid, the majority leader of the Senate. This grandstanding by Whipple and Dean did nothing good for the system. The petty games played by some of the regents would embarrass a middle-schooler running for student council. They tried to embarrass me and enlisted the help of Ron

Knecht, another amateur member of the board. He's an interesting fellow: world-class education (a graduate of the University of Illinois), a mathematician with an MA in Engineering from Stanford who also graduated from law school, although he never took the bar exam in any state. I always wondered about this aspect of his education. It appeared strange to graduate from law school and never take a bar exam. In any event, he didn't pursue the practice of law. He became an employee of the Public Service Commission, from which he was fired. If there weren't something terribly wrong with Knecht, he would be making $500,000 a year. Knecht is one of those types who carries a grudge forever. When he ran for regent initially, I supported his opponent with a $20,000 donation. Unfortunately, his opponent had an illness and was unable to complete the campaign. Knecht won by default, and is still viewed as one of our worst regents of all time. He attempted to have the Board of Regents pass rules that those who were employed by the system could not give money to a candidate for office if they did not fully disclose that contribution. I had fully disclosed the contribution. I later commented publically that it was a mistake to give his opponent only $20,000. I should have given him $100,000.

An additional problem that is apparent when you're dealing with the political aspirations of a member of the board is the relationship that a person has with the governor and/or the legislature. Knecht, Dean, and Whipple all curried the favor of former Governor Gibbons who was, to say the least, the most incompetent governor the state of Nevada has ever suffered under. As incompetent as he might have been, however, Whipple, Dean, and Knecht supported Gibbons' every move and every position, without regard to the interests of higher education. At the Board of Regents meetings, every individual knew how incompetent Governor Gibbons was. It stuck out like a sore thumb. Knecht, who talked more than all of the other regents combined, reportedly told the board that he thought the governor was doing an outstanding job and that the board should listen to and follow the governor's recommendations. On budgeting, Knecht from time to time talked about the inefficiencies of higher education to pave the way for supporting the governor's budget, which was devastating to the higher education system. Dean told me from time to time that he would support raising taxes for education – but at no time did he ever publically support this position. Dean remained in lock step with the governor on every issue, including taxes.

Whipple was a very strange duck. He ran for a second term. An unknown (also as incompetent as anybody in the history of the system) ran against Whipple, spending only $100 on his campaign, and he beat Whipple. Whipple is a series of contradictions. He has absolutely no judgment, even though he has great intellect. He is a graduate of the Wharton School of Business, a CPA and lawyer – probably a pretty good lawyer – but his own view of the world was so unrealistic, and he was so inflexible, the board and the public quickly discovered his shortcomings and voted him out of office. He was also a strong supporter of the governor, probably believing the governor was going to appoint him attorney general. Obviously that never happened.

The complications of running a higher education system with about 14,000 employees and 110,000 students, on a budget that is totally inadequate for a system still growing, are enormous. The governing body meets four times a year and is prohibited from meeting informally. They don't get much done, and my experience with them led me to conclude the Board of Regents has no positive effect on education. As I hope these examples show, Nevada's education system certainly has serious problems. The state of Nevada cannot afford to have a Board of Regents whose loyalties are split between their political ambitions and the welfare of the state. Regents who have strong political ambitions will never take a stand in favor of education. I call these matters to your attention not because these actions made a hell of a lot of difference in the operation of the system, but because the board participates so little in the system that their actions make no difference. The Board of Regents could be disbanded or dissolved and the system would not know the difference.

When I became chancellor of the NSHE system, my relationship with the Board of Regents, many of whom I'd known for 20-25 years, was very good. Some of them came to believe I was too independent, but I think they understood I had the best interest of the system at heart. I was very open with them about what I thought on all education related issues. I wrote weekly memos about the system and its problems. Over the last three years of my tenure, I wrote 16,000 pages of analysis of what was going on in the system, what needed to be changed, and what I intended to do about it. I hope at least some of them read my memos.

*

The NSHE system office is not overpowered by a large staff. However, that staff is first class. I would compare the competence and compatibility of the group in the chancellor's office with the group I had practiced law with for 20 years. There were a lot of very smart people, highly educated, very compassionate, very caring, a group that worked very hard and never looked at the clock. One serious problem I encountered was the need to be visible and active in both Las Vegas and Reno. Splitting time between the two cities was very difficult – a third of the chancellor's work time is spent travelling. Five people were my closest friends, allies and supporters while I was chancellor. While I spent most of my time dealing with institution presidents, my core administration was vital, and I want to talk a bit about them.

*

Dan Klaich

The position of general counsel for the system had serious problems. It was necessary to change leadership and I did so. I had been hearing about Dan Klaich for many years – he had an excellent reputation as an attorney. Dan had grown up in Nevada, had been the president of the student body at UNR, attended the University of Washington College of Law, and had earned a Master's degree in taxation from NYU. Several years earlier, Dan had been the chairman of the NSHE Board of Regents. He had been so intense and committed that he turned the chairmanship into a full-time job. Numerous people whose opinions I valued called me to recommend I hire Dan as general counsel. I interviewed Dan and decided he was the perfect man for the position. He was smart, well educated, sophisticated, and a man of great integrity. He was also an excellent lawyer and he became an outstanding general counsel. As time passed, I learned he had such a broad understanding of the system that he would be perfect as vice chancellor and chief operating officer.

Dan's appointment as vice chancellor solved several problems. Because Dan lived in Reno, he could stay there the majority of the time and not waste time going between Reno and Las Vegas. His being my right arm in Reno was a total success. The relationship was very productive and curtailed much of the jealousy between the north and the south. In dealing with any person, including my law partners, my business partners, and my mentors, I never felt more comfortable than I did when dealing with Dan. I never got half the story. I was never manipulated. I never felt I was talking with someone not fully prepared. Dan is a superman. His integrity is absolute. Dan served as the vice chancellor for several years. When I retired in 2009, there was no question who my successor would be. The transition between us was smooth.

> Jim has a passion for the state of Nevada, in particular for southern Nevada. I don't think that is necessarily a geographic statement, it's just a matter of where his sphere of influence is. But I think he understands very clearly how good this state and southern Nevada have been to him. He feels a strong sense of obligation to give back to that community and to other communities that he is a part of – the University of Arizona or University of California.
>
> It takes the form of thinking, "How can I give back to that community in a way that will live well beyond me?" I don't think he has an interest in just giving money to universities, per se. He does have a desire to create opportunities for people in return for all the opportunities that were given him. That naturally translates to education in his mind.
>
> When you take that and combine it with someone who is a born leader, then I think his passion for education and educational leadership just makes sense. You throw in his impatience and his frustration with baloney and stupid regulations and stuff that doesn't make any sense – I think he

looks at education and thinks, "I love it, I want to help it, and doggone it, it needs some change and I'm just the person to kick it in the tail."

Now that I'm chancellor, Jim and I probably talk every couple of weeks or so. I give him a call when I'm in town, and we go to breakfast and talk about how things are going. If ever a person were going to take over an office with a larger-than-life predecessor, then no one could ask for more support from him than I get from Jim Rogers. He promised me that he would never attack me publicly, no matter how much he disagrees with me, and he has offered his support on every issue at every time.

I am lucky as I can possibly be to have followed Jim Rogers as chancellor, which is not to say that he isn't annoying as hell. Jim can drive you crazy, but he generally drives you crazy because he is impatient to get the right thing done. He doesn't like to hear it can't be done or that it will be done tomorrow, or a whole bunch of gobbledygook. He gets impatient with that and he does push back.

Dan Klaich, Chancellor, Nevada Board of Regents

*

Bart Patterson

The legal department of the system, when I began as chancellor, had some very serious problems. It was ineffective, constantly in trouble because of open meeting law violations by the Board of Regents, and had no credibility. The system stonewalled all requests for information. Changing that policy was one of my first actions. Once Dan Klaich became general counsel, everything in that office changed for the better. When Dan Klaich moved from general counsel to vice chancellor, the system was fortunate to find and hire Bart Patterson as general counsel. Bart was totally compatible with Dan and me, a fine lawyer with excellent judgment. Bart was always very ambitious, which I mean in the most positive way. In my 50 years of practice, I've known many lawyers – Bart is one of the best. He not only knows the law, but he is always able to see beyond the law to its implications. His creativity led him to undertake several initiatives

beyond that of chief counsel. We all knew from the very beginning he
was destined to higher positions in the system. A self-starter, Bart was
always looking for new problems to solve. His work ethic was a major
driving force. All of us knew from the day Bart was hired that he was a
superstar with presidential qualities. We were right. He now serves as
president of Nevada State College.

*

Jane Nichols

Jane left the chancellor's position in 2004 because of health
problems. When those health problems were resolved, Dan Klaich
asked that she return to the system. Jane was a perfect complement to
Dan and me, having risen through the faculty ranks. She knew what
Dan and I didn't know about education (because our backgrounds
were in law and business). She also had superb political instincts. She is
a delightful, charming, substantive person with a national reputation in
higher education, and was welcomed by everyone. Beneath that charm
is a strong, independent woman with roots in Tennessee – she was
truly a steel magnolia on our leadership team. She is now retired and
I'm sure the system misses seeing and working with her. Not
surprisingly, she is still working on very important projects for the
system. As chancellor, the issues I wrote about and publicized weekly
could not have been handled without Jane's constant support and her
keen knowledge and insight into higher education policy.

*

Maurizio Trevisan

The NSHE Health Sciences System was established in 2005 to
bring together more than 150 medical education courses throughout
the system. It was the first of its kind in the United States. A search for
its leader garnered the interest of more than 80 prominent doctors.
Fortunately, Dr. Maurizio Trevisan, then Dean of the School of Public
Health and Health Professions at SUNY Buffalo, applied for the job.
All applicants were qualified by education and experience, but the one

critical qualification was a personality who could coordinate 150 programs. The most daunting problem that faced the new leader was bringing the University of Nevada Medical School into this new partnership. Dr. Trevisan stood out because of his warmth, understanding, and persuasive abilities. He was offered the job and took it.

During his four-year tenure as the head of the Health Sciences System, he was faced with an uphill battle. Academics are slow to adjust to any change, and medical doctors are at the top of that list. In spite of the foot dragging of many of the medical-related programs and institutions, especially the medical school and some of the seven nursing programs in the system, Dr. Trevisan made great strides. It is unfortunate that the Nevada legislature, which has no understanding of the Nevada higher education system and certainly had no understanding or appreciation of the efforts and successes of Dr. Trevisan, stopped funding his position. Dr. Trevisan is now Dean of the Sophie Davis School of Biomedical Education in New York. It's a great loss for Nevada.

> What Jim was trying to push was really, really a great thing to do. Unfortunately, six months into my tenure we hit the state financial crisis. We had no room to maneuver; everybody hung on to their own resources and stayed in their own sandbox. We had no toys. I remember the conversation we were having about the Dental School – on Shadow Lane campus next to the UMC. That campus was basically supposed to be one at which different programs would be housed together and share resources. But UNLV was so entrenched and didn't want to connect with or support that venture; they put up all sorts of obstacles. I remember now from a distance the amount of time discussing the opportunity; the regents got involved and they wanted to do it, but we were not able to move a stone.
>
> I remember one of the positive things that happened is the idea of the public health program. Both UNLV and UNR have a School of Public Health (both of them created in the traditional system of competition against each other). So we had a retreat – Larry Ruvo had a retreat up on Lake Tahoe at his place for two days. And at the end we managed to get

something done - the Ph.D program in public health was put into place after that. It was unbelievable.

Maurizio Trevisan, Dean, Sophie Davis School of
Biomedical Education and Interim Provost,
City College of New York

*

Marcia Turner

Marcia was a key figure in the operation of the system. As a lobbyist she had been very effective in dealing with the legislature. An expert in the practice of medicine and the operation of hospitals in southern Nevada, she was a key figure in creating the Health Sciences System. Marcia understood all the difficulties in the practice of medicine in southern Nevada. She had dealt with the fighting, the competition, and all the petty problems that had arisen in southern Nevada's medical profession. When she came to the chancellor's office she had not yet finished her Ph.D. I strongly urged that she do so, which would enable her to take on other major responsibilities in the system. She received her Ph.D, and when we established a single Health Sciences System for NSHE, Marcia became second in command. Marcia's many traits include loyalty, perseverance, and an ability to deal with every person, no matter what their political and financial interests are.

Because I demand a lot from fellow employees, including adjusting to new issues as they present themselves, it was very important that Marcia be flexible and creative. As we were entering previously unexplored fields, she adapted quickly and efficiently. Her experience in southern Nevada medical fields, coupled with her interest in tackling new and risky ventures, made her the perfect person to assume the position as vice chancellor of the Health Sciences System when Dr. Trevisan left. She now leads a state work force sector on health sciences. Marcia has also become a second set of eyes and ears in southern Nevada for the dean of the medical school, Tom Schwenk. Anyone who knows me knows I am committed to the expansion of the medical school in Las Vegas. I had serious reservations when Tom was hired as dean because I was not sure he fully understood the needs for the medical school to expand its presence in southern Nevada. Marcia, with her vast knowledge of the medical, hospital and labor communities, effectively presented southern Nevada's case for expansion of the medical school. To his credit, Dr. Schwenk recognized he had a valuable asset in Marcia, who knew all the critical players and how they could be brought together with the medical school to have a profound effect in southern Nevada. I predict that Dr. Schwenk will be highly successful as the dean to a great extent because of Marcia's knowledge and support.

*

John Kuhlman

John is one of the great gems of the system. He and I composed nearly all of the 1,600 pages of memos about the system. He did most of the work. John organized and published those memos. If one were to read every page, he or she would thoroughly understand every important issue in the Nevada System of Higher Education. In drafting those memos, with the intent to bring much needed transparency to the NSHE system and convince the public of its own vested interest in the state education system, I sought input from every substantive group in Nevada. Each week we asked those groups to support our position on the issue at hand. Of the more than 1,000 participants, only one person we asked failed to respond. I used those memos not only to inform and educate, but also to force those who had the power to support education to do so publicly. John never missed a deadline and never failed to have each and every person whose opinion we sought respond. Being compulsive about timing, which comes from running the six o'clock news at six o'clock, rather than six-fifteen or six-twenty, I pushed John to the limit. John is one of the most pleasant people I know. He never complained about my demands and never compromised on any task we undertook.

I think overall, Jim brought a very strong CEO ethic to the Board of Regents, and made them almost like a trade

240 · *Now, Let Me Tell You Something*

organization. He gave a vision of where they needed to be
going. He was able to communicate his vision. I saw some
people run afoul of him. I think in organizations you often
find that people will be operating on two different levels – not
necessarily a hidden agenda, but multiple goals that you may
or may not be aware of. When Jim came on board, people
were looking for that "other" agenda – I was just as guilty of
it – and it took a while to realize that there isn't one. What he
tells you is what it is.

John Kuhlman, Public Information,
Nevada System of Higher Education

*

As I look back on my five years as chancellor, my thoughts are
very positive. There were times when the job created immense stress,
primarily because of the lack of support from Nevada's citizens, its
legislature, and certainly its governor. In spite of all those problems, it
was a wonderful experience I would never have thought possible. I
think about it every day, and still closely follow the development of
projects I started or strongly supported.

Jim made some errors as chancellor, but he corrected them.
He sees an error or perceived error and doesn't brush it aside.
He might not let you know he's looking at it, but he does. I
think that's an innate quality. I'd say he is one of the top ten
most influential Nevadans. I'd put him up there with Gov.
Russell, Gov. Sawyer, Gov. Laxalt, Gov. O'Callahan, Sig
Rogich, Joe Brown, Kenny Guinn – I think Jim stands in that
group. I'd love to be in that group myself – I don't think I can
make it.

Mark Alden, Nevada Board of Regents

We also did a good job, I think, of helping the various institutions
in the system see themselves as part of the community. I was able to
introduce a couple of folks who went on to make things happen that
benefit everyone, and some of those stories are included here.

Jim was interested in partnerships and putting people together
to accomplish good things for the community. In our case, I
remember I got a phone call one morning that he and Lois
Tarkanian had just had breakfast and Lois was looking for a

site for a fire station for the city. I called Lois, at Jim's suggestion, talked to her a little bit about it and suggested we get together and talk about some synergies – a partnership that might benefit both the city and CSN. We had wonderful conversations and they resulted in a fire station that's right down here [gestures] on the campus. And along with it we have three classrooms that we use.

That partnership has blossomed into another relationship with the city that we'll be announcing shortly that involves training city employees and saving the city a lot of money. We're really excited about being able to announce that in the near future –there's some ink to dry there first. But it was Jim who got us on these pathways, these partnerships that have resulted in mutually supportive projects. I give Jim a lot of credit for that effort.

Mike Richards, President, College of Southern Nevada

/

I work in education as a consultant; I know education. So, at the end of the year, I did a report card for him and ranked him on a whole series of issues in higher education. I did it sort of for fun, because we had a good rapport – I told him, "I'm going to be paying attention to how you do this because you don't come from any background in higher education governance or leadership." He was so good-spirited about it and laughed and laughed – particularly because I used to chide him when we flew around in one of his planes – it was a prop plane – and I'd say, "Jim, please! Won't you get a jet so we can get there? Instead of this plodding old propeller thing?" Anyway, that was on the report card. It was kind of a list of things where he had a positive score and a list of things where he fell short. He came off on the positive side, over all, but one of the deficiencies was that he had a prop plane that took forever to get places.

Jill Derby, Former Chair, Nevada Board of Regents

/

Jim really, at a time when Nevada needed it, was a compass. He did a tremendous job. No question about it – he had a vision of what the state's education could be and should be, but it didn't happen. He didn't get support from the legislature, he didn't get support from the Board of Regents, he didn't get support from the governors. That's not typical in most states. He was doing this job for no pay, which is why he was able to reach out and tell people how he really felt. He didn't care about the Board of Regents or how people looked at him. He only wanted to do the right thing.

Harry Reid, U.S. Senator

Chapter VIII

Preserving America's History: Personal Collections

Movies were one of the thrills of my young life. I still watch movies on a daily basis and love them all. When my family returned to the United States from Costa Rica, the western movie industry was in full swing. The war had just ended and Gene Autry had returned to the U.S., along with many of his cowboy buddies, including Roy Rogers. Because I had the same last name, Roy Rogers became my hero. Roy and his beautiful horse Trigger captivated me. Trigger was a magnificent horse, and his backstory is quite interesting. He was owned by a rental agency that provided horses to the movies. Trigger was Maid Marian's horse (Olivia de Havilland) in *Robin Hood* with Errol Flynn.

When Gene Autry entered the military and was shipped off to war, Roy Rogers – who had always played a bad guy – started to play good guy roles to fill the void. Roy's real name was Leonard Slye and he had several stage names before he became Roy Rogers. He had always admired Will Rogers. When the studio wanted to give him a new stage name he chose Rogers. When Roy rode Trigger, a new cowboy hero was born. Like Gene, Roy was a singing cowboy. He had a better voice than Gene, and he was certainly better looking. Roy was a rather small man, about 5 feet 9 inches, but he could ride a horse like no one else. Trigger was seven-eigths Tennessee Walking horse and one-eighth thoroughbred – a very large horse with great speed.

At the end of the war Roy was called into the studio and was told that because Gene was returning, Gene would revive his good guy roles and Roy would return to his villain roles. There were discussions about Roy continuing to ride Trigger. Whoever was running the studio said, "We can put anybody on that horse and make him a hero." Roy replied, "I've bought the horse." He paid $2,500 for Trigger – I have the bill of sale for that horse in my western memorabilia collection – in 1944. At the time, this amount was three times the cost of a new car. There were two Triggers; the smaller one, Trigger Jr., did all the dancing and would kick Roy every time Roy rode him. When Trigger senior died, they stuffed him and put him into the museum, but when Trigger junior died, they put him in the ground and let him rot. Roy said, "That horse would wait a week to kick me once." The stuffed Trigger was just sold at auction because the museum in Branson, Missouri, closed and sold everything. Roy's Bohlin silver saddle sold for $450,000. There were bidding wars over his guns and all the prices went sky high – if you ever want to sell anything, do it at an auction.

In 1992, I was talking with a very close friend, Charlie Thompson, who had been two years ahead of me at Las Vegas High. Charlie had adopted Roy Rogers as his hero and father figure, and he remained a steadfast fan until Roy's death. Charlie came to me one day and said, "Why don't we go to the Golden Boot Awards?" I had no idea what those awards were. He told me the Golden Boot Awards were for actors and directors of westerns. The group had been formed by Roy Rogers, Gene Autry, and Pat Buttram. They sponsored a dinner once a year at the Century Plaza in Los Angeles, and all of the old Western stars came and received awards for all of the movies they had made. It was delightful. We went to the gala. There were 1,000 people and we mingled with as many as we could. We chatted with Roy Rogers and Dale Evans, Gene Autry, Pat Buttram, and all the usual movie stars from westerns.

At the end of each annual dinner, Buddy Rogers, who had been married to Mary Pickford, donated $50,000 to a retirement home for all of those who had been in western movies. That home had been started by Mary Pickford and her husband Douglas Fairbanks. Those who had been in the movie business for 20 years and retired and needed help could move into that home without cost. Unfortunately over the last five years, funding for that home had dropped off. I visited several times over the years. One day Beverly and I had lunch with Janet Leigh, chairman of the home. In the following years I became more and more involved in the Golden Boot Awards project.

We gave money, and I was elected to the board and became a very substantial supporter.

It became apparent after several years that the ability of the Golden Boot committee to raise money was becoming more and more difficult. Buddy Rogers died and his $50,000 donation disappeared. We found that the number of people attending the event declined from 1,100 to 900 to 700. Many of the regular participants had died, and many simply were not able to come to the event. Because Beverly and I enjoyed the event and looked forward to it every year, we decided to donate money for their dinner and assume Buddy Rogers' place in annual support.

Once I get involved in a good cause, I usually stay with it until the end. The first year Beverly and I gave $50,000, and after that we raised our gift to $150,000 each year until the dinner was eventually discontinued. The dinner introduced us to many people including Cheryl Rogers-Barnett, Roy's oldest child; she was one of the six children he and Dale adopted. Cheryl has become a close friend. She lives in St. George, Utah, and visits us several times a year.

> I met Jim through a mutual friend, Chuck Thompson. I think it was up in Lone Pine – Chuck might have brought him to an event at the Roy Rogers museum.
>
> In the beginning it was more through the Roy Rogers museum; Chuck brought Jim to an event at the Roy Rogers museum, the first fundraiser we did for dad's museum. He's just wonderful. Almost from the beginning of our acquaintance he was so generous with the museum. Of course he loves the old cowboys. He was just super. He had an RV that he loaned us, so we could take some of the artifacts on the road. And he put some graphics on the outside that said The Roy Rogers Museum. People thought it was just a traveling museum. But that was just wonderful because we went to Texas, Ohio, Tennessee, and we were able to reach people who couldn't have gotten to our museum in California, so that was just super.
>
> We're so thankful for Jim's friendship. It has meant a great deal to my family, especially to my mom. Some of the greatest memories I'll treasure the rest of my life are those dinners;

listening to the old pros, the people they knew in common, their experiences. We're so thankful that he's included us in that stuff.

Cheryl Rogers-Barnett, Board Member,
Western Music Association

I was fascinated by the people who attended the Golden Boot dinner. Ernest Borgnine, who recently died, was one of my favorites. I got to know A.C. Lyles, who had been head of one of the major studios for over 50 years (also recently deceased). At age 94, he met my wife Beverly and fell in love with her. We still see A.C. on the movie channel because he is the most knowledgeable historian of American movies. Dale Evans became a very good friend. When she'd attend various western events, we often flew her in our plane.

Charlie then asked if I had ever been to the Lone Pine Film Festival in Lone Pine, California. I'd never even heard of it. Lone Pine is located at the foot of Mount Whitney, and was a favorite location for filming westerns. Approximately 600 films, mostly westerns, were made there, including more than half of the Hopalong Cassidy movies and many of the Roy Rogers and Gene Autry movies. *Gungadin* was filmed there. It is still used as a film location; more recently, *Tremors* was filmed there. Lone Pine is known for its famous rocks, which seem to appear as the backdrop in almost every western movie. Ford and other companies' truck ads are still filmed there. Charlie asked if I'd like to go to the film festival for the weekend and I said of course, so he and I went. Dave Holland was running the festival at that time.

> The festival got started in 1989. Dave came along and bailed me out, and the next year I told him, Dave, I don't have the nerves for this, I'm not an executive, you'll have to be the director from now on. I can't do this – I had a young grandson living with me because his mother died and all kinds of things going on, but I could back him up because I was aware of what we needed. We needed police coverage, we needed port-a-potties all over the Alabama Hills, we needed support from the county, from the road department to close the road during the parade, I had to write to these agencies to get permission for all these things that we did.

When the people came, they loved it. We had hay bales all along Main Street — we still do — and they thought it was a little Disneyland, they could walk from one event to another, from the park to the town hall then back to the high school for the movies before we got the museum. It worked out they really enjoyed it; all the scenery, and all the people walking around in costume, the character that came along with it. We went from the $1,000 allowance I had ready to needing $4,000 for the buses and bodyguards, so I had to go back to them to get more money; after two or three years, they said you're on your own now, you have to generate your own money, so we needed to figure out how to make the events pay for themselves, which we could do with the tours and everything. Now it's grown to a $90,000 a year event.

Kerry Powell, Founder, Lone Pine Film Festival

Many of the old stars including Barbara Hale, Roy Rogers, Dale Evans, Gabby Hayes, Randolph Scott, and Gregory Peck appeared for panel discussions. Those discussions usually drew about 3,000 people. Lone Pine is a town of about 2,400 people, so it was difficult to find a place to stay. Many attendees brought their camping gear and motor homes. It became apparent to me after I started attending the event that it was struggling because of a lack of money. It was difficult to charge admission to a group of elderly people who had been retired for many years and lived off Social Security. They simply didn't have any money to support the film festival. Kerry Powell, a long-time resident of Lone Pine, initiated the festival. Dave Holland, who had been a promotion director in Los Angeles, moved to Lone Pine to develop the festival. As Beverly and I became more and more involved, we began to offer funding for the festival as well.

I started the film festival because we had the Frontier Motel, my husband's family, and we were going to build ten new units at the motel and I wanted to decorate them with pictures from the movies that were made here. I was born and raised here, across the dry lake from Keeler, and lived in the town most of my life, and I wanted to decorate those rooms with pictures from those movies. There was a restaurant in town that had posters from the movies, so I asked him where he got them. He said on Sunset Boulevard in Hollywood, so

Raymond and I headed down to Sunset Boulevard in Hollywood, to these poster places, these rundown old shops along Sunset there, and I went in and asked them for a movie that I remembered – I didn't remember a whole lot of them at the time. He brought me these manila folders with pictures from our mountains with movie stars in front of our mountains and our hills and I thought, "This is amazing."

They had different pictures, these shops I went to, just snapshots, 8x10s, small ones. Hardly any color posters, just small pictures. So I found and bought all of these and told Raymond that I wanted to have them made into sepia prints, larger sepia prints, 16x20s, that we could actually use in the motel. I thought I could make a plaque inside the door labeling it where it was in Lone Pine – all these movies were made in Lone Pine – and it was really exciting.

Kerry Powell, Founder, Lone Pine Film Festival

Beverly and I fell in love with the beauty of Mount Whitney and the friendliness of all of the old movie stars. I have never known another profession that cared so much for its own, had so much fun together and developed friendships that were life-long. The age of the attendees illustrates this – Ernie Borgnine was an attendee until his 94th birthday. Peggy Stewart, who is 91, has attended every year. Roy Rogers and Gene Autry, while their health allowed, came to the event regularly.

I met Jim up here (Lone Pine) at the Old Dow, at the cocktail party on Friday nights. Dave Holland, who ran things, came up and said the video camera is in the back. So I grabbed a glass of wine and went back and was introduced to Jim, and he was so nice. I thought he was just one of the crew! He introduced me to his mother and she's a kick – a lot of fun. And that was that.

Then another festival came along – maybe one or two later – and Dave could draw pictures of you, in charcoal and he drew one of me and said "now, I want you to sign this and present this to Jim at the Pheasant Club." So I did – I don't know what happened to it [It is framed and hanging on the wall at Channel 3].

Actually, all I can say – have you ever met somebody for the first time and just clicked – a certain rapport? That's the way it was with Jim. I just knew the minute I met him that we clicked. I don't know a thing in the world about him . . . I didn't know about any of the cable stuff. Just Jim. All I can say is Jim Rogers? Oh, I love that man!!

Peggy Stewart, Actress

The Lone Pine residents continually talked about building a museum. They were in love with these old movies, but didn't have the resources to build a real museum. Town leaders believed they could build the museum for about $500,000. That amount would include the cost of the land, which was in the center of the town on Highway 195. Little did they know that the Los Angeles Water and Power Company owned every square inch of that area. When a group of us went to Los Angeles to meet with Los Angeles Water and Power about buying two acres, the water company said it was reluctant to sell, but it could part with the land for $250,000. Everyone had apoplexy when they heard that figure, but we began to make plans to raise that money.

Beverly and I told them that if they could buy the land, we would contribute $500,000 for the building. They did raise the money for the land and the Lone Pine Film Museum, which is called the Beverly and Jim Rogers Lone Pine Film Museum, was built. It cost us $1,250,000 to construct. It is open to the public and has been very, very popular because it is on the main highway from Los Angeles to Carson City. Approximately 250,000 people drive by it every week, and many stop. The building is 12,000 square feet. It has a movie theatre that holds 150 people and shows old western movies. While the museum was under construction, our group gathered memorabilia from that period. Many of the old stars contributed their clothing, saddles, etc. Beverly and I bought a stagecoach that had been used in movies during the 1940s and gave it to the museum. I had a substantial collection of movie posters and other art related to western movies which we donated to the museum, as well as a large gun and saddle collection.

Jim's a real western movie buff, but I think what he would like to see demonstrated by people is the creed – the code of conduct that you see in western film. All the old western heroes had their personal code of conduct and when it came to a marketing plan, someone like Roy Rogers or Gene Autry or Hopalong Cassidy, they had this creed that would be in the cereal box or whatever.

I think that probably fits Jim's code of conduct in many ways, his expectations of life and what he expects from other people. All of us in this particular age group grew up with the Saturday matinees and the B westerns, the bad guys with the black hats and the good guys with the white hats.

I think that's what brought Jim to Lone Pine. The story I remember is that he walked up to Dave Holland and said, "I want to be involved – or I can help you guys" – something like that. He doesn't make himself that noticeable, but he's observant and if it's something that he has a passion for, he'll step up and get involved. That's what he did.

Jaque Hickman, Entrepreneur

The museum covers the history of the western movies for a 40 year period. We have had many people outside the museum project group give us western items. Gene Autry's family and Roy Rogers and his wife Dale contributed clothes to the project. The museum now has a 1937 Plymouth exactly like the one Humphrey Bogart drove through town to the top of Mount Whitney. In the 1937 movie *High Sierra*, Humphrey Bogart comes to the one stop light in Lone Pine while he is attempting to get away from the police; he turns left and goes up the road toward Mount Whitney, where he is shot. We redid the car; when we bought it, the car only had 17,000 miles on it. It's amazing what you can find – people really take care of these things. The very talented staff at our car museum returned this car to its original condition. The Lone Pine collection also has a 1941 Buick Roadmaster Convertible exactly like the one that Peggy Stewart was lying in (on the front seat) when Gene Autry jumped the breadth of the car with his horse Champion.

The stagecoach had been restored by an older gentleman, and I bought it from him 15 years ago. This is an original, and I can't imagine going across country in one of these damn things! You only made 10-15 miles a day. I've got another stagecoach that was Ronald Reagan's. I just sent that to Lone Pine. We've gotten clothes from everybody; all the clothing in the museum is on loan from the families who own them. They don't want to give them away, but we don't care as long as we've got them. People approach me or the museum and say, "Hey I have this, can you exhibit it?" We're very careful with everything, and we tell them, "If you want it back next week, you'll get it back."

> Jim and I are on the same page when it comes to the Western film genre. Like me, he believes that, one day – well, I believe that one day my grandson will write his doctoral thesis on the western film genre of the 30s, 40s, and early 50s.

> When Tom Brokaw retired, he wrote *The Greatest Generation*, but in my opinion, what Brokaw left out of the book was where those three generations of men and women got their morality; I believe, as does Jim, that they got it from Rex Allen (my dad), Roy Rogers and Gene Autry. When I met Jim, I was trying to gather all of those films and digitize them and get them ready to air on television because there are a million people in China who have never seen a Rex Allen or Roy Rogers film. So, our coming together was on the preservation of the heritage of those films and what they mean to so many people.

> I met Jim and he told me I needed to come down to his office and talk to him, so I did. I was, quite honestly, flabbergasted by what he had collected. I had no idea. I sold him some pieces of my dad's stuff that he didn't have. He has been extremely forthcoming in advice, especially about how to deal with museums (this was before the Lone Pine museum went up). After my first meeting with him – this was 10, 15 years ago – he said, I want to see your dad's museum in Willcox, Arizona. I said okay. So, we got into his plane and flew down to Willcox and went through the museum.

> He was impressed because it's a nice, small museum – it's not a big thing like they have in Lone Pine – and it's dedicated to my dad. My dad NEVER wanted a museum, but he did it for the city of Willcox, which was his hometown. They said they wanted to generate tourism and he said, okay, but only if you call it the Rex Allen Cowboy Museum. That's because, he

said, there are local heroes — ranchers, cattlemen — and just
because I'm a film star doesn't make me any different. So they
set up a separate hall of fame just for local people — Jim
thought that was interesting.

Rex Allen, Jr., Singer, Song-Writer

I ended up, through a strange series of events, with a saddle out
of Tex Ritter's museum. Someone mistakenly sent it to an auction and
I bought it. Tex's museum tracked it down; Patsy Smith came to me
and said, "They don't know how that saddle got out of there but gosh,
they'd like to have it back." I gave it back to them and they put it on
display. I'll never ask for it. The University of Wyoming has all of
Hopalong Cassidy's clothes. We went there and took a look at their
collection. They had it in boxes. They took it out, and it just fell apart
at the touch. We said we didn't want to touch it. If we put it in a box
like that, three weeks later it will turn to dust, and that's a shame. They
have Hopalong's saddle also. We asked them to lend it to us and when
they wanted it back they could have it. They told us "no." They have it
in a basement, and that's not right.

I have many Bohlin saddles. Bohlin was the man who made all
the best and fanciest silver saddles, bridles, breast collars and gun
holsters. All the horse equipment was made and owned by companies,
which then rented it out to movie producers just like they rented out
horses. To date it has cost over $2 million dollars to outfit the
museum, but it was worth it. The museum is open every day and does
an excellent business; its income pays the bills each month. I don't
know of any collections that are larger than ours. I don't think
anybody has a larger silver saddle collection than I do. In our house in
Montana there are over 60 silver saddles.

Beverly and I have been blessed with meeting so many old-time
movie stars. In every instance we've been pleased to find how warm,
loving and caring they are. That feeling is certainly evident every
October at Lone Pine when the western stars gather. The relationship
has been a lot of fun, especially when the stars talk about how films
were made. For example, Kathryn Grayson told us that when she
made *The Kissing Bandit* with Frank Sinatra, they shot the scenes out of

sequence, so she had never understood the plot. She'd never seen the entire movie until I showed it to her. Kathryn went with us to the Lone Pine festival four times. Of course Kathryn has passed on, as have Dale Evans and Ernie Borgnine.

One of the most interesting people we brought to Lone Pine was Gregory Peck. He had made a movie, *Yellow Moon* with Ann Baxter. We were celebrating the anniversary of that movie. He said he'd be happy to come; initially he said he'd like to come for lunch, but return to Los Angeles in the middle of the afternoon. We started talking to him about his career, his education at Berkeley, his interest in becoming a doctor and how he abandoned that to become an actor. His voice was magnificent, even though he was 82. We continued to talk throughout the entire day; at about eight p.m. we put him in our plane and sent him home.

Hopalong Cassidy, Roy Rogers and Gene Autry had radio and TV programs on which they advised kids to be good, follow what their parents said, and do well in school. Those values were pounded into American kids by the heroes they worshipped. While times have changed, and pop stars have replaced movie heroes, the western movies of the post-World War II years defined an important, idealistic time in American history. We're happy to have been so successful at collecting substantial memorabilia from that period, and to have built a permanent museum to house such an important part of American film history.

Along the way, we also started collecting movie posters. By the mid-1930s, movies shown in theaters throughout the United States were a major American economic engine. There was no television. There was very little radio, and newspaper ads were somewhat limited. How then would this booming movie business advertise its products? How would it excite the public to attend movies at night and on weekends in theaters that had sprung up all over the United States? Some of the major theaters, for example in New York, cost more than opera houses. The surroundings in the movie theaters were designed to excite and entice moviegoers to come to the movies again and again. The public was nearly hypnotized and excited in a way never before possible because life could be put in pictures, rather than just as words on a page. The movie poster was born and it took many diverse forms. They had to be large enough for people driving by the theater to see the name of the movie, the stars in the films, and some indication of the movie's story line. The outdoor posters were put in glass cases along the sidewalk, so that passersby would read them and get excited about going to the movies. Several sizes were designed. The "one sheet" was three feet wide and six feet tall. The "three sheet" was six feet wide and six feet tall. The "six sheet" and the "twelve sheet" are proportionately larger.

The development of the American automobile from the 1930s to the 1970s paralleled the development of the movie industry. While the automobile has been replaced with many types of transportation, the movie poster has been replaced by advertising on radio, television, Internet and every other conceivable type of electronic media. One cannot be interested in the history of the automobile in the United States without being interested in the development of our entertainment industry. New cars and new movies go hand in hand. Consistent with our collecting automobiles built from 1932 through 1972, we have collected our movie posters from that same period. We had each of them framed and hung in the two classic car museum buildings. There are over 250 posters. The cost of the posters and their framing has reached approximately $1,000,000. It is sometimes surprising to us that visitors to the car museum find the movie posters more interesting than the cars. In any case, the combination of the cars and the posters creates a very entertaining atmosphere.

*

The Automobile Collection

My family returned from Costa Rica in April or May of 1945. The following school year, I went to second grade in Paintsville, Kentucky, and lived with my grandparents. I had never seen an American car before September, 1945. Whether my love of automobiles was genetic or was an acquired taste, I fell in love with the American automobile.

When the Second World War began in December of 1941, all of the car manufacturers converted their plants from making cars to making tanks, airplanes and other war machinery. The 1942 models had just begun to be sold in September of 1941. By January or February of 1942, production of American cars had stopped. The automobile plants remained war plants until June of 1945 when the Second World War ended. In September, 1945 the major manufacturers – Ford, Chrysler, General Motors, Packard and Studebaker – began manufacturing and selling cars again. Even though production began in 1945, they were all called 1946 models. The number of cars produced (through 1947) was so limited that if one ordered a car, he or she would not receive that car until six months to a year later.

When we returned to the United States, my father was employed at Los Alamos, New Mexico, by the company that built and maintained the entire town of 14,000 people. My father was very fortunate in that during the war he had dealt with the War Powers Commission and was familiar with its rules. When he went to work for Robert E. McKee, he learned that McKee was owed a great deal of money by the War Powers Commission. Unfortunately, McKee was not aware that if the money were not collected by a certain date, the amount would be forfeited. When dad informed Mr. McKee of the problem, Mr. McKee immediately called his representative in Washington and the money was paid. Until this time, my father had been relegated to driving a 1937 Dodge Coupe because he could not buy a new car anywhere in the United States. In return for dad's timely advice, McKee found a 1947 two-door Chevrolet and gave it to my father.

From September, 1947, through the mid-1960s, like many other Americans, I looked forward to the introduction of new models of American automobiles. Cars manufactured in the 1930s, 1940s and 1950s had severe problems with wear. It was ordinary for a car to need extensive engine work after only 20,000 miles. Most people, rather than repairing the car, simply bought a new one. That habit led to the average American buying a new car every September when the new models came out. Unfortunately, as a college student, I didn't have the

money to purchase a new car, and as a young practicing attorney, I
didn't have the funds to purchase expensive cars – but that didn't stop
me from admiring each year's products. In the 1980s, when I was in
my early 40s, I had accumulated sufficient monies to be able to
purchase several automobiles. I began my collection with the purchase
of a 1940 Ford Coupe, which was similar to the 1940 Ford Coupe I
had owned during college. That car cost $250.

> Jim has always loved cars. I can remember my grandfather
> telling me – when they lived in Louisville – they had a purple
> Plymouth, and Jim would just go down and sit in that car. I
> think that Jim actually has a car identical to the one that our
> grandfather had in his collection. And you know, you don't
> refer to them as "cars" with Jim, they're "automobiles." I
> found that out the hard way. Also, when you bring the
> automobile home, you always raise the hood to let the heat
> dissipate to take better care of that car.
>
> I have one of the cars that was in that car barn. I had come
> out for a meeting and got together for breakfast with Jim at
> the Four Seasons, and he looked at me and said, "Bob, how'd
> you like to have a red Thunderbird?" I said that'd be great,
> and asked what it cost. He wouldn't take any money. That's
> just the way he is.
>
> Bob Savage, M.D., Family Physician, Cleveland Clinic

Habits like acquiring automobiles can be very expensive, and
there seems to be no limit to the number of automobiles one wants.
Over the last 25 years, I've purchased over 300 classic cars. I've fallen
in love with every one of them and other than a few duplicates, I have
not sold any of these classic cars. Collecting automobiles, like
collecting anything, starts with the collector wanting to be conservative
in the amount spent for each item. I initially set a limit of $25,000 on
any car I bought. That limit didn't last very long. As soon as I'd talked
myself into believing that these cars might someday be valuable, and
therefore a good investment, thinking about price limits ceased. That's
the way we rationalize the ridiculous things we do. As time went on
and I moved up the ladder of the cost of vehicles, I finally topped out
by buying three very expensive automobiles – each over $600,000.

I'm going on 14 years with Jim now. I've been building cars for over 50 years. I was a Shell Oil distributer for 35 years; when I sold that and came out here, I got a job running a service facility. (Revamped and got rid of graft – this place serviced Jim's cars.) I took over and saw how they were billing – I had to fix all that.

One day I was invited over to talk to Jim about his cars. At that time he only had 30-40 cars. So I came out to talk to him, and he said, "I want to build a unique car collection," which is the old "If you've got the money, I've got the time" conversation. He said, "I've got the money." So I said, "Let's do it." We started building the collection, and I began hiring guys.

Mike Pratt, Operations Manager,
Jim Rogers Automobile Collection

Collectors tend to find there are many items they buy that make their collections special. The first year of my collection is 1932, the first year that Ford made a V8. As I mentioned, the collection goes from 1932 until 1972, which represents a 50-year history of the American (and British) automobile. Collectors also develop special loves for items. For example, all the American cars manufactured in 1946, 1947, and 1948 used pre-war designs. It was not until 1949 that the entire industry rolled out modern designs for its products. It was not until 1949 – considered a milestone year for American automobiles – that the first hard top convertible coupe was built. It was the first year that automatic transmissions became commonplace in GM automobiles. Similar transmissions in Ford, Chrysler and Studebaker also appeared. The styling of the 1949 vehicles remained the styling for the respective brands.

In 1953, another milestone year, the Cadillac Eldorado, Oldsmobile Fiesta, Buick Skylark, and a variety of Ford and Packard automobiles came onto the market. This was the first year that air conditioning was offered, even though very few of the cars initially came with air conditioning. From 1953 through 1958, each manufacturer's vehicle was unique to the extent that it was easy to determine which car was a Cadillac and which car was a Lincoln. Over the last 20 years or so, all the cars have come to look alike, and therefore very few collectors buy cars produced after 1970.

Our cars can be broken down into the following groups: American and British cars from 1932 through 1972; Mercury convertibles from 1939 [the first year Mercury was built] through 1958. The Mercury collection stops at 1959 because after 1959 the Mercury models looked like every other car. Milestone cars – this group is limited to American cars for the year 1949, and convertibles built in America in 1953. There were 27 American convertibles built in 1953. We have one of each. In 1958 there were five cars – Chevrolet, Pontiac, Oldsmobile, Buick and Cadillac – that had so much chrome on them that, although beautiful, were ultimately ostentatious. The trunks could hold at least six bodies if you were in the business of accumulating bodies. They all got about 8-10 miles to the gallon. The quality of their manufacturing was far less than excellent, but they were all beautiful.

Our collection of Rolls Royces is world class. Contrary to the belief that it is not necessary to change the oil in a Rolls Royce, the Rolls Royce engine is like any other engine and must be maintained. Other than the myth about the "sealed engine" of Rolls Royce, they are magnificent works of art. An American car will be manufactured entirely over a two-day period. The Rolls Royce, because of the extensive handwork necessary, requires about six months to manufacture. They are designed to last a lifetime. Their bodies are aluminum, which does not rust. The woodwork is of a quality better than any household furniture. The paint is perfect. Wanting one of these cars is a special kind of sickness; there is no way to justify their purchase. A car costing $400,000 cannot be driven anywhere and cannot be parked in a parking lot for fear of the car next to it nicking the Rolls Royce paint. For example, I have a 1999 Bentley (which is a Rolls Royce) convertible. The car cost, with taxes, slightly over $400,000. It is 13 years old and has 4,200 miles on it. When you say Rolls Royces never wear out, that they last a lifetime, one of the primary reasons is that no one drives them enough to wear them out.

I'm often asked which of the 300 cars in my collection is my favorite. My response is that I love them all equally. I'm also asked how often I drive them and how I like driving them. My response is that I never drive them and have no interest in driving them. They don't drive or ride well. The quality of manufacturing was generally very poor on those early models: the doors rattle, the springs don't work properly, the engines overheat, and there is always something wrong with them. In the few instances when I have taken one of the cars for a ride, I've always called the shop to tell them it's likely they'll have to come get me.

> The uniqueness of this collection is really – we picked the year 1953 and as far as the convertible for the year of '53, we have every American produced convertible for that year: Fords, Chryslers, Pontiacs, Buicks, Olds – not only the original model, but every model that was produced. In 1953, you had a Buick Special convertible, you had a Buick Super convertible, a Buick Roadmaster convertible, and a Buick Skylark convertible. So we have all four of those. We have a lot of Oldsmobiles and Packards, too. That was our goal. We always bought high-end cars – we talk several times a day, every day. He's a unique man to work for. He has so many things on his plate.
>
> I think what makes us work in such continuity is that we think almost on the same track about cars and how to do things. My background is a strong one in building – homes, cars, buildings – and I really enjoy that. We literally save hundreds of thousands of dollars by using our mechanics and painters to do construction projects around the station. We set up new news units, use oil (racing oil), and different things. I have eight guys here – I tell them, "When you walk, don't look down and wonder where you're going. Look up and see what you can change while you're getting there." We're not going to reinvent the wheel, but we can make it run smoother. All my guys have been with me seven to ten years. They can do several different things: paint, build, and do mechanics.
>
> Mike Pratt, Operations Manager,
> Jim Rogers Automobile Collection

We store the 300 automobiles in two separate buildings. One building has 150 four-door hardtops, coupes, and station wagons, while the other building holds 150 convertibles. When I bought the cars and built the buildings, it never occurred to me that anyone would want to see the cars. While people do not line up on a daily basis, when we do offer to let a group see the automobiles, we have no problem convincing people to come to the museum. For anyone under the age of 45, the cars have little interest. My children's generation doesn't know anything or care about old cars. They have such scant interest in automobiles, if you tested them on which end of the car houses the engine, they'd be wrong 50 percent of the time. My grandchildren, strangely enough, *LOVE* them. The automobiles are works of art. My grandson and his sister decided they wanted to do an internship at the television station and car barn last summer. I thought they'd last about 20 minutes and then go home. Maren spent two weeks in the newsroom, and Aiden went to the car barn and decided he wants to be a mechanical engineer, designing car engines. The guys in the garage were putting a car back together and they couldn't get a bolt into a hole; their hands were too big. Aiden said, "Well, I can do that" and stuck his hand in. Now he's a hero with the guys in the shop. He fixed the car.

For those born after 1930 but before 1970, the cars produce a nostalgic effect that is difficult to describe. It is a love affair and each person who sees the cars remembers when their uncles, aunts and grandparents bought the cars and what they did with them.

> The car collection should be kept together. You can't put a value on that collection and to keep it intact is really important. He has at least one series that is unique – nobody else, well, maybe one other, has that series of cars. This collection is something that is really something that should be one of the "prides" of Las Vegas. I would love to see it preserved. It could easily be another non-gaming draw for tourists. I hope somebody can make that happen.
>
> Alan Kaercher, Insurance Agent

In looking over a list of the 300 cars, certain individual cars are particularly special to me. I have a 1932 Ford Roadster. This was the first year that a V8 engine was built in the United States. This same V8, which had only 80 horsepower, remained the central power source in Ford Motor engines for the next 20 years. The engine was called a "flathead" and in 1953 was replaced by the overhead valve engine. In one form or another, this initial engine was used in all Ford products for years. For example, in the 1946/47/48 Lincoln Continental, although those cars weighed nearly 5,000 pounds, Ford was determined to put the small V8 or a modification thereof in that car. The 80 horsepower engine would not have been able to move the car. Ford took the V8 engine and added four more cylinders to make the V12, which, with only 110 horsepower, proved inadequate in moving the Continental. In 1953, a milestone year in automobile production, Ford, not being able to purchase the three-speed hydramatic transmission from General Motors, built what was known as the Fordomatic two-speed transmission, which also was inadequate. Ford's lack of engineering creativity put it far behind General Motors.

I've got Mercury convertibles too. The first year the Mercury convertible was built was 1939. It should be noted that not only was the Mercury convertible built as a two-door coupe; it also had a four-door model. That car, like the Ford convertibles of that date, had the small V8 engine. Production had barely begun on the 1942 model cars when the Second World War began. We don't know how many 1942 Mercury convertibles were built, but in our research we could only find six. For nearly 10 years we attempted to purchase one of those cars. The owners sold them only when the price was so high they couldn't afford to keep them. In shopping for these convertibles, we found we could not purchase one for under $175,000. After 10 years of looking, we finally purchased a 1942 (in 2010).

I also own a 1945 Ford Convertible. The initial thought when car production resumed after the war was to call those cars 1945 models, but as noted, they were designated 1946 models. That is with the exception of one car – a Ford convertible with the year of production stamped on its body as a 1945 model. I don't know how many of these 1945 models there are, but we were only able to find one.

Cadillacs are exceptional cars. In 1939, the Cadillac V16 Limousine was launched. Keep in mind that in 1939, there were only a few highways that went more than just a few miles. Certainly there were no 4-lane highways. But given the limited amount of highway driving that could be done, the car companies, beginning in the early 1930s and continuing through 1939, built larger and larger cars that required larger and larger engines. The V8 became the V12, and was used by Lincoln, Packard and Cadillac. Cadillac had to do the industry one better – it produced the V16. The average engine in a car today weighs approximately 400 pounds. The V16 weighed 1,800 pounds and required a behemoth of an automobile to carry it. The next to last year of Cadillac's production of the V16 was 1939. We own one of those limousines with a V16, and we have a separate V16 engine with its transmission on display at our car museum.

In 1949, all the motor companies abandoned the pre-Second World War designs and went to more rounded, fluid, "pretty" cars. The automatic transmission then became standard equipment on Buicks, Cadillacs and Oldsmobiles. The automatic transmission was an extra on Pontiacs and Chevrolets. Buick had developed the overhead valve engine, a very heavy but very productive engine. In all of the Buick models, that engine, being a straight 8 engine as opposed to a V8 engine, propelled Buicks from 1949 through 1952. Cadillac continued its use of a flathead V8 through 1952. In 1953, General Motors produced the overhead valve V8 engine, which has remained its standard since then.

We have every American convertible produced in 1953 – 27 cars. This includes the 1953 Corvette, which was a cute, speedy-looking car. It was one of the first made of fiberglass. The problem with fiberglass is that it doesn't bend – it only breaks and is very difficult to repair. The 1953 Corvette was a disaster for anyone above average size because the top of the windshield prohibited the driver from seeing the road. The driver could not slouch enough to compensate. The car was impossible to get in or out of. John Wayne was reputed to have gotten into a Corvette, and couldn't get out until the front end was disassembled. In the last five years, with only about 70 left of the original production of 300, the price of these cars went from $250,000 to over $1,000,000.

I also have a 1955 Mercedes 300SL convertible. The car was built with a closed body whose doors swung upward when opened. The car was named the Gullwing Mercedes. The engine was a small three-liter engine, but with Mercedes engineering, the car had a top speed of slightly over 140 miles an hour. It has remained one of two mass produced sports cars whose values range from $750,000 to $1.5 million. Our blue 1955 Roadster has never been equaled in beauty and engineering.

From the early 1950s through the early 1960s, the contest among American car manufacturers was to see which company could build the largest, heaviest car with the most chrome. The chrome bumpers on some of the 1950 cars, especially the Buicks, could not be carried by fewer than three men. Detroit made the mistake of putting beauty before engineering, so the cars from the 1940s, 1950s, and 1960s advanced only slightly mechanically and in quality. If you close the door of a 1958 Buick, the open seam between the door and the fender may be nearly three-quarters of an inch; doors did not align with bodies. The doors were so heavy they began to sag and wouldn't close. We have the only set of the highest line of General Motors convertibles produced in 1958. The trunks of these cars are so large that if you chose to move from one house to another, you could probably put all of your belongings in the trunk.

Another one of my favorites is the 1962 Rolls Royce Convertible – I believe this car is the most beautiful car ever manufactured. Its horsepower is "adequate," as Rolls Royce describes it. Rolls Royce has never published the horsepower ratings of any of its cars. Of the 1962 convertible models, of which there were less than 50 built, the convertible we have is the most magnificent.

Beginning in 1959 and through the present day, the automobile industry became very conservative and timid in producing automobiles that were other than plain and boring. In other words, all the world's cars now look alike. The engineering in every production car is now superb. The cars perform as never anticipated in the 1940s, 1950s, and 1960s. Our collection represents examples of mid-line, mid-price, American (and a few English and German) cars from the 1930s through the 1970s. We do not have a Duesenberg, which would cost between $1.5 and $4 million dollars. We do not have a Mercedes 5K, which was built in the late 1930s, and which would now sell for $5 million. There are many cars far more expensive than any of our cars, but our cars represent those that could be afforded by the working man from the 1930s through the 1970s.

When people between 50 and 80 come through the museum, every one of them has very clear recollections of members of their family or neighbors who purchased American cars like those in our collection. Each visitor remembers the excitement of every September from 1946 through 1985 when the new models came out. Those who visit the museum generally intend to stay a half hour, but we often find that after three or four hours, they are still calling attention to some minor extra that these old cars have on them.

For the most part, the hunt for the car is more enjoyable and exciting than owning the car. We spent at least five years looking for our 1942 Mercury convertible. We discovered there were six in the world and it took us five years to persuade an owner to sell his to us. Mike Pratt has been with me for 15 years. I talk with him every night, and have talked to him every night over the last 15 years, about the cars we have and the cars we want. At this point, the collection is complete with the exception of those cars we've bought that require extensive restoration (because fully restored models are rarely available). The value of the 300 cars is approximately $17 million dollars. We have title to every one of those vehicles, and we keep the keys in the ignitions and they are all "gassed up" and ready to go. I point out our possession of a title to each vehicle because in many instances buying the car was easy, but getting title very difficult.

I'd really like to see the collection stay together, and see the public have access to it. It's taken a lot of time and patience to build, and for me, it's a masterpiece of American history. There are a few larger private collections in the country, but I don't think any of them focuses the way we do on the "common" American automobile.

*

The Pullman

Like most kids who grew up in the 1930s and 1940s, a railroad train was a major method of travel. Riding in a Pullman car, in which you could actually sleep on a bed, was really living in tall cotton. I love railroad trains. When the stations became very successful, it seemed a good idea for me to invite 150 of my closest friends on a train trip from Los Angeles to Chicago or San Francisco to Chicago. I've never had so much fun. As one thing led to another in my life, it seemed to me that having my own railroad car would be better than renting a train from Amtrak. Therefore, I bought a Pullman caboose which was manufactured in 1930. It is 88 feet long, has a 25 foot living room, three bedrooms, a full kitchen, and a room for a cook and butler. Being the caboose, it also had a veranda on the back where you could sit and watch the track go by under you. When we used the caboose, which we attached to an Amtrak train, my friends and I would sit on the back and wave to those we passed.

> Jim one year got a bunch of people together for a great train trip – people who had worked for him for a certain amount of time, some old time movie people like Anne Francis and Peggy Stewart, and my mom and her sister. I got to invite a friend. We left on a Friday afternoon from Seattle and got to Minneapolis on Sunday. It was a leisure trip. He wanted to familiarize his employees with trains, because he loves trains. It gave me a new appreciation of them. We went through some beautiful places.
>
> Don Barlow, Brother-in-Law

After many years of trying to deal with Amtrak, which is certainly an industry unions destroyed, we gave up and donated the railroad car to the railroad museum in Carson City, Nevada.

Chapter IX

Retirement: A Summary Death Sentence

I've never been a person to sit still and enjoy my leisure time. I like to build. It's hard to imagine peace and quiet. I've lived my life in the public eye, fighting for causes I believe in. I've tried to help develop public projects. When I stepped down as chancellor of the NSHE system, I maintained my interest in many of the programs I started. They're all a bit different, but they keep me going.

*

Executive in Residence

Yash Gupta was the dean of the USC Business School and I was on his board. I gave a commencement speech to the graduating class one year. When Yash went to Johns Hopkins (a strange place in that it's never had a business school or a law school because it looks at both of those as "trades"), he called me and said, "Why don't you come here for a month. We have an Executive in Residence program. You would talk to students. Many of them don't have any idea what goes on in the real world. You can give them advice, and then you can also talk to the faculty because many students don't know what goes on in the day-to-day business." I think Yash invited me because of our friendship and because he thought I was bored. I can't work eight-hour days anymore; I get too tired. I said I'd come in at eight a.m. and leave at two p.m. He wanted me to go to lunch every day with one of the professors and talk about my experience. Talk about high-powered brain intellects. I went to lunch every day and had productive discussions about the business world.

> I invited Jim to join the inaugural board at Johns Hopkins, which he did. Then he came to spend a month with us through the Executive in Residence program there (twice). He started with coffee meetings/receptions with small groups of students. Then we started small meetings with the faculty.

He always said he was learning a lot from the students and faculty with whom he mixed. But the reality is, his wisdom and his words of encouragement – and that's what he was doing, making sure that the young assistant professors knew the difference between vocation and profession, not just simply yet another job. In the process, as he spent so much time with these students, he would say, "Let me share with you what the television industry means; what advertising means; let me tell you how you can connect the community to your audience." Then he attended classes and gave lectures. Not only lectures to the business school; he gave talks to the school of education, and the medical school, and a bunch of other schools. The Dean of Education enjoyed Jim's company a good deal.

Yash Gupta, CEO of SDP Telecom

Let me give you an example of what I did and what I learned Yash assigned a class to me. I began talking about lessons I'd learned in everyday life. One night a young man said he wanted to ask a question. He said he was a medical doctor, and explained that doctors, as sole practitioners, could no longer buy malpractice insurance. I asked the rest of the class how many of them were medical doctors – a great majority raised their hands. I asked a grey-haired man what he was doing in this class. He said he was a plastic surgeon and had gone into medicine because he wanted to be a sole practitioner. Now he couldn't get insurance unless he joined a group practice. He said he'd never analyzed a financial statement. We talked about these problems. I learned as much from them as they learned from me.

I had office hours every day. I had a hell of a good time. The first time I went to Hopkins, I was restricted to the business school. The second time I went to Hopkins, I'd been the chancellor of the NSHE system. That opened doors to visiting other colleges. I visited the dean of the education college and the dean of the medical school. Johns Hopkins students are heavyweights, yet they came to listen to this Arizona grad who is certainly not an intellect or a scholar. I lectured to the faculty and thought, "What the hell am I going to talk to these people about?" I started out by saying, "I want you to know that I've never gotten into business solely to make a profit. That was never my purpose. My purpose was to do something in a business that I liked, and I *hoped* I made a profit." I talked about the importance of reputation. I told them I'd been broke four times, and the only thing that saved me was my reputation for honesty. If I hadn't had a good relationship with my bankers, who knew I was honest, I wouldn't have made it. The faculty seemed to like my approach for picking a business to enter. I spent a lot of time talking about the problems of working for someone else. I told them: "Never work for someone else, because you're at their mercy." If they don't like the color of your shirt, you may go down the road.

When I finished the second stint at Johns Hopkins, I asked the people at the University of Arizona why they didn't do something similar there. No one had ever done an executive residency program, but I thought it would be a great experience for everyone. It was interesting to see how they set it up and got the word out. I volunteered to be the first Executive in Residence, but they've had several successful visitors after me. The dean of the education college came to see me and wanted to chat, as did the dean of the business school. The dean of the medical school talked to me. Of the two full weeks I was there, I spent two days at the medical school. I called Marcia Turner at the Nevada System of Higher Education and told her to bring some of the regents from Nevada to see how the University of Arizona medical school was working together with other universities in the Arizona system. The regents came to Phoenix twice and walked around, looking at ways similar collaborations could work in Nevada.

> I talked to Jim about doing a similar program at the University of Arizona and I talked to the Johns Hopkins people and they told me what he liked and how he liked to be staffed. He had mentioned that he wanted to look at medicine because he's really interested in the technologies and he wanted to do a lot with education – and there happens to be a lot going on – and he wanted to do business, and we saved a little time for law.

> What I had him do here was talk to some of the new professors he had never met. Some of the old-timers have seen him throughout the years and he knows their projects a

little bit – and they know him and that's neat . . . but there are six or seven new people. He spent time the very first day he was here talking with some of the new people and looking at some of the places they are invested. He told me he wanted to be of use to the university and the students, to the extent that he could come in and talk, teach a class, talk privately. Then he wanted to learn. He wanted to go out with a faculty member or small group for lunch every day, if he could. He delivered a lecture over at Eller [the business school] and we had him at an informal coffee with students here.

Nancy Stanley, Assistant Dean for Advancement,
James E. Rogers College of Law, University of Arizona

I told a class of about 250 sophomore business students: "Your values are everything. If I'm sitting across the table and you're talking to me, I have no idea if what you're telling me is true or not. I'm going to make a decision based on what you tell me, and your credibility is what will sell you. I'm at your mercy, at least the first time. Your integrity is everything because flawless integrity is the only way anybody will deal with you a second time. The first time it gets out that you're not honest, you're done. It's like losing your virginity – you can't get it back. You can't do enough to make up for the doubt you've created. Don't ever lie to anybody about anything." I've never dealt with anybody at any level who I didn't trust, because their reputation always preceded them. If I have any doubt, I refuse to work with them. I don't want to worry about things I can't control. I don't think people are fundamentally dishonest, but when pushed you'd be surprised how many fold.

I've been talking to people at Gonzaga about trying out an Executive in Residence there, which I'd like to do. We also instituted the same program at UNLV, a few years back, which has been very successful. I enjoy being with students, and I'm always pleasantly surprised they want to talk to me and ask me questions. It's been a great experience, and I'll keep doing these visits as long as the universities invite me.

*

Nevada Health Sciences System

It's no secret that I took a keen interest in the state of medical care and the lack of coordination of Nevada's health science programs while I was chancellor. While I was able to start some coordination, since I've left the system it is beginning to show some real results. From time to time I'm able to help out in that growth.

As County Commissioner, I asked Jim to look into UMC financial structure. At the beginning it wasn't about getting the county to work well with other organizations; that was the second step. First it required the county to have a sense of its own direction. UMC historically lost an enormous amount of money. It was a huge drain on the county. And I thought that it was at least partially due to the governance structure – how it was organized – and I knew it needed to change. And nobody agreed with me. So I just called a press conference and said what I thought needed to happen. But before I did I'd talked to Jim, because he agreed with me, and I know Jim well enough to know that he's not very shy, and when he thinks he's right he's pretty dogged in the pursuit of whatever it is. I figured it would be harder for my colleagues to criticize him than to criticize me. With the TV station, Jim's a prominent guy and they didn't work with him every day like they did me – so I announced that we were working together on this joint effort, kind of as a buffer. That's how that started.

As I expected, Jim got in there and rolled up his sleeves and immediately started to throw elbows. He suggested within days that the county commission had no business running a hospital – which is true. And he said that seven politicians didn't know anything about running a hospital, and he called for the creation of a separate board to deal with it (and I believed in that too, but it was easier for him to say it publically than for me). So that was the first step to getting the county headed in a better direction. That was at least four years ago; and they're just now getting to the point of asking the city legislature to give authority to create a new governing board and do all the things that we talked about. Jim was an integral part of that. I don't think it would have worked if some of the commissioners weren't concerned about crossing Jim Rogers.

Rory Reid, Attorney

I know I've said this elsewhere, but the state of Nevada isn't willing to pay for quality medical care. It never has been. Our medical school in Reno is among the lowest ranked nationally. Local public hospitals are run by boards made up of members who know nothing about medicine or medical education. Medical governance needs a major overhaul.

I had moderate successes as chancellor getting the various institutions in the state to work together, particular in the health sciences. There were duplicate programs that couldn't fill class seats, expensive equipment that went unused or was under-utilized, and so on. While some of those programs now share equipment and facilities, I don't believe Nevada is anywhere near where it *should* be in the development of medical education and care.

> As chancellor, Jim was right on about the health sciences project. It could help put Nevada on the map, medical tourism – he was right on the issue, but his vision was too grand to match reality. I'm sure that was very frustrating to him (and to me). He's somebody who doesn't compromise on his vision. Sometimes that works for you, sometimes it doesn't. It's great that they're still trying, but that (health sciences) project is still nowhere near where his vision was. Nevada is so far behind in medical development. Our cancer center closed. I don't want to sound too cynical, but you get what you pay for. We're not willing to pay. We're not willing to make corporations who set up here pay. That's why we don't have top quality medical care capable of attracting top doctors . . . you would think that this being Vegas, the medical tourism idea is fantastic, if we had the infrastructure to support it. Jim wanted better than state of the art. He wanted top of the line. But you can't get there with our taxes. And if the state isn't willing to invest, the private sector isn't going to make up the difference. The bottom line is that Nevada hasn't recovered from Jim Gibbons, and isn't yet willing to pay for what's needed.

Sheila Leslie, Former Nevada State Senator

Until we make medical care in Nevada meet the highest standards, people will continue to go to California and Arizona and back east to get quality care when they can afford it. That leaves a large population of locals without the funds to go elsewhere, but until everyone agrees to do something to improve it, we'll wallow in mediocrity or worse.

*

Black Mountain Institute

Bev and I have always supported the liberal arts. She's a very avid reader, and has become closely involved with the Black Mountain Institute (BMI) housed at UNLV. Directed by President Emeritus Carol Harter, who established the literary institute when she stepped down from UNLV's presidency, the Black Mountain Institute has, in its short tenure, garnered national and international acclaim. It does a variety of community oriented lectures and readings, bringing local and national writers to UNLV and the Las Vegas audience. It also sponsors doctoral students and writer fellowships. As with all privately funded organizations, it has had to cut back in recent years. Bev and I decided to make a substantial contribution to BMI to enable it to pursue all the visionary goals it has.

In November (2013) we announced a $10 million commitment to BMI, to enable it to significantly expand its literary programming. In recognition of the gift, BMI will be renamed the Beverly Rogers, Carol C. Harter Black Mountain Institute. We've structured the gift to support BMI with $500,000 to $800,000 periods over the next 15 years. This will allow BMI to increase existing support to doctoral students and fellowship programs, enhance its public programing and outreach, and reinstitute and expand its acclaimed City of Asylum program, which provides a safe haven for writers from oppressive countries. The gift will also help establish the Black Mountain Institute Prize for Fiction. We're very excited about all the support BMI will be able to give writers and the community.

We joined a group, City of Asylum, and Las Vegas was the first city in the United States to have an asylum program – which is so ironic because people don't see Las Vegas as a literary sanctuary. But Richard Wiley and Wole Soyinka asked the mayor and there was support from the city and we became one – Pittsburgh is one, Ithaca is one, there is supposed to be one at the University of Iowa – I don't know if that one is defunct now– but at the beginning we had a writer from Sierra Leone who was able to go back to his country after the civil war was over. He was effectively on the wrong side. Then we had a Chinese poet – he's still here, somewhere, and his wife is working at the Post Office. He can't go back. And of course we had Moniro [Ravanipour] from Iran for three years because there was so much trouble going on there. She was arrested right before she came and knew that it was going to be long. She stayed for three years, but we just didn't have any more money after that. We just weren't raising money.

So now we are reconstructing the program and even hoping to host two exiled writers at a time. There is a Syrian writer that we're trying to get out of Damascus – we're having a hard time. And there's an Afghani writer, but he has six kids and none of these places are large enough to accommodate them. If we bring them, it's our responsibility to figure out how to do that. I would love to sponsor a Syrian and an Afghani writer because they are two of the most difficult places in the world to have free expression. So, it's a very exciting part of what the new money is going to do. We want journalists and creative writers.

We try to get three writers each year – we have a partnership with the Library of Congress, so one is always going to be there, and we've had some terrific people: Daniel Brook, Judith Nies, Sally Denton. Plus, we do two Ph.D fellowships – so we have six altogether and that gets very expensive. We are going up to $25,000 from $20,000 (for the students) and that's very competitive, nationally. All of those extra dollars make the extra difference.

We have a couple of new things – an alumni writers' workshop and that will be funded as a new program. Then we have a new award we're starting. BMI already has an award for fiction, which is a $50,000 award (the national book award is $10,000), and we will pay $15,000 each for three established writers to make a judgment on that year's books; we'll also have built into the budget a big reception to announce the award. We think it will put BMI way up on the international stage because of the size of the award. Some are bigger, of course – the Nobel and perhaps the Pulitzer. Our award will be every other year, though – not every year.

Everything BMI does is all community based. We never charge for any public event we do; we subsidize it all. We try to keep everything we do free and open to the public. Adding the alumni writing program will also have a positive effect on the students. We hope it is a very collegiate outreach to the community.

Carol Harter, Executive Director,
UNLV Black Mountain Institute

Beverly is also going to build a library/reading room. Literary magazines and journals will be purchased and made available to students and faculty. The gift will assist developing a public alumni reading series as well, featuring UNLV graduates from the award winning creative writing program. We'll also see some money go toward BMI's free public program, the Readings and Panels Series. Some money will also go to support BMI's highly regarded literary magazine, *Witness*, as well.

Jim and I are so proud of Carol and of what she has accomplished at Black Mountain Institute. She brought together fragments of the former International Institute of Modern Letters, the City of Asylum, and a fledgling fellowship program for writers. We encourage and strongly support "pockets of excellence" within UNLV that both open doors for scholars and writers world-wide, and link the university with the community by way of lectures and discussions. We're thrilled to be able to help BMI progress and welcome in a new era of expansion to help put Las Vegas on the map.

Beverly Rogers, Family

We're eagerly anticipating what BMI does with this gift, and how it will work with the university and the community to enhance awareness of global issues, as well as foster local talent. We expect BMI to do wonderful things.

*

Channel 3 – Doing All News, All the Time

Free speech means far more than simply having the right to express one's views. The right to express one's views can only be preserved and protected if one exercises that right. Exercising that right means more than giving lip service to general theories about how we should all live. Free speech means speaking the truth and speaking that truth, without any fear of having that truth repressed. All of us have an obligation to speak out and speak loudly. Our primary avenue for doing that is by participating in our government's activities. If we do not actively participate via holding a government position, we must express our views and then vote with those views in every election.

I do not view our television station's primary role to be to entertain those who watch our station. We who have FCC licenses enjoy a spectrum of communication that is limited in capacity. Those of us who have television stations must use those television stations to educate and persuade our communities to participate in resolving society's problems. We must do far more than entertain viewers. I entered the television business because I had an obligation to inform the public of life's important issues, not by pushing my views down the throats of viewers, but by pushing those thinking individuals into a thought process of substance. That's my one and only duty as a broadcaster.

Back when I was the chancellor of the Nevada System of Higher Education, I began to plan discontinuing the purchasing of syndicated programming. I wanted to move toward an all-news format. Jon Ralston, an outstanding political, social and economic interviewer on our competitor Channel 8, would often call me when he couldn't find anyone else to beat up on, and I'd let him interview me. I said, "I'm probably going to do something as I go forward with more and more news, and I'm going to try to stop broadcasting syndicated programming." Jon thought that was a good idea.

My first cancellation of syndicated programming was *Access Hollywood*. When we removed it from its six thirty p.m. slot, Jon Ralston came to work for our station and filled the half hour following our six o'clock news. We then persuaded CBS (the owner of syndicated programming) to move *Judge Judy* to another local station. We also notified CBS we would not be renewing other syndicated programming. Fortunately Channel 8 jumped on the opportunity to pick up *Wheel of Fortune* and *Jeopardy* and starting this last September, that station began to run them. What is all this reformatting going to do for us? It may bankrupt us – it is high stakes gambling – but it will allow us to produce very extensive news analysis.

When I was at Johns Hopkins, I talked to the faculty about the 30-second sound bite. This generation relies upon the 30-second sound bite for its total understanding of national and political issues. We've gotten so accustomed to the idea that news can adequately be delivered in these little bites that we actually believe it is all the information we need. Our company is unique because it has no shareholders. We believe we have an unlimited opportunity to broadcast programs that everyone should have been broadcasting during the last 50 years. As licensees of the FCC, we were sworn to provide the public substantive programming that raises the quality of life of all southern Nevadans. We are going to do just that.

We believe we have such an understanding of this community that no one can duplicate our efforts. We're going to take advantage of that because we want to satisfy our legal and moral obligations to inform and educate our viewers.

TELEVISION STATION

At KSNV-TV
Channel 3 station,
Las Vegas

Sunbelt
Communications'
first company plane,
a Cessna, 1997

The *Dawn & Jim*
show, with guest
Harry Reid

Jim Rogers in his television station office, Las Vegas

PHILANTHROPY

James E. Rogers

Jim and Beverly
Rogers at home

Jim Rogers with
Bill Boyd and Cary
Wright

Jim Rogers speaking to a
group at a charity event

Jim Rogers with
Marcia Turner at Black
Mountain Institute
gift announcement,
November 2013

National Atomic
Testing Museum,
Las Vegas

Frank H. Rogers
Science and
Technology
Building, Atomic
Testing Museum

Frank Rogers' desk
at the National
Atomic Testing
Museum

William S. Boyd
School of Law,
UNLV

Jim Rogers opening
the Thomas
& Mack Moot
Courtroom, William
S. Boyd School of
Law, UNLV, 2007

James E. Rogers Center for Administration
and Justice, William S. Boyd School of Law,
UNLV (above and left)

James E. Rogers
College of Law
entry, University of
Arizona

James E. Rogers
College of Law,
University of
Arizona

James E. Rogers College of Law,
University of Arizona

Library, James E. Rogers College of
Law, University of Arizona

Donor wall, James E. Rogers College
of Law, University of Arizona

James E. Rogers Circle, University of
Arizona

Black Mountain
Institute panel, Arab
Spring, February
2013

Jim Rogers and
Mark Whitehead
at Black Mountain
gift announcement,
November 2013

Dr. Carol Harter
opening a Black
Mountain Institute
event at Bauman
Rare Books,
Las Vegas

Nobel Prize winner
Wole Soyinka

Harriet Anna Mayor
Fulbright, Wole
Soyinka, and Carol
Harter (left to right)

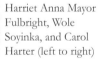

Beverly Rogers,
Carol Harter, and
Nobel Prize winner
Toni Morrison (left
to right)

The Chancellor Era

Jim Rogers speaking at a UNLV event

Two UNLV press photos of Chancellor Rogers

Chancellor Rogers introducing Carol Harter at UNLV event (above) and speaking (below, left)

James E. Rogers official KSNV portrait

Chancellor Rogers speaking to press and university body

Beverly and Jim Rogers with Carol and Mike Harter at a charity event

Chancellor Rogers with NSHE Regents at UNLV commencement

NSHE Regents presenting Chancellor Rogers with an honorary doctorate

Chancellor Rogers speaking to media at a student budget rally, 2008

UNLV students protest state budget cuts, 2008

Jim Rogers at his final NSHE Board of Regents meeting as chancellor

Chancellor Jim Rogers' service award presentation from NSHE Board of Regents (at left)

Maurizio Trevisan, Jim Rogers, and Marcia Turner (below)

Auto Collections

Jim in his favorite car, a 1931 V-16 Cadillac Roadster

Mike Pratt with Jim and 1931 V-16 Cadillac Roadster

1958 Cadillac Biarritz

1962 Rolls Royce
Drophead Coupe

A row of front ends
in auto barn

A row of back ends
in auto barn

WESTERN COLLECTIONS

Jim in his office with
western memorabilia

Western boot wall
at KSNV Channel 3
station, Las Vegas

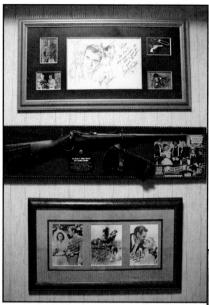

Western memorabilia on the walls of KSNV Channel 3 station, Las Vegas

General George S. Patton guns

Roy Rogers' receipt for Trigger

The Beverly and Jim Rogers Museum of Lone Pine Film History, Lone Pine, California

Jim being interviewed about the Lone Pine museum collection

Lone Pine museum gift shop

Jim admiring a
Bohlin saddle in the
Lone Pine museum

Humphrey Bogart's
car from *High Sierra*

1941 Buick
Roadmaster
convertible from
Peggy Stewart film,
Trail to San Antone

Dale Evans Rogers

Lone Pine dinner
with Dale Evans
Rogers and Kathryn
Grayson

Fire truck in the
Lone Pine museum

Doctor's Bag
carriage

Gene Autrey on
horse, signed by
Peggy Stewart

Alabama Hills wagon. Photo taken in Lone Pine on Jim and Beverly Rogers' first anniversary.

Chapter X

MY GREATEST ACCOMPLISHMENT:
I'VE NEVER SAID THE WORDS, "IF I'D ONLY"

The worst words in the English language are: "If I'd only." I have to tell you that statement has probably been one of the most influential in my life. I made a conscious effort never to put myself into that position. When I was younger, I'd hear people say, "If I'd only bought this property," or "If I'd only gotten into this business," "If I'd only taken advantage of education," and so on. It became kind of a thing with me that I swore I would end my life never having said, "If I'd only." And I think that's probably been one of the great motivating factors in my life – deciding that "If I'd only" would not relate to me. I would take chances from time to time, major chances, really, but when it was all over I doubted I missed anything. I'm 75 now. As I look back, I can tell you I've never said to myself, "If I'd only." I've taken some big risks, and gambled a lot of what I've had, and I've been broke four times. But I have never said "If I'd only," and of that I am truly proud.

I grew up in a time when history was passed from one generation to another through family members sitting on the porch at night, telling stories about what this person or that person had done in their careers. The communication system among people in the 1940s and 1950s was probably a hell of a lot better than it is now. You paid attention to each other, and you learned from each other. I remember being 10 years old and listening to my grandfather and other relatives talk about what they had done. No one in the state of Kentucky has told the truth in the last hundred years, but they tell these stories about their lives. My grandmother once said, "You know Jimmy, a few years ago a fellow came through town and he was selling stock in General Motors and I could've bought "x" number of shares in Coca-Cola for

$5 and I would be a millionaire now." For the first time in my in my life I heard this statement: "If I'd only . . ."

I remember as a kid, and I must have heard the story 20 times, people saying, "When Coca-Cola started, my father had the opportunity to buy into the company. There was a salesman coming through town, selling stock in Coca-Cola. And nobody believed in the stock. And if I had just bought $200 worth of stock, blah, blah . . ." I don't want to hear those stories. I'm sure there have been a lot of opportunities I've missed because I didn't know about them, but I've never gone back to the "If I'd only" mindset. If I thought a project had potential – even if it were only a 10 percent chance, if I liked the project I jumped in head first.

When I go to Johns Hopkins every second or third year, I teach a class for a month. From time to time I talk to the faculty. John Hopkins is really one of the elite universities in the world. I was speaking to the faculty, which was about 85 people, and I said, "I want you to understand that I've never gotten into a business solely to make a profit. I always got into it because I liked the nature of the business." I went on to say, every business I've ever gotten in to, I got into because I liked the business; I thought it was valuable, that it provided some social value, and I prayed it would be successful. I have not always been successful. I've had real financial problems over the years. And it was only through the grace of God and a fast infield that we pulled out of it. From time to time I put my family in financial jeopardy because I was willing to gamble everything we had. Fortunately the gamble paid off.

Let's get back to the "If I'd only." I've been very lucky in the television business. We were the second or the third station in the country to buy *Wheel of Fortune* and *Jeopardy*. We bought them, by the way, for $125 a week. We now pay $40,000 a week – but we are now substituting news in their place. I never had any desire to take credit for someone else's program success. When NBC was number one, people would say to me, "Aren't you really pleased that NBC is number one?" I'd say sure, I'm glad, and we sell ads and make money on them. But I can't take credit for the programming they produce. I want to produce as many programs I can. Being a lawyer, and a flaming liberal, I believe in the First Amendment. I believe in saying what I want on the air, and I say it. But I also believe in letting everyone with opinions far different from mine have access to our broadcasting facilities.

I've talked about this generation's increasing reliance on the 30-second sound bite for all of its national and international information. We've come to expect that news can efficiently and fully be delivered in these little bites. Our company is unique. We are interested in and connected to our community. We have an opportunity to produce the types of programs that every broadcaster should have been producing over the last half a century. When we won the license in the 1970s, we swore we would provide public service to our communities. We will do that with all news, all the time.

You will never hear me say: "If I'd only done more news."

I hope I have expressed at least one thought in this book that will be useful to you. I am honored and pleased you have read it.

AFTERWORD

by Heather Lusty

Jim lost his battle with cancer on June 14th, 2014. We'd finished the manuscript about two months prior. I had encouraged him to write the retirement section, to sketch out the "small" things he was still working on, because to me it seemed as though the book stopped midway through his story. While he didn't want to give away the types of programming his station was creating, he in fact worked every day preparing for and guiding the transition of KSNV to a new, community focused, all news format. In addition to the station, Jim continued to give time and money to education, to the Nevada Health Sciences System, and to other endeavors. He'd just discovered that a dozen of his relatives had been involved in the Kentucky Wesleyan University during its early days, and that tickled him – being a crusader and philanthropist for education was an inherent trait, and he wanted to keep up his family's tradition and name even though he had no personal association with the school. He had also discussed, with Nevada Governor Brian Sandoval, donating his entire automobile collection to the state as a museum; although the planning hit turbulence and fell through, his love of automobiles is one he'll share with thousands of people who come to see it. Jim didn't understand what "retirement" meant.

*

When Jim first approached me about helping him organize this project, it sounded like an interesting opportunity – because more than anything, Jim was a fascinating man. In the two years we worked on his memoirs, I came to know him very well. He enjoyed being able to roll his sleeves up and get involved in issues; he didn't understand the idea of rest or vacation, but always looked at what he was going to accomplish next. He loved getting people riled up, provoking reactions from political and educational figures, and would offer himself up as a target to get a conversation rolling. He knew there were those he worked with or against who held grudges – but he was always be willing to talk with his adversaries, because getting someone to the table was always his end goal. Despite his larger than life stature – his influence in education, in media, in the community, and in the state was enormous – Jim was an incredibly humble man.

What Jim didn't want in this book was his soft side – he didn't want stories about the hundreds of students who had gone through college and graduate/law school on scholarships he provided, who wrote him letters regularly thanking him and detailing the differences his support made in their lives. He didn't want to discuss the dozens of employees, employees' children (and siblings and parents) he put through school privately, out of his own pocket and out of the limelight. Jim was fond of saying, "Everyone ought to go to law school to learn how to think – but nobody should ever be a lawyer." In fact, he's encouraged numerous people to do just that. These personal contributions were the real Jim – a man willing to hand you his own jacket or car if he thought it would help you be more comfortable or get somewhere. I think Jim was always conscious of the way people viewed him – as a wealthy man who had to prove his worth. Louie's life lessons were not just lessons for Jim, who lived them to the letter, but they were lessons he passed on, encouraging others to give back in any way they could, just to do it, to care, to be a part of something, even if their contributions were not rewarded. He was far more successful than he realized.

Despite his enormous accomplishments, Jim prided himself on being accessible; he answered his own office phone, and took meetings with anyone who asked. He treated his employees at the station exactly the way he describes his father as an employer in this book. Jim knew every one of his station employees – their families, their hobbies – he managed to become the same personal, caring boss Frank was, and I think he took pride in that. I think he was less aware of the influence he had on others he came into contact with. Jim was a mentor and a father figure to scores of people over the years, whether he realized it or not. Many of the interviews here attest to that, but many more preferred their personal feelings be set aside in favor of highlighting his accomplishments. Some shared the enormity of his impact on them as individuals, their families, their professions, and their departments or schools. He encouraged everyone he spoke with, people he knew well and people he had just met, to get an education, and saw the championing of education his most important calling. Jim became one of the mentors he so admired, and to whom he credited for helping him become who he was and achieve what he did. Perhaps this is his most important legacy to the community – the legion of students and citizens he mentored, who are now working to affect change in education, in the health system, in their own and others' lives. His impact on others as a mentor is almost impossible to really measure, but it lives on in others far more than his philanthropy.

In a few dozen of the interviews I conducted for this book, I asked people, "How do you think history will remember Jim Rogers?" Their answers were astute, measured, and thoughtful. Jim read these (unaware that I had asked and compiled them) towards the end of the writing process in the spring of 2014. While he didn't comment on them specifically, and didn't want them included because he felt that it would be arrogant to include praise about himself, he went back and reread them on several occasions. He was flattered and pleased that people he respected and worked with, and on whom he was occasionally hard because he thought they weren't doing enough or pushing hard enough, saw him in the bigger picture, and understood what he hoped to achieve and change – and he wasn't finished. I include the comments at the end of this section because I can, and should – because they made him proud.

*

"How do you think history will remember Jim Rogers?"

> History: I think it'll treat him well. Philanthropically he's been as good as it gets. It's tough to think they'll treat him as kind of a guy who was hard hitting, but had his heart in the right place. No one can say that what he did was self-serving. He had all the resources in the world that he needed—he's given

most of that away, as you know. How can you not admire that? I certainly do.

Sig Rogich

I think Jim played and is playing a very significant role in fashioning the public's attention and awareness of critical issues, particularly in education as a whole. I think that when you take strong positions like Jim does, it's kind of like being in politics whether you want to or not; some people are going to agree with you and some are not. Whether people remember Jim and agree with him or not, they will always remember him as a person who put it out there, and who really made sure that everybody knew exactly where he and the people he was representing stood. He's not afraid to tackle tough issues and that's a rare quality.

Nevada Governor Bob Miller

In the end, Jim made Clark County a better place to live, and the Nevada System of Higher Education would not be anywhere near where it is today were it not for his efforts. He took on strong personalities and made it work. Thank goodness he did.

Steve Sisolak

How will history remember Jim: If Jim would have been able to have his dream, it would have been completely different – we would have a much stronger academic health institution. It would have been very different. People will remember him as a major pain in the neck. But his motivations were always good. He may not have the smoothest approach, but he's a man of high integrity.

Maurizio Trevisan

I think Jim is a great person. He's what people should aspire to be. Just by being him, he's changed my life. Some of his philanthropy has rubbed off on me (not that I have the same kind of money). It's always been important to me to help other people, but now, I have his encouragement. I think Jim's made me a better person because I really look up to him, and look at the things he does. He's sincere about everything. He's a pretty straight shooter. He fights for what he believes in. He stands up for what he believes in and backs it. He's been a really good inspiration for me.

Don Barlow

I think Jim will be remembered as someone who really cared, and cared enough to put his own personal reputation and his physical well-being on the line.

Carol Lucey

I think Jim will be remembered as a great pioneer, in television, in education. He accomplished a great deal for [Nevada], he really truly did. I think of Jim as someone that you can go to, and talk with, and be really direct with, and he has a mind that sees all different types of things. I think he has a good heart. And he's sincere. You don't find that in people much these days. And of course he's very intelligent, and a very hard worker. Put all those things together and in addition to that he's persistent. You know what they say: persistence is the key to success.

Lois Tarkanian

I think Nevada history will remember Jim as the chancellor who was most vociferous in his advocacy for his higher education, who was an uncompromising advocate for the university system. I'm not sure we'll have another man like him for a very long time.

Sheila Leslie

I think history will treat Jim very, very well. He is a great human being, but he had tremendous gifts and passion for the betterment of society, and the human condition. You don't find those ideals in young executives today. To them, it is not about the place they live, because they can be living anywhere around the world. That's not Jim. He sincerely believes he has a role to play in Nevada. Nevada really did not take advantage of this very smart, very generous, very driven man. It's a shame. It's a lost opportunity.

Yash Gupta

Nevada history probably won't treat Jim as well as it should. I don't think people understand what he's done. It's rare that somebody goes into a public position because of ideas. Jim had no ambition. He wasn't trying to prove anything to himself or anyone else. Jim's been very successful; he can do whatever he wants. And because he believed he was right, he's spent a lot of time donating his time and energy to the public good – for no salary. That's an incredible example that should be followed. I don't think people appreciate that. I think it hasn't been as widely recognized as it should be, and if it has been recognized, he's not as appreciated as he should be.

Rory Reid

Jim will probably be remembered more so in terms of his tenure as chancellor and his philanthropy more than for his earlier years in the law firm, although he was successful. His philanthropy is unparalleled. And then his focus on education; I think in all those respects, Jim will always be remembered as someone who spoke his mind. There are people who have felt that the brunt of his rhetoric or felt a little trampled on by him. But you always know what Jim was thinking; he doesn't pull any punches. He can be brutally honest, and that can be a positive or a negative (if you're on the receiving end), but it's a characteristic that helped Jim succeed in all of those areas. I kind of always put Jim in the category (in Nevada) with Steve Wynn, as a builder. Jim always had to be building, expanding, growing. If he wasn't adding on to his house, he was expanding his car collection, or expanding the law firm; Jim is a master builder.

Bob Woodard

Jim is a unique person in the history of the state of Nevada. His legacy is significant. He's known all over the western United States. He has business interests in Idaho, Montana, Arizona. He's really been an attraction to Nevada for how to be a business person and how to be extremely ethical, but yet not be a shrinking violet. He's never been afraid to speak his mind.

Harry Reid

I think he'll be remembered for his passion for the city of Las Vegas and his passion for the university. When it's all said and done, he's touched a lot of people. I think one of the things is that Jim gets as much joy out of people achieving their goals and being happy in their lives as he has been in his. He understands the true meaning of "share the wealth" – a wealth of knowledge and a wealth of experience. I can't imagine anyone else thinking anything different of him. His passion for life, and his passion for the university, and just Las Vegas in general, and the people who are connected to it, was just fantastic.

Reggie Theus

I think Jim will be remembered for three things: 1) He made a lot of money and was very successful, but he didn't choose to just pass it on to his children. He wanted to give it away to see the world become better; 2) His ability to link the north and south of our state and the university systems; the articulation of K-16 education never existed before, and he is the author of that; 3) Here's this western loving guy, who with his own grit, his own perseverance and vision, ends up contributing to law schools, and having an impact on the best and brightest students in the country, inspiring and challenging people all over. I don't think people see that yet – it's too close. His range of impact and influence is so much greater than we know, and people who have had the privilege of working with him recognize it.

Judy Steele

This man is all positive in my book. You know, there are very few people – the glass is sometimes half empty with me – but this guy is wonderful for this community. My God, if we didn't have Jim Rogers I don't know where this community would be, especially Clark County, and the whole state when it comes to education. You know, here's a man who really cares about education. I wish everybody had the same type of philosophy as him. And also when it comes to philanthropy, there are very few people who are as generous as [Jim]. I just can't say enough positive about what he's done for the community.

Mike Cherry

If you were going to have to name the top 100 people in Nevada history, it's a no brainer that Jim makes that list. If you were going to name the top 50, he makes that list. I don't think it would take a great lawyer to successfully argue that Jim Rogers is top ten. If you think in terms of his role in education, and the media as a tool for education, he has really been (at least as far as Nevada is concerned), I would have to say that Hank Greenspun and Jim Rogers are, and will be recognized as the two most important, most influential media people in the history of this state beyond any doubt. Jim Rogers is a rugged individual. He's not going to patronize the establishment, nor is he going to rail against it. Beyond any doubt, Jim is one of the greatest men in Nevada history in regards to media.

Dominic Gentile

There are a great many reasons to admire people. You can admire them for financial success, but to me that's not nearly as important as admiring them for what is in their heart. For that reason, I believe that Jim Rogers is one of the most admirable people, if not the most admirable person I've ever met. He's a wonderful man and I am proud to call him a friend.

Rex Allen, Jr.

History is written based upon the press an awful lot, and Jim gets good press, so I think he'll be remembered as a major influence in Nevada, especially in education. It's interesting how history is written, so I just don't know. He certainly has his strengths and his weakness, and some of the weaknesses will probably not be written in history, so you know, I think he'll be remembered as an important figure in building education in Nevada.

Jane Nichols

It's really poignant that you ask me (how Nevada history will remember Jim) now, as Nevada is going through a real transformation. I think Nevada will remember Jim, and cherish Jim, for being one of the fathers of modern Las Vegas. They will remember him for his passion for the community, for his passion for higher education, and for that sincere desire and willingness to put himself on the line to improve the quality of life in southern Nevada. That is an incredibly rare thing. A lot of people will talk a good talk, but to put your own skin on the line, to put yourself in harm's way, to be willing to fight the tough battles, there aren't a lot of those types of people around. They emerge, rightfully so, as the quintessential leadership for the community. I think that Jim embodies that and his life and his work represent that (idea) in an incredible way.

Pat Mulroy

Honorary Degrees and Awards

Honorary Degrees
Carroll College, Helena, Montana
College of Southern Nevada
Gonzaga University
Idaho State University
Kentucky Wesleyan University
University of Arizona
University of Idaho
University of Nevada, Las Vegas

Chair of Fundraising Campaigns:
Idaho State University (chaired campaign; raised 80% more than original goal)
Nevada State College (initial foundation chairman)
University of Arizona, with Karl Eller (exceeded goal by several hundred million dollars)
University of Nevada, Las Vegas, with Don Snyder (doubled original goal and met that goal)

Law School Boards:
Gonzaga University College of Law
New York University, New York City
University of Arizona, James E. Rogers College of Law
University of Colorado College of Law
University of Idaho College of Law
University of Nevada, Las Vegas, College of Law
University of New Mexico College of Law
University of Southern California Gould School of Law
Washington University in St. Louis, Missouri

Other Boards:
Albertson College, Boise, Idaho
University of Nevada, Las Vegas, College of Business

Interview Citations

All titles listed are from the time of the interview.

Mark Alden, Nevada Board of Regents, interviewed by Melisé Leech, Las Vegas, NV, 5 October 2012.

Rex Allen, Jr., singer song-writer, interviewed by Melisé Leech, Las Vegas, NV, 13 June 2013.

Stavros Anthony, mayor pro-tem, City of Las Vegas, interviewed by Melisé Leech, Las Vegas, NV, 6 February 2013.

Dan Ayala, entrepreneur, interviewed by Melisé Leech, Las Vegas, NV, 13 November 2012.

Don Barlow, family, interviewed by Heather Lusty, Las Vegas, NV, 31 January 2013.

Shelley Berkley, former US Congresswoman, interviewed by Heather Lusty, Las Vegas, NV, 11 February 2013.

Dick and Connie Bowen, former president, Idaho State University and wife, retired, interviewed by Melisé Leech, Boise, ID, 16 November 2012.

Hannah Brown, community developer, interviewed by Heather Lusty, Las Vegas, NV, 27 February 2013.

Richard Bryan, attorney and former Nevada governor, interviewed by Melisé Leech, Las Vegas, NV, 7 March 2013.

Barbara Buckley, former Nevada state assemblywoman, interviewed by Heather Lusty, Las Vegas, NV, 28 February 2013.

Michael Cherry, Justice Nevada Supreme Court, interviewed by Heather Lusty, Las Vegas, NV, 18 March 2013.

Rob Correales, professor of law, UNLV, interviewed by Heather Lusty, Las Vegas, NV, 20 February 2013.

Sondra Cosgrove, history professor, College of Southern Nevada, interviewed by Melisé Leech, Las Vegas, NV, 24 October 2012.

Adam Cronis, associate Vanguard Financial, interviewed by Heather Lusty, Phoenix, AZ, 12 December 2012.

Michael Crow, President, Arizona State University, interviewed by Heather Lusty, Phoenix, AZ, 22 March 2013.

Jill Derby, former Chair, Nevada Board of Regents, interviewed by Heather Lusty, Las Vegas, NV, 10 March 2013

Thalia Dondero, Clark County commissioner, retired, interviewed by Melisé Leech, Las Vegas, NV, 10 October 2012.

Suzanne Ernst, public relations, retired, interviewed by Melisé Leech, Las Vegas, NV, 11 October 2012.

Vicki Fleischer, assistant dean of Seton Hall law school; former senior director of development University of Arizona Eller College of Management, interviewed by Heather Lusty, Newark, NJ, 25 March 2013.

Dominic Gentile, attorney, interviewed by Heather Lusty, Las Vegas, NV, 18 March 2013.

Dawn Gibbons, senior vice president of communications and government relations, Intermountain West Communications, interviewed by Heather Lusty, Las Vegas, NV, 16 November 2012.

Shelley Goings, general manager KPVI, interviewed by Heather Lusty, Pocatello, ID, 16 November 2012

Josh Griffin, lobbyist, interviewed by Melisé Leech, Las Vegas, NV, 30 October 2012.

John Guedry, president, Bank of Nevada, interviewed by Heather Lusty, Las Vegas, NV, 29 April 2013.

Yash Gupta, CEO of SDP Telecom, interviewed by Heather Lusty, Baltimore, MD, 14 February 2013.

Carol Harter, exec. director UNLV Black Mountain Institute, interviewed by Heather Lusty, Las Vegas, NV, 14 February 2013.

Jaque Hickman, entrepreneur, interviewed by Melisé Leech, Lone Pine, CA, 26 July 2013.

Lisa Howfield, executive assistant, KSNV-TV, interviewed by Heather Lusty, Las Vegas, NV, 16 November 2012.

Alan Kaercher, insurance agent, interviewed by Melisé Leech, Las Vegas, NV, 31 October 2012.

Dan Klaich, chancellor, Nevada Board of Regents, interviewed by Melisé Leech, Las Vegas, NV, 25 April 2013.

Jane Korn, dean, Gonzaga University School of Law, interviewed by Heather Lusty, Spokane, WA, 19 February 2013.

John Kuhlman, public information, NSHE, interviewed by Melisé Leech, Las Vegas, NV, 18 October 2012.

Sylvia Lazos, professor of law, UNLV, interviewed by Heather Lusty, Las Vegas, NV, 20 February 2013.

Jim Lenhart, physician, interviewed by Heather Lusty, Las Vegas, NV, 15 October 2012.

Sheila Leslie, former Nevada State Senator, interviewed by Heather Lusty, Reno, NV, 17 April 2013.

Pete Likins, president University of Arizona, retired, interviewed by Melisé Leech, Tucson, AZ, 26 October 2012.

Jessica Lucero, former graduate student body president UNLV, interviewed by Heather Lusty, Las Vegas, NV, 1 December 2012.

Jim Livengood, athletic director UNLV, retired, interviewed by Heather Lusty, Las Vegas, NV, 7 March 2013.

Carol Lucey, president, Western Nevada College, interviewed by Heather Lusty, Cason City, NV. 11 September 2013.

Joyce Mack, trustee, UNLV Foundation, interviewed by Heather Lusty, Las Vegas, NV, 18 February 2013.

Toni Massaro, former dean, University of Arizona James E. Rogers College of Law, interviewed by Heather Lusty, Tucson, AZ, 19 January 2013.

Bob Miller, former Nevada Governor, interviewed by Heather Lusty, Las Vegas, NV, 8 March 2013.

Earl Monsey, attorney, retired, interviewed by Heather Lusty, Las Vegas, NV, 25 February 2013.

Dick Morgan, former dean, UNLV School of Law, interviewed by Heather Lusty, Las Vegas, NV, 12 February 2013.

Pat Mulroy, general manager, Las Vegas Valley Water District, interviewed by Heather Lusty, Las Vegas, NV, 3 April 2013.

C.L. Max Nikias, president, University of Southern California, interviewed by Heather Lusty, Las Vegas, NV, 8 May 2013.

Jane Nichols, vice chancellor, Academic and Student Affairs, Nevada Board of Regents, interviewed by Heather Lusty, Las Vegas, NV, 19 February 2013.

Kevin Page, Nevada Board of Regents, interviewed by Melisé Leech, Las Vegas, NV, 11 March 2013.

Bart Patterson, president Nevada State College, interviewed by Melisé Leech, Henderson, NV, 7 November 2012.

Kerry Powell, founder of Lone Pine Film Festival, interviewed by Melisé Leech, Lone Pine, CA, 26 July 2013.

Mike Pratt, operations manager, Jim Rogers automobile collection, interviewed by Heather Lusty, Las Vegas, NV, 16 February 2013.

JoAnn Prevetti, director of operations, Griffin Communications Group, Nevada, interviewed by Melisé Leech, Las Vegas, NV, 30 October 2012.

Park Price, president, Bank of Idaho, interviewed by Heather Lusty, Idaho Falls, ID, 19 November 2012.

Cheryl Rogers Purdue, family, interviewed by Heather Lusty, Las Vegas, NV, 22 March 2013.

Harry Reid, US Senator, interviewed by Heather Lusty, Searchlight, NV, 18 February 2013.

Rory Reid, attorney, interviewed by Heather Lusty, Las Vegas, NV, 18 February 2013.

Beverly Rogers, family, interviewed by Heather Lusty, Las Vegas, NV, 10 December 2012.

Mike Richards, president College of Southern Nevada, interviewed by Melisé Leech, Las Vegas, NV, 11 October 2012.

Cheryl Rogers-Barnett, board member, Western Music Association, interviewed by Heather Lusty, St. George, UT, 16 February 2013.

Sig Rogich, president, Rogich Communications Group, interviewed by Heather Lusty, 11 March 2013.

Jerry Rourke, attorney, retired, interviewed by Heather Lusty, Las Vegas, NV, 10 January 2013.

Walt Rulffes, superintendent Clark County School District, retired, interviewed by Melisé Leech, Las Vegas, NV, 6 March 2013.

Larry Ruvo, vice president and general manager Southern Wine and Spirits, interviewed by Melisé Leech, Las Vegas, NV, 20 April 2013.

Michelle Sanders, accountant, Intermountain West Communications, interviewed by Heather Lusty, Las Vegas, NV, 15 November 2012.

Bob Savage, physician, Cleveland Clinic, interviewed by Heather Lusty, 14 February 2013.

Jack Schofield, Nevada Board of Regents, interviewed by Melisé Leech, Las Vegas, NV, 3 October 2012.

Thomas Schwenk, dean, University of Nevada School of Medicine, interviewed by Heather Lusty, Reno, NV, 25 March 2013.

Joel Seligman, president, University of Rochester, interviewed by Heather Lusty, Rochester, NY, 4 April 2013.

Steve Sisolak, Clark County commissioner, interviewed by Melisé Leech, Las Vegas, NV, 14 March 2013.

Neal Smatresk, president, University of Nevada, Las Vegas, interviewed by Melisé Leech, Las Vegas, NV, 14 December 2012.

Nancy Stanley, assistant dean for advancement, James E. Rogers College of Law, University of Arizona, interviewed by Melisé Leech, Tucson, AZ, 26 October 2012.

Judith Steele, president, Public Education Foundation, interviewed by Heather Lusty, Las Vegas, NV, 20 March 2013.

Peggy Stewart, actress, interviewed by Melisé Leech, Lone Pine, CA, 5 October 2012.

Bob Stoldal, executive vice president of news, KSNV Channel 3, Las Vegas, NV, interviewed by Melisé Leech, Las Vegas, NV, 29 March 2013.

Tom Sullivan, president, University of Vermont, interviewed by Heather Lusty, Burlington, VT, 25 March 2013.

Jim Snyder, journalist, news anchor, Channel 3, interviewed by Heather Lusty, Las Vegas, NV, 20 January 2013.

Lois Tarkanian, city councilwoman, interviewed by Heather Lusty, Las Vegas, NV, 12 March 2013.

Reggie Theus, head coach, Cal State Northridge, interviewed by Heather Lusty, Las Vegas, NV, 12 March 2013.

Pauline Thiros, director of planned giving, Idaho State University, interviewed by Melisé Leech, Pocatello, ID, 16 November 2012.

Kent Tingey, vice president of university advancement, Idaho State University, interviewed by Melisé Leech, Pocatello, ID, 16 November 2012.

Ralph Toddre, president and COO, Intermountain West Communications, interviewed by Melisé Leech, Las Vegas, NV, 17 October 2012.

Maurizio Trevisan, dean, Sophie Davis School of Biomedical Education and Interim Provost, City College of New York, interviewed by Heather Lusty, 17 February 2013.

Marcia Turner, vice chancellor of health sciences, NSHE, interviewed by Melisé Leech, Las Vegas, NV, 15 October 2012.

Art Vailas, president, Idaho State University, interviewed by Heather Lusty, Pocatello, ID, 29 April 2013.

Vic Welbourne, engineer, Interview by Heather Lusty, San Francisco, CA. 8 December 2012.

Steve Wells, Desert Research Institute, interviewed by Heather Lusty, Las Vegas, NV, 2 April 2013.

John White, executive vice president and provost, University of Nevada, Las Vegas, interviewed by Melisé Leech, Las Vegas, NV, 3 December 2012.

Mike Wixom, Nevada Board of Regents, interviewed by Melisé Leech, Las Vegas, NV, 6 November 2012.

Bruce Woodbury, attorney, interviewed by Heather Lusty, Boulder City, NV, 15 March 2013.

Buck Wong, entrepreneur, retired, interview by Heather Lusty, Las Vegas, NV, 21 February 2013.

Tim Yock, CFO, Intermountain West Communications, interviewed by Melisé Leech, Las Vegas, NV, 17 October 2012.

Index